Beginning Blender

Open Source 3D Modeling, Animation, and Game Design

■ ■ ■

Lance Flavell

Apress®

Beginning Blender: Open Source 3D Modeling, Animation, and Game Design

ISBN-13 (pbk): 978-1-4302-3126-4

ISBN-13 (electronic): 978-1-4302-3127-1

Printed and bound in the United States of America 9 8 7 6 5 4 3 2 1

President and Publisher: Paul Manning
Lead Editor: Frank Pohlmann
Technical Reviewer: Luca Bonavita
Editorial Board: Steve Anglin, Mark Beckner, Ewan Buckingham, Gary Cornell, Jonathan Gennick, Jonathan Hassell, Michelle Lowman, Matthew Moodie, Duncan Parkes, Jeffrey Pepper, Frank Pohlmann, Douglas Pundick, Ben Renow-Clarke, Dominic Shakeshaft, Matt Wade, Tom Welsh
Coordinating Editor: Tracy Brown
Copy Editor: Damon Larson
Compositor: MacPS, LLC
Indexer: Potomac Indexing, LLC
Artist: April Milne
Cover Designer: Anna Ishchenko

Distributed to the book trade worldwide by Springer Science+Business Media, LLC., 233 Spring Street, 6th Floor, New York, NY 10013. Phone 1-800-SPRINGER, fax (201) 348-4505, e-mail orders-ny@springer-sbm.com, or visit www.springeronline.com.

For information on translations, please e-mail rights@apress.com, or visit www.apress.com.

Apress and friends of ED books may be purchased in bulk for academic, corporate, or promotional use. eBook versions and licenses are also available for most titles. For more information, reference our Special Bulk Sales–eBook Licensing web page at www.apress.com/info/bulksales.

The source code for this book is available to readers at www.apress.com.

To Christal

Contents at a Glance

Contents

About the Author

Lance Flavell is a fully registered teacher from the Kapiti Coast of New Zealand, with a sideline interest as a 3D animator/freelance artist. At the time of writing this book, Lance is teaching a full-time workload as an IT tutor at the Paraparaumu College secondary school. Lance has a passion for open source programs and has run Linux as his primary operating system for the past decade. He has gained a few academic degrees over time, and is especially fond of having earned his animation diploma from the Media Design School of Auckland, New Zealand. Lance has contributed to online publications such as BlenderArt magazine and he is frequently involved in holiday programs teaching computer graphics, where he usually specializes in Blender. Lance can often be found in the BlenderArtists forums (http://blenderartists.org/forum) or at www.nzcgi.com under the username "Lancer".

About the Technical Reviewer

Luca Bonavita is an Italian engineer and special effects supervisor.

During his studies at the Politecnico of Turin, he worked as a freelance camera operator in broadcast television, and later on as a motion control specialist in the advertising and film industries.

As his job, he makes extensive use of Blender for designing visual effects (previsualization, animatics) and for sharing 3D data with motion control rigs on the set. He uses Blender for the postproduction of his project, at www.mindrones.com.

Acknowlegements

There are a number of people I would like to thank who have made this book possible in their own way.

The book was written in a time of extreme business and stress, so I owe thanks to God for answering my prayers and finally allowing it to be completed.

I would like to thank Adele Flavell, my mother, who has always been a rock of support, and still is today. Thanks also to Winston Flavell, my father, for dropping by and checking how things were going.

I would also like to thank Roger Feron, Simon Heath, Mike Ogle, Emil Polyak, Don Smith, Kyall Thompson, Leon Woud and the others at Media Design School for everything they have taught me while I was studying there.

Thanks also to the team at Apress, particularly Tracy Brown Collins, Matthew Moodie and Luca Bonavita for their continual assistance and advice while pulling these pages together.

Introduction

Welcome to the world of 3D! The fact that you are reading this book means that there is a good chance you are interested in 3D animation. You have heard that Blender is a freely available program capable of making such animations, so now you want to know how to use it, and fast! But then, it's dangerous for me to guess this scenario. Perhaps it's 3D games you're interested in making. Perhaps you're not into the animation side of things, but you want a good reference on how to get started on making your own 3D models. Maybe you've heard that Blender has some powerful video-editing capabilities. Well, Blender can do all these things and so much more.

When I started using Blender, I was soon overwhelmed with the many controls it has. Buttons just seemed to be arranged all over the place! When I pressed one button to see what it did, sometimes all the other controls around it would change, but I had no clue as to what the button I had just clicked was supposed to be doing.

What I needed was direction. I didn't want a manual explaining what every button does (I didn't have the patience), but a guide to explain just the few important options needed to get me started. I'm hoping that this is the kind of book I have written for you.

This book does not aim to be exhaustive, and yet it is not written to an overly simplified manner so as to insult your intelligence. 3D animation by its very nature is not simple. What you have with *Beginning Blender* is a book that covers a good range of the many different areas of Blender, with practical examples to get you fast-tracked into using those areas. Whether you are wanting to learn 3D modeling, animation, game-making, or movie production, this book will get you started the area you want to go.
The following sections outline what we'll cover in each chapter.

How This Book Is Organized

The first two chapters introduce Blender, with essential information that you really need to know before digging into the program.

Chapter 1 starts off with the background of Blender, explaining what Blender is and how it came to be, including some sample artwork from talented Blender users. I don't like "practical" books that turn into history lessons, although once you see what Blender can do, you're naturally going to get curious about how such a powerful program could possibly be free, so I decided the information was relevant. I have also included information on where you can get the latest versions of Blender and how you can install it on most common operating systems.

Chapter 2 contains key information to understanding Blender in terms of the user interface. It is important that you get a mindset for thinking in terms of 3D space. Everything you do in Blender will be affected by your understanding of the base concepts in this chapter, making it a must-read before any of the remaining sections of the book.

The remaining chapters of the book branch out into the different areas of Blender, before concluding with some resources you can look to for continuing your learning. The sections are progressive in terms of complexity, although I have made each chapter independent from the others, in order to cater for readers who like to skip a head and flip to a particular section of interest.

Chapter 3 contains information on basic modeling. Blender has many mesh modeling tools that can prove overwhelming to the beginner, so I have outlined the ones I believe are going to be the most important; and this chapter is designed to be a reference you will want to return to as you come to grips with the most essential tools. I have included instructions on how you can set up a mirror modifier for the times when you need to build anything symmetrical. Modeling is an art, making it a difficult task even for experienced Blender users, so I also included information on how you can use Blender's sculpting tools to make modeling as easy and as enjoyable as working with clay, including how you can integrate the different modeling techniques together.

Once you can make models, Chapters 4 and 5 are concerned with using lighting and texturing to make your work look good. In Chapter 4 you will learn how to set up a camera and lights to effectively display your model, and there is information on how you can design your own procedural textures to enhance the surface texture and the color of your models. Chapter 5 takes your texturing to the next level with UV-unwrapping techniques, showing you how to make very realistic textures created from photographic sources. The chapter then outlines normal mapping techniques, a valuable skill in games modeling, where you can use texturing to make low-detail models look as though they are highly detailed.

Chapter 6 returns to the earlier emphasis of modeling, this time outlining more unusual techniques than those presented in Chapter 2. The techniques presented here include lesser-used techniques, specifically for modeling with curved surfaces.

Chapters 7 and 8 look at animation. This is where your creations will be transformed from static models into moving, lifelike creatures. You will learn how keyframe-based animation is used in Blender and how you can set up your models so that they bend, and what you need to know in order to make them walk. Chapter 7 contains the basics of what you need to know to get started in animation, whereas Chapter 8 goes onto more advanced techniques, right up to how you can prepare the mouth shapes of characters for lip syncing animation.

Chapter 9 looks at how movies are can be made with Blender. You will learn how shots can be mixed in Blender's compositor, including greenscreen techniques. You will also learn how to use Blender's cutting room—the Video Sequence editor—in order to edit the shots of your own movies.

At the advanced end of the book, Chapter 10 looks at Blender's particle capabilities, which give you the power to generate special effects like water, hair, and smoke, while Chapter 11 explores how you can get started in making your own games, all completely within Blender!

Finally, Chapter 12 concludes the book by answering common problems users often face when they first use Blender. You will also be shown a range of resources you can use to continue to develop your skills, even after reading this book.

A Note on Blender Versions

This book was written at a time when Blender was undergoing some massive changes. The official Blender version is currently 2.49b, although the Blender Foundation has been working hard on a complete bottom-up rewrite of the code, and Blender 2.49b will soon be superseded by the 2.5 release of Blender, which is currently available as an optional download to the 2.49b release. I started writing this book when Blender 2.5 alpha 2 was available. During the time of writing, this "cutting-edge" release progressed through Blender 2.53 beta and then 2.54 beta, which is available now. There are significant differences between Blender 2.49b and the developing 2.5 version of Blender. In order to future-proof this book as much as possible, I have avoided addressing issues specific to the 2.49b release. Instead, emphasis is on the 2.5 branch of Blender. It is likely that by the time you hold this book, yet another update of Blender will have been released; however, given that the Blender this book is based on is the next version in the making, much of what I have covered should remain relevant through the next few versions to come.

Extras for This Book

This book contains many examples of many different things you can do in Blender. Various illustrations throughout the book show examples of what it being taught, taken as screenshots from my own computer while I was writing each section. I have tried to write the book in a way that makes the material directly applicable to your own work, although having access to example files can make understanding the exercises much easier. For this reason, you can download many of the example files used for my illustrations from the Source Code page on the Apress web site, at www.apress.com.

I very much hope that this book provides a key learning experience for people who will continue to enjoy Blender for a long time.

Please e-mail any feedback or suggestions to blenderbook@orcon.net.nz.

I would love to hear how this book has helped you, or how I could improve things in a future edition.

Lance Flavell

CHAPTER 1

■ ■ ■

History and Installation

First and foremost, Blender is a 3D modeling and animation studio package. If you are familiar with Autodesk Maya, Autodesk 3ds Max, NewTek LightWave, or other 3D modeling/animation applications, you'll have an idea of what Blender is like. If not, don't worry, you're in for a treat.

Think of animated cartoons, along the lines of those produced by DreamWorks, Pixar, and so forth. Think in terms of *Shrek, Toy Story, The Incredibles, Finding Nemo, Kung-Fu Panda, VeggieTales,* and so on. While those movies may not have actually used Blender (I'm throwing out random examples that most readers have heard of to give you an idea), they are in the genre of 3D animation that you would typically expect from Blender. Some clever computer graphics people spent time creating all the 3D characters in those movies, lovingly rigged them for animation, and rendered off the final film mix. To do this, they needed some pretty powerful computer programs known as *3D animation packages*. And that is the kind of program that Blender is.

Often, production pipelines require several powerful packages: one for modeling, another for texturing, others for animation and compositing. Fortunately, Blender is kind of a Swiss Army knife program in that it can do many of these tasks.

- Blender is a 3D modeler, which can make characters for movies.
- Blender has powerful texturing tools for painting the surface of the models.
- Blender has powerful rigging and animation functions. The models you create can then be made to move around and act.
- Blender has its own rendering engine and can be thought of as a complete lighting studio for a film. It also provides support for external renderers such as YafaRay and LuxRender.
- Unlike other 3D packages, Blender has its own compositing module, so movie "shots" can be mixed. Blender also has a unique video sequence editor, making it possible to cut and edit movie strips without having to rely on extra third-party applications for the final editing stage of production.
- Besides all of this it also has a full-blown game creation suite.

Now that you know what Blender is, the rest of the chapter will cover the following topics:

- A small sample of artwork made in Blender by experienced Blender users
- The history of how Blender originally came to be and how it has developed over the years
- How Blender has been used in real-life projects
- How to download and install Blender on your own machine

■ **Note** Blender is also an *open source* program. We'll see what that means later in the chapter.

Sample Blender Artwork

While Blender may have a steep learning curve, this book is designed to introduce you to the program in a logical and relatively painless way. That said, Blender is a very big program, providing many hours of ongoing study even after you have a good understanding of the basics.

To start, Figure 1–1 shows some artwork made with Blender from people at the BlenderArtists forums (www.blenderartists.org).

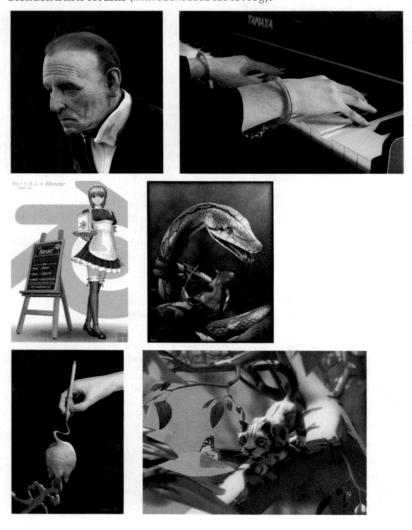

Figure 1–1. From left to right, Old Guy, by Kamil (maqs) Makowski; About Freedom of Speech, by Enrico Cerica (www.myline.be); Maid San, by FEDB; Snake and Mouse, by Anna Celarek (www.ania.xibo.at); Digital World, by Fabian Fricke (http://frigi.designdevil.de); and Mothbiter, by Derek Watts

Visit the BlenderArtists galleries at http://blenderartists.org/forum/ forumdisplay.php?f=27 for more.

Blender has been used in the making of TV advertisements and also some high-quality short films. *Elephants Dream* and *Big Buck Bunny* (see Figure 1–2) are Open Movie projects where only open source software (discussed in the next section) was used (as a rule), making Blender the primary choice. A third Open Movie, *Sintel* (see Figure 1–3), is set to be released at the same time this book is published.

These open projects, which are the initiative of the Blender Foundation, were made in order to stress that Blender is valuable at a professional level; each movie focuses on a different aspect of Blender (e.g., *Big Buck Bunny* focuses on Blender's particle-based hair and fur features).

Figure 1–2. Movies from the Blender Foundation: Elephants Dream (left) and Big Buck Bunny (right). © 2006 and 2008, Blender Foundation / www.elephantsdream.org, www.bigbuckbunny.org

Figure 1–3. Concept art and test model for Sintel. © copyright Blender Foundation | durian.blender.org

Blender History Timeline

Figure 1–4 shows the history of development from which Blender was born. In a nutshell, Ton Roosendaal, the cofounder of animation studio NeoGeo, was in charge of its in-house software. However, the company hit financial problems, and in 2002, with investors beginning to pull assets, Ton took the radical measure of offering the Blender software as public domain, on the proviso that the community of Blender enthusiasts could raise 100,000 euros to relinquish the debts. Blender had obtained a loyal following, and the bid succeeded within a few weeks. As promised, Blender was released as open source under the GNU General Public License (GPL), and Ton has since dedicated himself to ongoing development of the software. Blender has grown because of a strong following of users and developers who tirelessly work on improving the application and its uses.

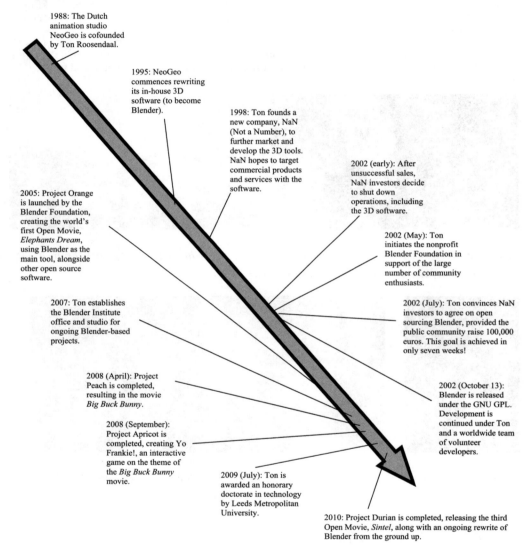

1988: The Dutch animation studio NeoGeo is cofounded by Ton Roosendaal.

1995: NeoGeo commences rewriting its in-house 3D software (to become Blender).

1998: Ton founds a new company, NaN (Not a Number), to further market and develop the 3D tools. NaN hopes to target commercial products and services with the software.

2002 (early): After unsuccessful sales, NaN investors decide to shut down operations, including the 3D software.

2005: Project Orange is launched by the Blender Foundation, creating the world's first Open Movie, *Elephants Dream*, using Blender as the main tool, alongside other open source software.

2002 (May): Ton initiates the nonprofit Blender Foundation in support of the large number of community enthusiasts.

2007: Ton establishes the Blender Institute office and studio for ongoing Blender-based projects.

2002 (July): Ton convinces NaN investors to agree on open sourcing Blender, provided the public community raise 100,000 euros. This goal is achieved in only seven weeks!

2008 (April): Project Peach is completed, resulting in the movie *Big Buck Bunny*.

2002 (October 13): Blender is released under the GNU GPL. Development is continued under Ton and a worldwide team of volunteer developers.

2008 (September): Project Apricot is completed, creating Yo Frankie!, an interactive game on the theme of the *Big Buck Bunny* movie.

2009 (July): Ton is awarded an honorary doctorate in technology by Leeds Metropolitan University.

2010: Project Durian is completed, releasing the third Open Movie, *Sintel*, along with an ongoing rewrite of Blender from the ground up.

Figure 1–4. Blender history timeline

■ **Note** For a more detailed breakdown of the timeline, see www.blender.org/blenderorg/blender-foundation/history.

Also of significant note is that, since 2007, the Blender developers have been hard at work on a complete bottom-up rewrite of the Blender code, with the goal of renewing the internal architecture and the user interface as well: this Blender series is called 2.5. You can find the development roadmap at www.blender.org/development/current-projects/blender-25-project.

What this means is there are currently *two* versions of Blender you can download:

- The current "stable" version, Blender 2.49b, which is the default download.

- The 2.5 release. This version, which is the new, rewritten Blender project, currently has some incomplete features, as it's still under heavy development; however, it is certainly very usable. Instructions throughout this book are based on the 2.5 version, as it will soon supersede the 2.49b release.

At the time of this writing, the very latest available version is 2.54 beta (see Figure 1–5 for the current release timeline). Ultimately, when all the version 2.5 features have been implemented, Blender will work toward a grand 2.6 series. As with the previous open projects by the Blender Foundation, project Durian (the *Sintel* movie) is being made to demonstrate that Blender 2.5 works at a professional level.

Figure 1–5. The Blender 2.5 development roadmap (courtesy of www.blender.org/development/current-projects/blender-25-project)

As you can see from Figures 1–6 and 1–7, the newer 2.54 beta version of Blender looks quite different from the 2.49b version.

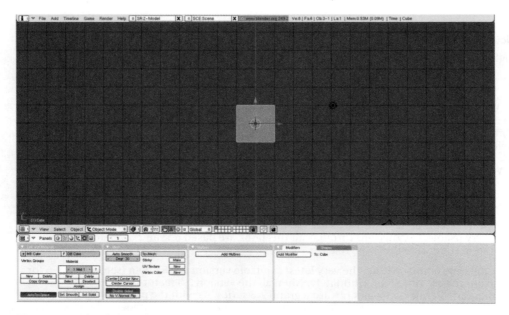

Figure 1–6. Blender 2.49b

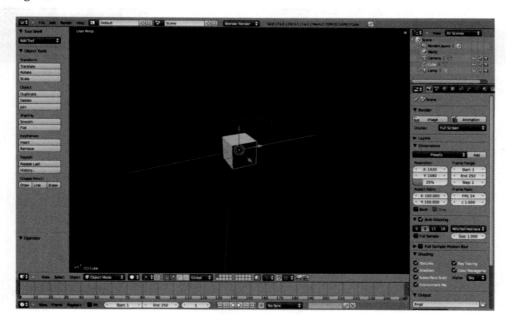

Figure 1–7. Blender 2.54 beta

Due to the free availability of Blender, many Blender artists are 3D graphics hobbyists and enthusiasts. However, Blender is increasingly being used by computer graphics industry professionals for commercial work. Some examples of this are shown in Figures 1–8 and 1–9.

Figure 1–8. Studio 125 used Blender in its pipeline for its animated TV series Me and Jessie D.

Figure 1–9. ProMotion Studio (now Red Cartel) has been using Blender alongside 3ds Max for a number of years.

■ **Note** The music video for "All Nightmare Long" (directed by Robert Schober), a song from the legendary metal group Metallica, used Blender for some of its animations and 3D special effects. About the animation, Schober says, "Most of it was done in ZBrush and Maya, but the bomber and giant walking robots were done using Blender" (see `www.blendernation.com/blender-used-in-pipeline-for-metallica-video`).

There are many more people using Blender for their projects. See Appendix A for some examples, or look online at `www.blender.org/community/professionals`.

About Open Source

In the history timeline shown previously, you can see that Blender has really made ripples by becoming public domain under the terms of the GNU GPL (see `www.gnu.org/licenses/gpl.html`).

When software is released as open source, it means that the software follows some very special copyright conditions, as dictated by whichever open source license is attached to the software. In the case of Blender, that license is the GPL (authored by Richard Stallman);this section will describe how the GPL makes Blender open source.

Essentially, open source works by acknowledging that the original author holds copyrights over the software, but that as the original owner, they give the rest of us permission to make copies on as many machines as we like. They give us full distribution rights to the software (we can give it away to our friends and we can also sell the product if we like). What we can't do is add extra conditions when distributing the software. We can't say to our friend, "I sold that to you so therefore you can't give it away." Once they have their copy, the GPL dictates that they have all the rights that we do.

What makes the GPL open source is how it affects the distribution of the program code. When released under the GPL, the conditions state that the uncompiled source code written to create the working program must also be freely available. If you are a developer (i.e., a programmer) and you see something you want to change, you can modify the code and build your own version of the program with the changes you want. This is different from the typical concept of copyright, where the original form of the program must be protected. It encourages programmers to get actively involved in contributing improvements to the software. The GPL has the restriction that your modified version should also be released as open source under the GPL (not all open source licenses require that the modified version be covered by the original license). Some like to call the freedoms given by the GPL "copyright reversed" or "copyleft" for this reason. It's better than just making the software "free of charge," because without the well-thought-out GPL, "free of charge" risks having conditions attached somewhere down the line.

This may sound wonderful (and it is), but what does it mean to you? How does it affect your using Blender for, say, commercial purposes? Some companies fear that by using open source, they may inadvertently lose the ability to keep a commercial ownership on any resulting work. To put their minds at ease, the sections that follow provide a summary of what is and is not included in Blender copyrights.

For a more detailed breakdown of the GPL terms of use regarding Blender, see the following:

- Appendix B, which covers the Blender terms of use (see also `www.blender.org/education-help/faq/gpl-for-artists`)

- Appendix C, which covers the GPL (see also `http://download.blender.org/release/GPL-license.txt`)

Do I Owe Royalties If I Use Blender for Commercial Work or Otherwise?

You are free to use Blender for any purpose—from private renders in your own home to commercial movies. The Blender Foundation will not be asking for royalties on any of your own work.

Does the GPL Apply to All the Work I Do with Blender?

No, work created with Blender is your sole property and can be licensed or sold under any conditions you prefer.

If I Download Blender for Free, Can I Give It Away? Can I Sell It?

You can give it away to your friends. You can make multiple copies of Blender. You can install it on any number of machines you like. You can even sell Blender. However, you must include the GPL terms in the documentation, which give the receiver full permission to also distribute Blender as they please. In other words, if you distribute Blender to someone, you cannot then restrict them from selling, or even giving Blender away for free, regardless of whether you sold it to them or even gave it to them in the first place.

What About Making Changes to Blender Source Code? Can I Market My Own Custom Version?

Certainly; being licensed under GPL, Blender allows you to look into its source code and change what you like. However, if you want to distribute your modified version, the GPL terms state that your revamped version must remain as free to distribute as the original versions. You must include full documentation of the code and the GPL license (see Appendix C), along with your revised version of Blender.

Technical Caveats

There are a few extra technical caveats I have not mentioned. While games can be made using Blender, the games engine is actually a mini version of Blender, and thus must remain under the GPL even if the game itself is to be under commercial copyright. In such cases, it is best to keep the game file and the engine as separate (not embedded) files to avoid end user confusion about what may be freely distributed. Also, the Blender and Blender Foundation logos are registered trademarks and must be respected as such (see www.blender.org/blenderorg/blender-foundation/logo).

Installing Blender

Blender is a very complex program. It uses every key on the keyboard in about three different ways (e.g., holding down Shift, Alt, Ctrl, and so on can bring about different functions for each key), and it uses some uncommon keys, such as those found on the number pad (referred to in the keyboard combinations in this book as "numpad"). The interface relies heavily on the user having a mouse with a wheel that can be clicked as a third button. So, provided you have a computer with a good amount of RAM, a reasonable graphics card, and a three-button mouse with a wheel (this being the third button), you should be able to run Blender.

Hardware

These days, there is a vast array of different computer specifications for any user, so it can be difficult to guarantee that any program will run on a given system. Generally speaking, though, the installation requirements for running Blender are as shown in Table 1–1 (see also www.blender.org/features-gallery/requirements).

Table 1–1. Blender Hardware Requirements

Hardware	Minimum Performance	Medium Performance	Production Standard
CPU	300MHz	2GHz dual-core	64-bit quad-core
RAM	128MB	2GB	8GB
Monitor	1024×768-pixel display with 16-bit color	1920×1200-pixel display with 24-bit color	Two 1920×1200-pixel displays with 24-bit color
Mouse	Two-button mouse (with wheel acting as third button)	Two-button mouse (with wheel acting as third button)	Two-button mouse (with wheel acting as third button), plus tablet
Keyboard	Working number pad (optional but recommended)	Working number pad (optional but recommended)	Working number pad
Graphics card	Open GL graphics card with 16MB RAM	Open GL graphics card with 128 or 256MB RAM	Open GL graphics card with 768MB RAM, ATI FireGL, or Nvidia Quadro

You should have at least 20MB of hard drive space for the install, in addition to ample space for your amazing 3D creations, especially if you're intending to go into animation; all those movie frames can add up! Bear in mind that professional production studios often far exceed these recommendations, eating terabytes of storage space (and then there's the backups to think of as well!). That said, these recommendations should be sufficient to get you up and running.

Operating Systems

Blender is available on a wide range of operating systems, including

- Windows
- Mac OS X
- Linux
- Irix
- Solaris

As mentioned earlier, there are currently two Blender versions available: the stable 2.49b release, which can be downloaded from www.blender.org/download/get-blender, and the highly recommended 2.5 release, which is available from the main www.blender.org page (follow the Blender 2.54 Beta link on the right). Note that different versions are available depending on your operating system and in some cases the type of processor you run (e.g., 32-bit vs. 64-bit versions).

■ **Note** FreeBSD users can download a port from www.freshports.org/graphics/blender, after which they can follow directions given at www.blender.org/development/release-logs/blender-254-beta to see whether the 2.5 version is available. At the moment of writing, Blender is available to FreeBSD as a 2.49 release.

A NOTE ABOUT PYTHON

Blender 2.5 relies on Python 3.1, although it should be contained within the download. If menus are missing in the program, it could be that Python needs to be downloaded. Python is a freely available scripting language available from www.python.org.

Let's look at how to install Blender 2.5 on a Linux machine.

Installation Example: Linux

Until the 2.5 release becomes the default, downloading Blender from the Download Now link on the main www.blender.org page will lead you to a download of the current Blender 2.49b release.

If you would like the cutting-edge Blender 2.5 version, follow the Blender 2.54 Beta link (note that this may have been updated since publication). Depending on whether your machine is a 64- or 32-bit model, choose either Linux x86-64 or Linux x86-32.

Once you have the correct Blender package, you can either install it through your GUI window manager (e.g., Gnome, KDE, etc.) by double-clicking the file, or by using a command terminal.

Using the GUI

Right-click the file. A menu should appear with a choice of something like "Extract here." Select this, and a new `blender` directory will be created. To run Blender, simply go into this directory and double-click the Blender icon.

Using the Command Line

Navigate to where you downloaded the file, and then type the following at the command line, using the version you have downloaded:

```
tar -jxfv blender-2.5.tar.bz2
```

Note that the `blender-2.5.tar.bz2` in the preceding command will likely be something like `blender-2.54-beta-linux-glibc27-i686.tar.bz2`, but I've shortened the file name to make the instructions less confusing, as the actual version number may have changed by the time you read this.

This should create a similarly named folder containing the Blender files.

Now type

```
cd blender-2.5/
```

(or whichever directory was created), and then type

```
./blender
```

Blender should then start up.

Installation Example: Windows

Until the 2.5 release becomes the default, downloading Blender from the Download Now link on the main `www.blender.org` page will lead you to a download of the current Blender 2.49b release. This is fine, but you might choose to install the 2.5 version instead, since it will soon be the standard. To download the new version, click the specific link on the page.

There are two main things to note when deciding which Blender install file to download:

- It is important that you decide which version of Blender is right for your machine. You need to know whether you have a 64-bit or 32-bit model, since there are separate downloads for these.

- The next consideration is one of personal choice: do you want an easy autoinstaller (see Figure 1–10), or would you like a portable version? The difference is that the installer opens a wizard (i.e., where you click the Next button to perform successive steps) to guide you through installing Blender on your system. Take care to check each screen, as the last window asks an important question about where you want the saved Blender files to go. The portable version is a ZIP archive that unzips to a folder that can be run from your hard drive, or even placed on a USB stick to be run on a different computer (provided the target machine meets the required specs).

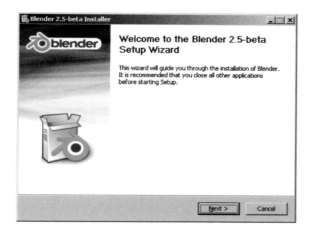

Figure 1–10. The Windows system installer

If you have decided on the ZIP version, simply unzip the files, go into the resulting directory, and double-click the Blender icon. If you do not have Python, you may like to visit www.python.org and download the version that your Blender release was compiled with.

If you instead download the system installer, double-click it and follow the prompts. Python will be bundled as part of the install.

Summary

This chapter covered Blender briefly and gave an overview of its history. Blender was not always free; it began as a commercial application that became open source when its founding company had difficulties. This move gave Blender a real surge in interest, and Blender is now supported by a strong and very talented community.

Now you should have Blender installed on your machine , and you should be ready to take your first look into what you can do with this incredibly powerful program.

CHAPTER 2

■ ■ ■

The Interface

This chapter will give you a hands-on tour of Blender. With an interface jam-packed full of buttons, Blender can be quite daunting at first. We will approach the interface slowly, and by the end of the chapter you should be able to navigate it well enough to make simple models from basics primitive shapes.

Please note that I will be using some abbreviated terminology to simplify instructions. Where you see the terms LMB, MMB, and RMB, these refer to the left, middle, and right mouse buttons, respectively, with the middle mouse button usually doubling as the mouse wheel (MW). Note that you have to be able to click your MW to perform MMB actions. Figure 2–1 shows the layout of the mouse I am referring to.

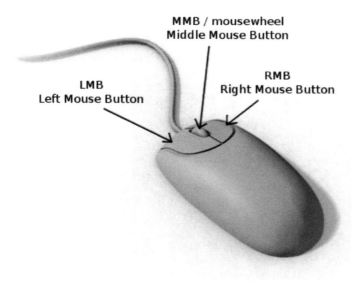

Figure 2–1. *The mouse buttons*

The Blender Interface

When starting Blender, you will be greeted with the splash screen shown in Figure 2–2.

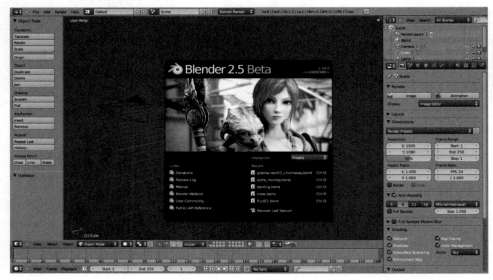

Figure 2–2. *Splash screen for Blender 2.5*

LMB-click to remove the initial title box, and you'll be left with the setup shown in Figure 2–3.

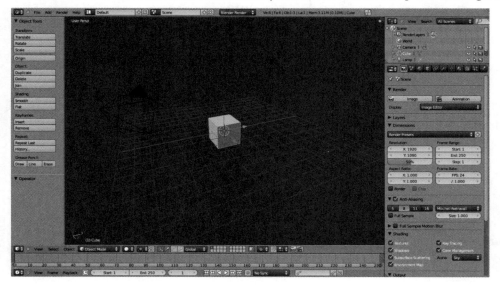

Figure 2–3. *Blender's default layout*

Blender has a *lot* of buttons. Thankfully though, you don't need to familiarize yourself with all of them before you can start using Blender. (That's the mistake I made when first trying to learn the program). For now, the main action is all done in the main 3D View window where you can see the cube, and the basic operations can be performed with simple mouse actions.

Changing the View

Blender has quite a list of controls for changing the view, which you will become familiar with over time. To get started, you should see which ones you think are the most useful. Try the following mouse manipulations in the 3D area:

- *MW roll*: Position your mouse somewhere over the main 3D view and roll the MW up and down to zoom your view in and out.

- *Shift+MW roll*: Rolling the MW while holding down Shift causes the window area to scroll vertically.

- *Ctrl+MW roll*: Ctrl works like the Shift key, but for horizontal scroll.

- *MMB drag*: Place your mouse over the middle of the screen, and this time hold the MMB/MW down. Without letting go of the MMB, move your mouse around. You should now be able to orient your point of view, trackball style.

- *Shift+MMB drag*: Hold down Shift and then perform the same MMB drag as before. With Shift held down, you will be able to pan the view. Make sure you press the Shift key before the MMB, and that you hold it down for the duration of the mouse movement.

- *Ctrl+MW drag*: Hold down the Ctrl key and then the MMB. Keeping both down, move the mouse vertically. This performs a zoom that is smoother than rolling the MW by itself.

Please note that the preceding actions are contextual in regard to where the mouse pointer is. For example, if you want to zoom a certain window, you should roll the MW *while the mouse pointer is over the target window*. If the mouse pointer is positioned elsewhere (e.g., over the side panels), you won't be able to zoom (and you might even accidentally perform an unwanted action on the window or panel immediately below the mouse pointer).

The View Menu

So far, you know how to zoom and rotate your point of view using the MW, along with a few other keys such as Ctrl and Shift. If you are working on a model and want to look at it directly from the front or side, it can be very difficult to precisely reposition the view with your mouse. However, there is a special View menu in the header strip at the bottom of the 3D window that contains presets for top, front, side, and camera views (I will discuss the camera in more depth later on). See Figure 2–4 to see what this menu looks like. Note that these views also have number pad shortcuts (e.g., hovering your mouse over the 3D area and pressing numpad 3 will snap to side view). Holding the Ctrl key makes the shortcut keys work from the opposite angle (e.g., numpad 7 gives the view from top, whereas Ctrl+numpad 7 gives the view from the bottom).

Make sure Num Lock is active if you're using the number pad key shortcuts.

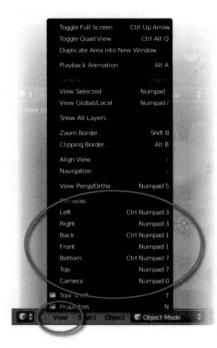

Figure 2–4. *The View menu, showing view shortcuts*

This View menu is especially useful for splitting the screen into different areas, which we will be looking at next.

REDUCING THE CLUTTER

Things can get very messy when you begin to split the screen, so I first want to mention how you can hide a couple of panels that can get in the way and confuse your perception of the views. With your mouse hovering over the main 3D view, you can perform the following actions:

Press T to show/hide the Tool Shelf panel.

Press N to toggle the Properties panel.

These panels are very useful and will be covered later on, but for now it may help simplify things by putting them away.

Now you should be able to change the point of view of a single window, as well as zoom in, rotate the point of view, and pan in different directions (up, down, left, and right), all via keyboard shortcuts and/or the View menu. The next step is to manipulate the screen windows themselves to customize your screen layout.

Splitting the Screen

This is a very important part of the Blender interface that makes Blender different from other 3D apps. Not only can you split windows into different layout arrangements, you can customize them by dragging around individual window edges and create new areas as needed.

Custom Window Splitting

In Blender 2.5, each window has diagonal stripes at the top-right and bottom-left corners (see Figure 2–5). To split a screen, position your mouse over this corner (when the mouse pointer changes to a cross, you are in the right position), hold down the LMB, and drag toward the center of the window (e.g., if you are using the top-right corner, drag either left or down; if you are using the bottom-left corner, drag up or to the right).

Figure 2–5. Diagonal stripes at the top right of the window border

So far, so good. You should now be able to split the screen into multiple windows and really clutter things up. But how do you separate them again?

Joining windows back together is very much the opposite of separating them. Place your mouse over the top-right (or bottom-left) stripes of the window next to the one you wish to remove. As with splitting windows, the mouse pointer will become a cross when you are on the right spot. This time, instead of dragging the corner into the window, drag it outward. This movement will expand the window so that it takes over the next area.

Maximizing Windows

Split windows enough times and you'll soon find each area becomes too small to reasonably work in, but you can snap any window to full size on demand (and then back again) as needed. Make sure the mouse pointer is over the window you wish to expand. Hold the Shift key down and press the spacebar. The window immediately underneath the mouse pointer will snap to full screen (press Shift+spacebar a second time to return it to its previous size). This is very useful when your layout becomes full of tiny windows. A spacious full-screen view of the window you want to work in is much better than a view the size of a postage stamp.

Blender Window Conventions

Notice that Blender has a variety of panels with lots of buttons. I'll discuss the specific panels later, but now is a good time to go over some basic fundamentals of how Blender windows and panels operate.

Every window consists of a large area (for now, you have been working with one that shows the 3D view), and includes diagonal lines at the top-right and bottom-left corners that you can use to split the window into more windows. You can also LMB-drag the edges of windows to resize them.

Each window also has a *header strip* running along the top or the bottom (see Figure 2–6). You can change whether this header strip is at the top or bottom of a window by RMB-clicking it and choosing Flip to Top or Flip to Bottom on the menu that appears.

Figure 2–6. Header strip with the window type set to 3D View (cube icon)

The menu options on the header strip may change depending on the context, but the most important button remains at the far left end of any header strip. This button is the Window Type button (as indicated in Figure 2–6). Clicking this button opens a menu of the different kinds of windows Blender can host, and selecting from this list changes the information that is shown in the larger window view. Among the views you can choose from are timelines and graph editors for animation (note that the default Blender layout includes a Timeline window along the bottom of the screen, with the Window Type button displaying an icon of a clock), a UV/image editor (most often used in texturing a model's surface), and a video sequence editor for editing movies. Also on this menu is a Properties option, which fills the window with buttons like the panel on the right of the default view.

At this point, you will mainly be interested in the 3D View window type. I am showing you the other options so that you know how to access them, as required in later chapters.

The default layout for Blender has a vertical set of panels at the far right of the screen. These are in fact two windows, each containing a number of panels.

The top one is the Outliner window (Figure 2–7), which displays a tree list of the items in your scene (you usually start off with a camera, a cube, and a lamp). Among other things, the Outliner is useful for efficiently LMB-selecting an object when you have lost it from the main 3D view.

Figure 2–7. The Outliner

Below the Outliner is a Properties window, which contains many buttons (see Figure 2–8). These buttons may change depending on what is selected and the kind of task being performed. The thing to take note of is that the top presents a row of tabs that group the many available buttons into various types of tasks.

Hovering your mouse over these tabs reveals headings for the kinds of settings each tab deals with; options include Render (camera icon), Scene, World, and Object. We will explore some of these in more depth in later chapters.

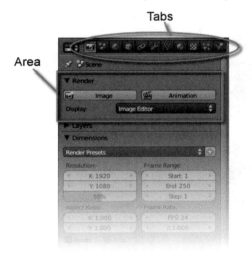

Figure 2–8. *The Properties panel*

Below these tabs are many buttons and slider controls. They are sorted into labeled rectangular areas that can be expanded or minimized by LMB-clicking the triangular arrow to the left of each respective label. The top-right of each area has handles (the diagonal lines) that allow you to LMB-drag the areas into a different order if there are some options you want to place at the top for easy access.

Take care not to confuse the Properties editor buttons, the Properties panel reached via the N key, and the Tool Shelf reached via the T key (these last two toggle on and off when pressing N or T with the mouse pointer over a 3D view). Admittedly, having the 3D view Properties panel and also the editor type named Properties is confusing; however, as long as you are aware of the places to look for options, you should soon get the hang of finding the tools you are after.

Multiple-View Setup

Now that you can create (or divide) new window sections and have seen how Blender windows work, you should be able to split the screen into separate areas for different views of your work. For example, you could divide the screen into four views and then use the View menu to show top, front, side, and camera angles in each section.

As it turns out, the numpad 7, numpad 1, and numpad 3 shortcut keys for the View menu we looked at earlier are not randomly placed. They form an *L* shape on the number pad of your keyboard, which corresponds to the onscreen positioning when making a classic four-planar view (top-left for top view, bottom-left for front view, and bottom-right for side view). Figure 2–9 shows a typical four-planar layout with the top, front, and side views matching the number pad hotkey layout.

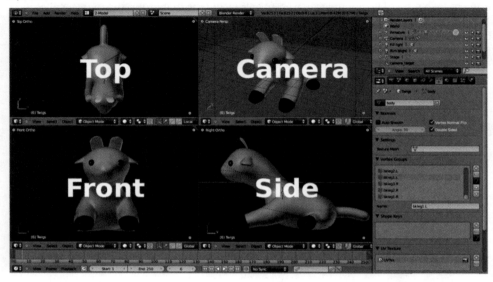

Figure 2–9. *Blender split into traditional four-planar view*

The button at the far left of the header strip of any window allows you to change the window type, as shown in Figure 2–10. This means you can specify whether the window area is for viewing 3D space, whether it is a panel of buttons or a timeline, and so on. For now, you will be working with the main 3D view, for which the Window Type button will display a cube.

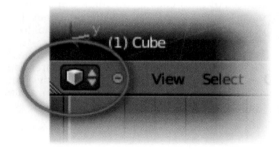

Figure 2–10. *Cube icon indicating the 3D View window type*

You should now be able to lay out the Blender windows pretty much any way you like. Blender is incredibly flexible in this area, and it is worth practicing the interface until adjusting windows becomes second nature. Often you will want to work in a traditional four-planar view, using Shift+spacebar to toggle which window you want to view as full screen.

Built-In Screen Layouts

In addition to creating your own window layouts, you can call up certain premade window arrangements from a drop-down list at the top of the screen (see Figure 2–11). The given layouts are useful for common purposes; one is optimized for animation, and so forth. These are adjustable as well; make alterations to one of the layouts and it will remain even after switching back and forth between others on the list. There is also an Add button (the + sign), which you can use to increase the number of layouts on the list.

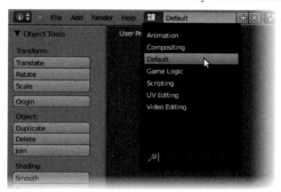

Figure 2–11. The Screen Layout menu

Adding New Objects

Now that you are getting to grips with the Blender interface itself, let's look at adding items so you can build your own 3D scene. Blender comes equipped with a certain number of *primitives*, which are basic shapes like cubes, tubes, and spheres. These are useful for starting modeling (covered in Chapter 3).

The Cursor

LMB-click random places around the 3D screen. You will notice that a target symbol appears wherever you LMB-click. This is known as the cursor, and is shown in Figure 2–12. It will becomes very useful later on, but for now, all you need to know is that it shows where the next object you are going to add to your scene will appear.

Figure 2–12. The cursor

Choosing a New Object

Once the cursor is in position, press Shift+A to bring up the Add menu (Figure 2–13). Once the menu appears, click Add ➤ Mesh, and select an object of your choice.

■ **Note** A *mesh* is a 3D object. The name "mesh" is descriptive of how Blender thinks of 3D objects, forming them out of connected *vertex points*. A cube, for example, has six faces, which are formed by a net of eight connected vertex points on the corners. I'll cover this in Chapter 3 in the discussion of editing shapes. For now, just adding mesh objects as they are is fine.

Figure 2–13. The Add Mesh menu

Of course, you don't have to be limited to cubes, just because a cube appears in every new file. You could have performed Add ➤ Mesh ➤ Monkey or Add ➤ Mesh ➤ UV Sphere, for example.

There are a number of points I would like to raise here:

- If you open the Tool Shelf (press the T key), extra options appear at the bottom for certain shapes. For example, if you add a UV Sphere, you'll have options for segments, rings, size, and so on. You can change these properties as you see fit.

- A transformation (movement, rotation, scaling, etc.) only happens to the currently selected item. To choose a different object to manipulate, RMB-click the object.

- You can select several items by holding down the Shift key while selecting each in turn.

- Press the A key to toggle between "select all" and "select nothing."

- To destroy a selected object, press the X key.

- Shift+D makes a duplicate copy of the currently selected object. This new copy tends to follow your mouse around until you LMB-click to drop it.

Moving Things Around

Once you can add objects, you'll be wanting to make something in Blender. But first, you need to know how to move objects around. As a general rule for any 3D program, you should at least be able to perform the following operations on any given object:

- *Move*: Moving a selected object where you want in 3D space
- *Rotate*: Turning an object to face a specified direction
- *Scale*: Resizing an object

Moving Objects

Start Blender (or choose File ➤ New in the top menu). RMB-click the cube to select it. Once selected, the cube will show colored manipulator arrows, as in Figure 2–14.

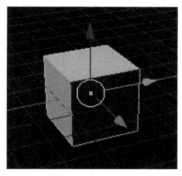

Figure 2–14. *Cube with manipulator arrows*

If the manipulator arrows do not show

- Make sure the cube is selected (RMB-click it).
- Make sure the manipulator icon at the bottom of the window is active (e.g., it is pressed down, as in Figure 2–15).

Figure 2–15. *Use this button to turn the visual manipulator on or off.*

- Make sure you are in object mode, and that the pivot mode is set to median point or bounding box center (Figure 2–16 shows the icons of these settings). If you need to change either setting, click the appropriate icon, and a drop-down list will appear, allowing you to choose other options.

Figure 2–16. *Object mode (left) and the median point setting of pivot mode (right)*

Moving the object is easy. Simply hold the LMB on one of the arrows and drag in the direction you wish the cube to move. Notice that you can only move the cube parallel to the arrow you are pulling. You can drag in all directions by LMB-dragging the circle where the manipulator arrows meet.

Notice that each arrow is a different color (red, green, and blue). These colors indicate different x, y, and z axis directions (red = x, green = y, and blue = z). To help you remember this, Blender has a small diagram of the axis directions at the bottom left of any 3D window, as shown in Figure 2–17.

Figure 2–17. *Axis diagram*

LMB-dragging the arrows can be tedious after a while, and the manipulator arrows are sometimes easy to miss. The shortcut key G (for "grab") can be used to drag a selected object.

■ **Note** Your mouse should be over the 3D view when pressing the G key, and preferably near the selected object. At first this makes the object follow mouse movements all over the screen.

While you are moving the object around, you can press the X, Y, or Z keys to move the object in the respective directions; it's just the same as if you had pulled the arrows.

Rotating Objects

Now that you can move an object, follow these steps to rotate it:

1. Place your mouse near the edge of the object.
2. Press the R key once.
3. Move the mouse around the object in circles to watch it rotate.
4. LMB-click to release the object in place, or press Esc to cancel.

Here's something different to try; normal rotation causes the object to rotate clockwise or counterclockwise as you look at it. If you press R twice, however, the rotation changes to trackball mode. This means that when you move the mouse pointer across the front of the object, it spins toward or away from the camera instead. The differences between normal and trackball rotation are shown in Figure 2–18.

Figure 2–18. *Normal rotation (left) and trackball rotation (right)*

Changing the Manipulator Arrows

As mentioned previously, you can use the manipulator arrows to drag objects around the screen. However, by changing the arrow type from movement to rotation, you can also use the manipulator arrows to rotate objects as well.

As shown in Figure 2–19, in the 3D window header ia a menu for the manipulator selection tools (look just to the left of the word "Global").

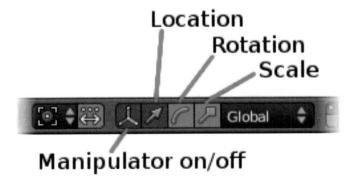

Figure 2–19. *Manipulator controls*

The leftmost button is a toggle for turning the manipulator on and off, and the other buttons are switches for manipulating location (movement), rotation, or scale (size). To rotate the selected object, select the Rotation icon (the curved line). The manipulator arrows on the object will change to rings, as shown in Figure 2–20, which can be used to rotate the object in much the same way as the arrows are used to move it.

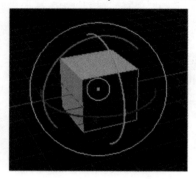

Figure 2–20. *Rotational manipulators*

The Difference Between Global and Local

Now that you can rotate objects (using either the R key shortcut or the manipulator tool in rotation mode), you should take special note of the difference between *global* and *local* coordinates. The difference is that with global coordinates, the x, y, and z directions are given in terms of world space. This means that z is always up, no matter which way an object is rotated. However, in local coordinates, z is up only in terms of the object itself. So if the object were rotated 90 degrees, then local z would be pointing out to the side. If the object were upside down, then the local z direction would be downward (even though global z direction is upward), as demonstrated in Figure 2–21.

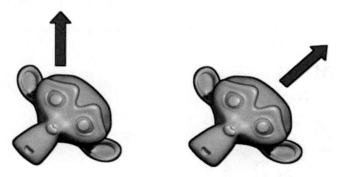

Figure 2–21. *Global up (left) and local up (right)*

Just to the right of the manipulator tool buttons is a drop-down list where you can change whether the manipulator arrows work on global or local coordinates (there are a few other options on the list, but for now Global and Local are the ones that matter). Notice that when you change from one to the other, the manipulator arrows change.

When moving objects with shortcut keys (e.g., G, R, or S followed by X, Y, or Z), the xyz direction moves according to global coordinates. However, if you press X, Y, or Z twice, it will toggle to local mode. Pressing X, Y, or Z a third time resets the movement (as though X, Y, or Z had never been pressed).

That may sound complicated, but it really isn't. Just to illustrate the point, try this:

Start with the default cube, and rotate it so it is not straight up and down.

1. Change the manipulator to local, so that the manipulators are diagonal (the same angle at which the object has been tilted).

2. Press G and then X, and you can see the movement is global.

3. Press X another time and watch the movement change to local.

4. Press X a third time to reset the axis movement. Pressing X again just steps through the cycle (it's like going back to step 3).

Hopefully this isn't too difficult to understand; but if so, don't worry, since most of the time you will be dealing with global coordinates anyway.

Scaling Objects

Now that we've examined moving and rotating, it's time to look at the third basic action, scaling. To get an idea of how to scale objects, perform the following exercise:

Select the cube (RMB-click it).

1. Place the mouse pointer near the edge of the cube.

2. Press S.

3. Draw the mouse pointer away from the cube (do not hold any mouse buttons) to enlarge it.

4. LMB-click to finalize the scale operation or press Esc to cancel.

Experiment with the same principles that you did with rotation. Look at what happens when you press the X key while scaling (it expands in global X direction). With a rotated object, examine what happens when you press X twice (if Local is selected from the drop-down list, then the scale will change to local).

Note that when using the manipulator tool with scaling, the manipulators look like they did with movement, except the arrowheads are squares, as shown in Figure 2–22. LMB-dragging each manipulator arrow will stretch the object along the respective axis, whereas dragging from the middle area (where the manipulator arrows are connected) will scale the object in all directions.

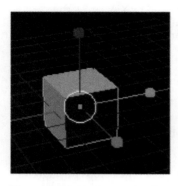

Figure 2–22. Scale manipulators

■ **Note** If you scale something small enough, it eventually flips to an upside-down state. This is because you've made it smaller than zero and have thus inverted the object. This actually turns the object inside out, creating a situation known as *inverted normals*. Not all textures work when an object is inverted, so it's generally best to avoid shrinking things to negative size.

Early in this chapter, we got rid of a couple of panels to make the screen less cluttered. One of them, the Properties panel, is now going to prove useful. Press the N key to bring up the Properties panel, which is shown in Figure 2–23.

This panel contains rotation, location, and scale information about any selected object. When you move the object around, the information in the Properties panel updates. You can also type numbers directly into the properties boxes, and when you press Enter, the object will adjust accordingly.

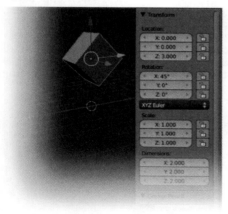

Figure 2–23. The Properties panel

While the Properties panel is a useful tool for examining and manipulating the positional properties of objects, it may also help you to understand what is happening internally to your object while we look at the undo commands (in the "Undoing Things" section later in the chapter).

Using Numbers

As mentioned previously, you can specify the direction to which a transform applies by pressing X, Y, or Z while the transform is being made. For example, pressing X while scaling a cube will make the cube scale/stretch along the global X axis, and pressing X, X while scaling the cube will result in the cube scaling along its own local X axis.

You can also type in numbers to achieve a similar effect on an object that is being moved, scaled, or rotated. Here are some examples:

- If you scale a cube along the X axis (press S and then X), and then type 4 and press Enter, the cube will move along the X axis a length of 4 Blender units. (A *Blender unit* is the size of one of the squares in the floor grid of the 3D view, and the default cube is normally 2 Blender units wide).

- If you are rotating an object and type in 45 or 90, the object will be rotated 45 or 90 degrees, respectively.

Use the Properties panel to study the result.

Layers

We haven't had a need to use layers yet because we have been working in a single view with only a few objects. Later on though, when dealing with many objects, layers will become very useful. The idea with layers is that you can set various objects to belong to different layers (layer01, layer02, layer03, etc.), and then turn those layers on or off to show or hide the objects.

Along the header strip of a 3D view is a section made of small squares representing the different layers (see Figure 2–24). By default, the top-left square (layer01) is activated. You can activate other layers by LMB-clicking the squares. Using Shift-LMB (hold down the Shift key while clicking different squares), you can turn on several layers at the same time. Note that the default cube is on layer01 only, and therefore seems to disappear when the view is switched to other layers.

Figure 2–24. *Layers in the header strip*

The ordinary number keys along the top of the keyboard perform as shortcuts to layers. Pressing 1 sends you to layer01, pressing 2 to layer02, and so on; pressing 0 sends you to layer10. Holding down the Alt key while pressing layers allows shortcut access for layer11 through layer20. For example, Alt+5 is the shortcut for activating layer15.

Some desktop environments (e.g., Gnome on Linux) have other uses for the Alt key that interfere with the preceding actions. In most cases, you can fix this by holding down a special key (e.g., the Windows key, next to Alt), while the Alt key is pressed. However, this has more to do with your individual desktop settings than with Blender itself, as Blender is designed to respond to the Alt key.

To move an object to a different layer, RMB-select the object and then press the M key. The Move to Layer dialog will appear (see Figure 2–25), allowing you to select the layer(s) on which you wish the selected object to appear. Again, you can use the Shift key to specify multiple layers. This is helpful when you want several objects to have their own layers, and also when you want to set up a final "view all" layer, where they are all present.

Figure 2–25. *Move to Layer dialog*

■ **Note** While you can use layers to hide objects (by moving them to a separate layer from the one you are viewing), you can also hide selected items by pressing the H key, and unhide them again by pressing Alt+H. Layers allow more flexibility, however, because they allow hiding/unhiding on a more selective basis.

Undoing Things

There are two types of undo in Blender:

- The standard undo allows you to take one step back in your working process. Each time you press Ctrl+Z, Blender goes back one step. Pressing Shift+Ctrl+Z is the opposite (redo), so if you undo too far back, just redo until you are at the right step. Needless to say, if you undo a few times and then make a change, you lose any redo from there.

- The second kind of undo is more of a refresh, as explained in this section.

Every object in Blender knows its rested state; that is, where it would be had it never been moved, resized, or scaled. Using the Alt key, we can tell any selected object to reset itself in terms of location, rotation, or scale. Following are the available reset options:

- *Alt+G*: Resets the location to the global center

- *Alt+R*: Resets the rotation so the object stands upright in global coordinates

- *Alt+S*: Resets the scale to the object's original size

Put simply, the Alt+G/R/S reset commands work by repositioning an object to its rested state of position 0,0,0, rotation of 0 degrees, or size of 1, respectively. You can verify this by examining the data shown in the Properties panel.

This is all very well, but what if you want to change an object's rested position? For example, you might want the rested position to be 45 degrees diagonal, or the default shape to be taller. The solution is to make the change to the object, and then lock it in its new positioning by selecting Object ➤ Apply ➤ Location/Rotation/Scale (depending on which you want to preserve) from the bottom menu. From then on, your object will reset to the new position.

Saving Your Work

To save your work, go to File ➤ Save or File ➤ Save As. The first time you save, and each time you perform a save-as, you will see a file manager allowing you to navigate to where you would like to store your file. The file manager works like it does in many other programs. There are a few things to take special note of, though:

- Standard buttons to navigate directories/folders are along the top of the file manager, followed to the right by buttons to control various aspects of the layout such as icon size, the order in which items are listed, and whether to show/hide various file types from view.

- In the left column of the file manager are useful bookmarks and a list of recent save locations.

- There are two text areas at the top. The first contains the file path (which directory/folder location the file will be saved in) and the second contains the name of the file.

- After the file name, there are + and – buttons (the keyboard shortcuts for them are numpad + and numpad –). Pressing these automatically adds a number to the name of a file so that successive saves are easy. For example, if your file is called `superdog01.blend`, pressing the + button will rename the save to `superdog02.blend`. (It is a good idea to keep copies of previous saves in the event that you make mistakes.)

  Be sure to click the Save As Blender File button when you are ready to save.

Exercises

Now that you have had some time looking at the basics of Blender, it's time to put them into practice. It is important that the functions of this chapter become second nature, so please take some time to complete at least one of the following exercises. I suggest you try one task, sleep on it, and then try the other.

Exercise 1: Making a Robot

Using primitive shapes (cubes, tubes, spheres, etc.), piece together your own robot (two of mine are shown in Figure 2–26). You can combine primitives together to make interesting shapes as needed (the smaller robot shown has a dome top, which was made by positioning a UV sphere over a tube). Make your robot as simple or as detailed as you like. When done, save it as `myrobot.blend`.

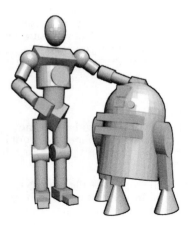

Figure 2–26. Robots formed from cubes, spheres, tubes, and a few cones

Exercise 2: The Ten-Cube Challenge

Another interesting exercise is to see what you can make from ten cubes, examples of which can be seen in Figure 2–27. This idea was used as a creative challenge on the BlenderArtists.org forums, where even seasoned artists participated for fun.

- For any model, use ten cubes maximum.

- At first, adding ten cubes can be cumbersome. You may prefer to duplicate the first cube with Shift+D.

- You may stretch the cubes directionally with scale, but only in rectangular directions; do not pull them out of shape. (If a cube has been rotated, be sure to scale it in the local direction.)

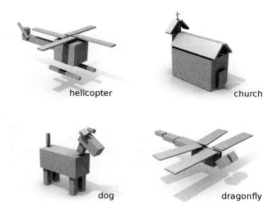

Figure 2–27. Models formed from ten cubes

Useful Keyboard Shortcuts

We've covered a lot of commands in this chapter, so let's round things out with a reference guide. Table 2–1 describes some useful keyboard shortcuts for manipulating objects.

Table 2–1. Some Useful Keyboard Shortcuts

Function	Description
Shift+A	Add a new object
RMB-click	Select an object
A	Select/deselect all objects
Shift+LMB	Select multiple objects
G	Move a selected object
R	Rotate a selected object
S	Scale a selected object

The G, R, and S shortcuts can be followed by pressing the X, Y, or Z keys either once or twice, depending on whether you want to move/rotate/scale in specific global or local directions.

This chapter also demonstrated how to use the manipulator tools to perform the equivalent actions to the G, R, and S shortcuts.

There are other useful keyboard shortcuts as well, such as those shown in Table 2–2.

Table 2–2. Other Useful Keyboard Shortcuts

Useful Key	Description
X	Delete a selected object
Shift+D	Duplicate (copy) a selected object

Using these and others shortcuts, you can create simple scenes by piecing together basic object primitives.

Summary

This chapter has given an introduction to the complex interface of Blender. You should now know how to split and join windows, and how to navigate the 3D view using the MMB/MW. Additionally, this chapter covered adding objects and moving them around. Table 2–1 describes some useful keyboard shortcuts for manipulating objects.

In the next chapter, we are going to look more in depth at modeling. You will learn how to make your own shapes from scratch, including how to model based on blueprints.

CHAPTER 3

■ ■ ■

Modeling

We ended the last chapter with making simple shapes by positioning premade mesh objects. This is fine if you want to make boxlike characters, but Blender can make much more realistic models. In this chapter, we are going to go to the next level and edit the mesh objects themselves.

We will be advancing from moving premade primitives around to making our own models. We are going to look at two different approaches:

- *Direct mesh editing*: A more traditional approach commonly used by professional modelers

- *Sculpting*: A fast and fun way of shaping a model, also useful for fine details like wrinkles

Finally, we will examine a way of combining both methods to make the most of the advantages of each. By the end of this chapter you will have learned the techniques to make full 3D versions of your imaginary characters and designs.

What Is a Mesh?

While the better models in Blender may look convincingly real, we know that the 3D objects in Blender are not real, but a 3D illusion. When Blender creates a 3D object, it has to think of the object in terms of a mesh. To make any polygon object, you need the elements described in the following subsections.

Origin Point

First you need an origin point. This doesn't affect the shape of the object itself, but is the location of the object as a whole. You may have already noticed an orange dot that appears in the middle of selected objects. This dot is the origin point (see Figure 3–1). The shape of the model is built around this origin point, and when it is moved, scaled, or rotated, the object follows along likewise. The origin represents the very heart of the object itself.

Figure 3–1. The origin point

Vertices

Around the origin point, the model takes shape as a series of dots known as vertex points or vertices. By themselves, the vertices merely form a cloud of floating points, and need something more in order to define a solid-looking object (see Figure 3–2).

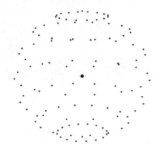

Figure 3–2. Vertices

Edges

The vertices are connected point to point by lines known simply as edges. This makes the form much easier to see, creating what is commonly known as a *wireframe* of the object (see Figure 3–3).

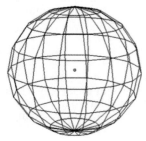

Figure 3–3. Edges

Faces

Three edges can form a triangle, and four can make a square; a *face* is made when those edges are filled in as a solid surface. When the mesh is made of faces, it finally looks solid (see Figure 3–4). Faces can be colored to make realistic textures on an object (this will be covered Chapter 4 and 5).

Figure 3–4. Faces

Edit Mode

In Chapter 2 we looked at the interface of Blender, how to split windows, how to move objects around, and so on. Obviously, editing our own objects is going to increase the complexity. The good news is that many of the skills involving moving objects around are reusable in the editing stage. Blender can seem very hard to learn at first, especially with the number of shortcut keys it employs, but is it very consistent with them, making new skills less difficult to pick up.

We are about to practice using some common mesh-editing functions. Start with the default scene by selecting File ➤ New or pressing Ctrl+N.

On starting Blender, you are in object mode. Click the list and change to edit mode (Figure 3–5). Alternatively, you can press the Tab key to switch between object and edit modes.

Figure 3–5. Switching to edit mode

USING THE TAB KEY TO SWITCH MODES

On starting Blender, Tab toggles between object and edit mode, but this is not always the case. The truth is that Tab switches between edit mode and whichever mode you were otherwise in. So, if you are in sculpt mode, pressing Tab will toggle back and forth between sculpt and edit modes, for example.

When going into edit mode the first time, often all vertices of the object will be preselected (e.g., the whole cube will be orange). Deselect everything by pressing A (toggles select all/deselect all) so that nothing is selected (the edge wires look black).

Check that you are in vertex select mode. You can confirm this by looking at the bottom of your 3D window and ensuring that the "Vertex select mode" button is depressed (Figure 3–6).

Figure 3–6. Vertex select mode

Now select one of the corner vertices of the cube by RMB-clicking it. Then you can move the selected corner vertex using the G key or by LMB-dragging the manipulator arrows, just as when moving objects in Chapter 2 (see Figure 3–7). You cannot scale or rotate a single vertex point. However, if you select several vertices (e.g., using Shift to select a few points), the selected area can be rotated and scaled.

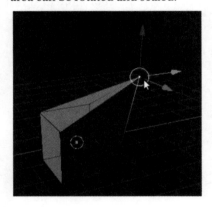

Figure 3–7. Moving a single vertex

Look at the other selection buttons near vertex select mode, as shown in Figure 3–8.

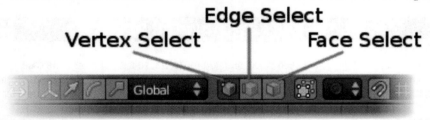

Figure 3–8. Selection modes

Enabling edge select mode allows you to select edges by RMB-clicking them. Likewise, with face select mode, the actual faces can be selected via RMB-clicking.

■ **Note** You can switch between vertex, edge, and face modes by using Ctrl+Tab+1 (vertex select), Ctrl+Tab+2 (edge select), or Ctrl+Tab+3 (face select).

Experiment with these modes and get used to moving parts of the cube around.

The "Limit selection to visible" button (Figure 3–9) is used to toggle whether a mesh in edit mode renders as a fully opaque solid, or whether the faces are slightly transparent, allowing you to see through to the other side (see Figure 3–10). It is useful to have this button enabled so that you can only see the frontmost faces, as this prevents accidentally selecting areas through the wrong side of a mesh.

Figure 3–9. The occlusion button (aka "Limit selection to visible")

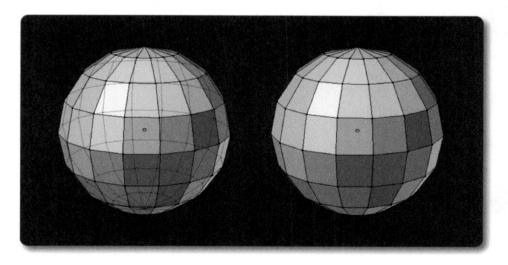

Figure 3–10. The effect of "Limit selection to visible." On the left, the option is off, allowing you to accidentally select vertices on the opposite side of the mesh. On the right, the option is on, hiding the vertices from the other side.

Some Mesh-Editing Tools

So far, so good; you can now move parts of the cube around. However, you still need to learn a few commands to really get to grips with modeling. It's all very well moving individual vertices, but what if you want to add new areas to the mesh? Selecting a row of vertices one by one can be very slow—is there a faster way to do it? What if there's a hole in the mesh—can we fill it in? How can we join two mesh objects together? Certainly, Blender has many functions to do all these things and more. For now, however, I'm going to briefly cover a few of the important ones. Play with them and see whether you can use them to make a small model from the cube Blender starts with. For the most part, these work best with face select mode.

Extrude

This is one of the most powerful editing features. RMB-select a face of your cube. Press the E key and then move your mouse slightly. You should find that the selected area extrudes out like a branch. Initially, extrusions only go outward at an angle directly perpendicular from the faces of the mesh. To confirm the extrusion, click the LMB; once you have done so, though, you can then use standard Move, Rotate, and Scale controls to precisely position the new pieces.

By selecting multiple faces (use the Shift key), you can extrude large areas from the mesh as one big section. Pressing Alt+E will give you a variety of options, such as being able to pull the surface out as individual faces. For example, instead of rising as a single big area, the selected faces will come out as separated squares.

Figure 3–11 shows a cube that has had its top face selected and then extruded upward. At one point, a side face was selected so a branch could fork off at an angle.

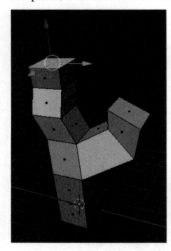

Figure 3–11. *Extrude in action*

Fill

The fill command (F key) creates a new face from selected vertices. Simply select three or four vertices and press F to make a face from the selection. It helps to have the faces resemble a square formation in order to prevent Blender from having to guess which vertices are connected (e.g., as opposed to in opposite corners). Figure 3–12 shows the effects of having four vertices selected around a hole and then pressing F to fill in the gap.

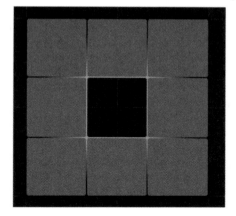 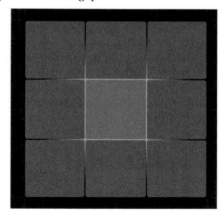

Figure 3–12. Filling a square hole

Selecting only two vertices and pressing F creates an edge.

You do not have to be in vertex select mode to create faces. Looking back at Figure 3–12, for example, selecting the two opposite edges of the hole in edge select mode is the same as selecting the four same vertices.

Add Edgeloop

An edgeloop is where a set of vertices are connected in a line, or sometimes in a circle. In the monkey in Figure 3–13, you can see a selected edgeloop around the eye (I'll show how to select edgeloops in the next section). This edgeloop has been added to the mesh using Ctrl+R, which creates a new edgeloop in the mesh, directly under where the mouse is positioned.

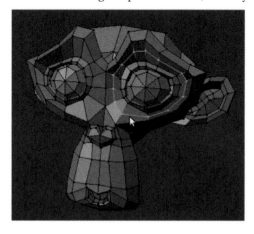

Figure 3–13. Adding a new edgeloop

When adding a new edgeloop with Ctrl+R, there are a few steps that occur:

1. At first, when you press Ctrl+R, a pink preview of the new edgeloop is shown. This allows you to move the mouse to different positions so that you can decide where the loop should go (the pink line moves with the mouse) before finalizing the move with a single LMB-click.

2. After the LMB-click, the new edgeloop is formed, and mouse movement now allows sliding the loop into just the right position (at this time press the 0 key if you don't want the line to be moved from the center).

3. A final LMB-click anchors the newly formed edgeloop into place.

The Edges Menu

Pressing Ctrl+E will bring up a special Edges menu (Figure 3–14) with numerous options. The following are some of the most useful:

- *Edge Slide*: This allows the selected edgeloop (or part of an edgeloop) to be moved from side to side.

- *Edge Loop*: If you have one edge selected, this option will continue the line to select the rest of the edgeloop until it comes to a fork in the edgeflow or a dead end.

- *Edge Ring*: If one edge is selected, using this option selects a parallel ring running perpendicular to the selected edge. In other words, two edgeloops are selected, running through the vertices of the selected edge.

Figure 3–14. The Edges menu

Edgeloop Deletion

In edit mode, the X key (delete) brings up a menu of options. For a selected area, you can choose whether you want to delete faces, edges, or vertices, and there are subtle differences in the results. Deleting vertices deletes all the faces that depend on those vertices; deleting edges deletes the respective edges and faces along the edge selected, leaving vertices attached to any edges not selected for deletion; and deleting faces leaves the connected vertices and edges behind, only deleting the solid wall. You can also delete edgeloops using this menu—a real time-saver when you want to get rid of long lines of vertices. Simply select the edgeloop (you can use the Edges menu's Edge Loop option to do this), press the X key, and choose Edgeloop from the pop-up menu.

Merging Vertices

In vertex select mode, you can select a number of vertices and then press Alt+M to bring up the "Merge vertices" menu. On choosing where the vertices should meet (e.g., the first vertex of the selected group, the last, somewhere in the middle, etc.), the selected vertices become fused together as a single vertex (see Figure 3–15). This function is very useful for stitching areas together, as with a zipper.

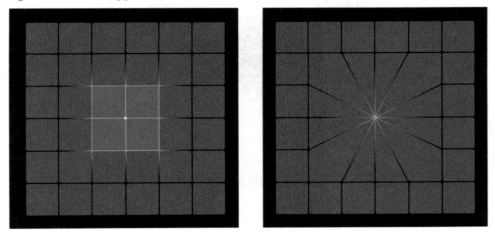

Figure 3–15. The selected vertices merge together under the "Merge vertices" option

Joining and Separating Mesh Objects

In object mode, it is possible to combine separate mesh objects into one by Shift-RMB-selecting them and pressing Ctrl+J. Likewise, in edit mode, it is possible to split a mesh into different objects with the P key. Generally, the workflow is to select the faces you wish to separate, press P, and choose Selection from the pop-up menu. Choosing "By loose parts" will make Blender separate an object into separate pieces, based on whether the mesh is made from separate islands (e.g., some parts are not directly connected to others and are therefore "loose").

Background Images

When making a model, it can be useful to have a reference image behind your work that you can model over for accuracy (see Figure 3–16). For any 3D view, press the N key to bring up the Properties panel. Toward the bottom is the Background Images check box; select it and then click the Add Image button in the same area (you might need to hit the black triangle to expand the Background Images area). A new area for the image will appear, saying that the image is not set. Click the white arrow to open a file dialog where you can navigate to find a suitable image for the view window. (See Figure 3–17 for example settings.)

This feature is useful for placing blueprints behind an image as a reference for modeling over. Note that background images only work when the view is *orthographic*, which means that the view is flat. This is opposed to a *perspective* view, where things that are close up appear larger. (Press numpad 5 to toggle between orthographic and perspective views.)

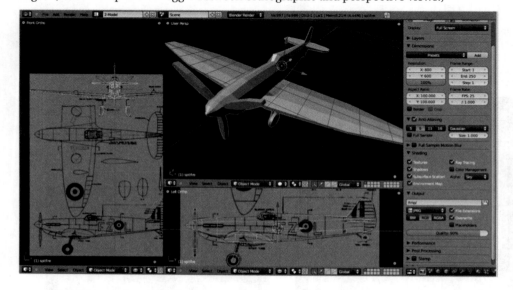

Figure 3–16. Background images from www.the-blueprints.com *being used to model an aircraft (left), and the Background Images panels (right)*

Figure 3–17. The Background Images properties in the Properties panel

Topology

When editing an organic model, especially one meant to be used in animation, it is important to consider the topology of edgeloops. *Edgeflow* is a term used to describe how the edges of a mesh should follow the form of the shape, and how they should be positioned along folds so that bending doesn't crease the faces. *Topology* describes the effectiveness of the edgeflow of the lines of a mesh, which can be good or bad depending on the following factors:

- How well the lines follow the form of the shape. Often, smoothing a model with multiresolution or subsurface modifiers will distort the overall shape if the topology is bad. Edges should be evenly distributed, and extra edges should be positioned at sharp corners.

- Whether the faces are quads (four sided), or triangles and N-gons (an N-gon has five or more edges). In most cases, especially when a mesh is designed to bend like flesh, quads are considered better because they twist easily (as opposed to triangles, which don't twist well, and N-gons, which often have so many vertices that they can warp into odd, unwanted shapes).

- Whether the lines available allow easy distortions for animation (i.e., there shouldn't be too many lines, they should be evenly spaced, and they should follow the direction of curves).

For shapes like the head, it is good edgeflow to have concentric circles around cavities like the mouth and eyes (see Figure 3–18). This allows for a lot of flexibility in terms of easy reshaping, opening, closing, and so on. For limbs that bend, such as elbows and finger joints, it is good practice to have three edgeloops or more around each bend in order to enable the mesh geometry to bend in a smooth curve. Poorly aligned edgeloops can make the desired surface deformations more difficult to create (e.g., imagine folding a piece of paper in half, and then unfolding it and trying to crease it along an imaginary line 10 degrees off from your crease).

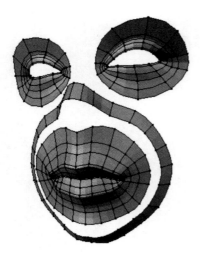

Figure 3–18. Edgeloops of a face should ideally form concentric circles around the eyes and mouth.

Example Modeling Through Mesh Editing

Modeling is fairly simple in terms of the number of functions needed, but it can take a lot of time to do well. Even at a professional level, modelers are always learning better ways of doing things, and the best teacher is practice. That is, make models, make more models, and then more until the process becomes second nature.

The Mirror Modifier: Making a Mirror Cube

Many objects are symmetrical (including people, animals, boats, cars, planes, chairs, tables, space aliens, and monsters). Thankfully, Blender provides a mirror modifier that can be used when modeling such objects, so you can model one side of an object while Blender automatically creates the other. Let's try it out:

1. Start with the default cube, and go to front view in edit mode (press numpad 1). Place your mouse over the top edge of the cube.

2. While still in edit mode, press Ctrl+R.

3. At this point, a vertical edgeloop should appear. If not, the mouse pointer may be in the wrong position; circle your mouse over the top edge until the vertical edgeloop appears, or repeat the last step until a pink preview edgeloop appears. When you are satisfied that the edgeloop is in the correct place, LMB-click *once only*.

4. As you move the mouse horizontally, the new edgeloop will slide back and forth. The header section will show an edge slide percent reading of how far out you are moving the line. To make it stay exactly in the center, type 0 (that's zero) to tell the edgeloop to stay put (move no distance). Alternatively, pressing Esc also works in this case. Note that this technique

of pressing Esc or 0 will likewise cancel other movements, scale actions, or rotations in Blender (for both parts of objects and whole objects). You can also type in numeric values to manually specify how much something is moved.

5. When the new edgeloop is in place, press Enter to anchor it in position. Your cube should now look something like Figure 3–19.

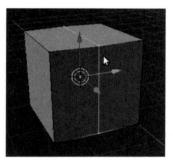

Figure 3–19. *New edgeloop at center position*

6. Now that you have a line down the middle, you only actually need one half of the cube to enter mirror mode, so you need to delete the other side. You can do this in one of the following ways:

    •   You can delete vertices one at a time (RMB-select a vertex point, press X to delete it, RMB-select the next, and so on.).

    •   In face select mode (Ctrl+Tab+3), you can delete each face of one half of the cube one at a time.

    •   You can select each of these vertices with the Shift key to delete them all in one press with the X key, as shown in Figures 3–20 and 3–21.

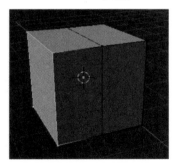

Figure 3–20. *Select the far side.*

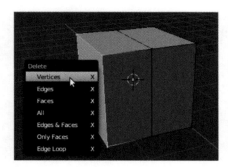

Figure 3–21. Four vertices selected and ready to delete

- Alternatively, the B key (block select) allows you to select a rectangular area by dragging diagonally with the LMB pressed. This way, you can simply drag the mouse to select the four vertices you want in one movement. Likewise, holding down Ctrl and LMB-dragging a circle around the area is yet another way of quickly selecting a group of vertices. These methods are faster than one-by-one selection, although you may want to simply select vertices one at a time if that is what you are comfortable with. When using multiple selection methods like these, you'll want "Limit selection to visible" to be activated (the mesh should *not* be see-through); otherwise, you risk selecting vertices from the wrong side of the mesh.

- You can select just the very end face, which is the same as selecting those four vertices from the last method, and use X key to delete vertices (using the pop-up list).

7. You should now have half a cube (Figure 3–22). Go to the Modifiers panel on the Modifiers tab (the spanner icon).

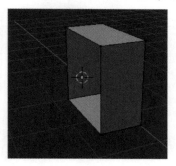

Figure 3–22. Half a cube

8. Add a mirror modifier (Figure 3–23). You should now see the cube in full. If you make any changes to one half, they'll be automatically reflected in the other. Note that the default settings for a mirror modifier are to mirror along the x axis, as marked in the Modifiers panel in Figure 3–24.

Figure 3–23. Adding a mirror modifier

Figure 3–24. Mirror modifier default settings

9. Click Clipping in the Modifiers panel. The clipping function welds the vertices at the center together. Without it you can tear open the mesh at the middle seam. There are times where you may need to temporarily switch it off, such as when extruding legs out in different directions.

10. It's a good idea to save this file (you can use Ctrl+S or go through the File menu) any time you want to start building something symmetrical. Save this file as mirrorcube.blend. The final result is shown in Figure 3–25.

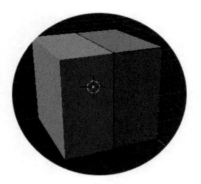

Figure 3–25. The finished mirror cube, ready to model something symmetrical

A Note on Modifiers

Mesh modifiers can be thought of as additions to mesh objects. They work like filters in that the actual mesh is unchanged while the modifier works its magic to complete the effect. They are a safe way of creating effects because of their nondestructive nature; only when the Apply button in the Modifiers panel is clicked do modifiers affect the real vertices of the final mesh.

The order of modifiers is important, as the top ones in the list in the Modifiers panel are applied before any modifiers further down the list. For example, if a multiresolution modifier (or any other that partially shrinks a mesh) is applied before a mirror modifier, the shrinkage may cause a gap in the middle seam of the resulting object; on the other hand, mirroring first (with clipping enabled in the Modifiers panel) and then smoothing creates no such seam. Some modifiers are fixed about their order. It is not possible to apply a multiresolution modifier after a mirror modifier, because it would create a buffer of separate resolutions that would be too difficult for Blender to accurately update if the modifiers were able to switch around.

Until it is applied, each modifier has show/hide buttons for different modes (Figure 3–26): whether the effect is shown in the final render, whether it is shown in the main 3D view, whether it is shown in edit mode, or whether new vertices created by the modifier are treated as normal vertices (meaning that the modified effect on the vertices is shown in edit mode and the vertices act as though they were real).

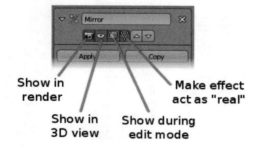

Figure 3–26. Options for where the effect is shown

There are so many modifiers to play with that it would be impossible to mention them all, and they may change for different Blender versions over time. You can experiment to discover whether some of the listed modifiers do what you would expect.

Smoothing a Mesh

Because mesh edges are straight, you need lots of vertices to make smooth-looking curves. Fortunately, Blender has a couple of methods for smoothing the look of your models. Both are modifiers, and they're described in the following sections.

The Subsurface Modifier

The subsurface modifier, which is used frequently by modelers, subdivides your mesh so that every face is split two ways, with each quad face becoming four faces. In the subsurface options on the Modifiers tab, there are View and Render options. The View field affects how smooth the mesh looks in 3D view, and the Render property specifies the degree of smoothness in the final render (e.g., how the model appears in the end product CGI movie. We will look more into rendering in Chapter 4). By bumping these numbers up, you increase the level of smoothness for your mesh. For convenience, you can set specific smoothness levels for a subsurface modifier to the keyboard shortcuts Ctrl+1 through Ctrl+5.

The Multiresolution Modifier

The multiresolution modifier works in a similar way to the subsurface modifier, but it is additionally compatible with sculpt mode, which we'll look at next. Generally speaking, most people use subsurface modifiers to smooth their models, and use multiresolution modifiers for sculpting purposes.

Box-Modeling a Man

Box modeling is a process by which you start with a cube, extrude face by face, and add edgeloops as necessary (see Figure 3–27).

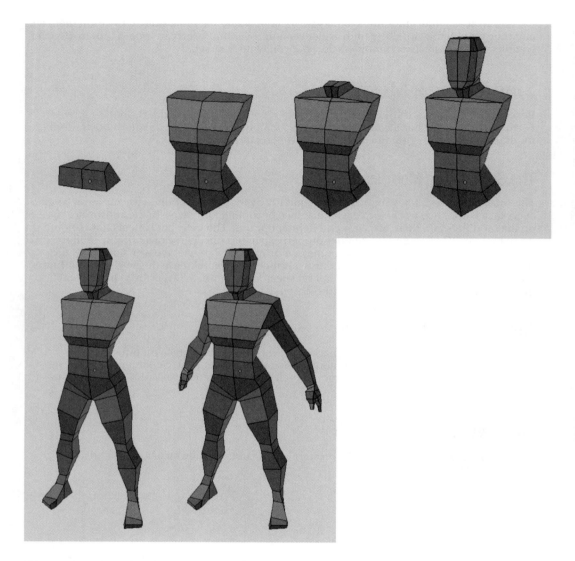

Figure 3–27. Example of box modeling. This model started as cube with a mirror modifier (see the following section), and faces were extruded out to form the torso and head, and then the legs and arms. Note that to get accurate shapes, some individual vertex positions had to be adjusted.

Sculpt Mode

With sculpt modeling, you use special brushes to warp the shape of the mesh. The workflow usually involves starting out with a general shape and then sculpting to add details. Sculpting can be used to get right down to the wrinkles of a character.

This example uses sculpt mode to change a cube into a cat's head. Realistically, a cube has nowhere near enough vertices to form anything like a cat's head (it only has eight, with one vertex point for each of the corners). For this reason, we are going to use the multiresolution modifier to increase the number of vertices while we sculpt the model into shape. By the end of the sculpting, we will have created a convincing model with a technique that is very similar to modeling with clay.

Start off with the default Blender scene. You should be looking at the default cube with the Tool Shelf open on the left, and the Main Buttons panel open on the right, as shown in Figure 3–28). If the Tool Shelf is missing, activate it with the T key.

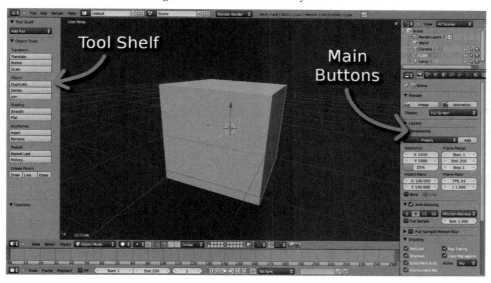

Figure 3–28. Default panels

Getting into Position

Go to front view (numpad 1), and then move the view slightly off center by holding down the MMB and dragging the mouse to one side. Have the y (green) axis/arrow pointing toward you; something like what is shown in Figure 3–28 is fine.

Roll your MW to zoom in so that the cube takes up most of the screen space. Make sure the cube is selected by RMB-clicking it.

Adding a Multiresolution Modifier

As mentioned, the multiresolution modifier is one of many modifiers available in Blender—there is a large collection of them, arranged into three columns (sorted into categories of Generate, Deform, and Simulate) under the Modifiers tab, as shown in Figure 3–29.

Click the Modifiers tab (the wrench) in the main Properties panel to the right of the screen.

You should see a button labeled Add Modifier. On pressing this you will be confronted with an extensive list of possible modifiers. In the leftmost column (under Generate), choose Multiresolution.

Figure 3–29. *Selecting the multiresolution modifier*

At this point, the Multiresolution panel should appear, as shown in Figure 3–30. Click the Subdivide button a few times. Every time you click Subdivide, each face of the cube will divide into four faces (this is essentially what multiresolution does—it increases the "resolution" of a mesh by multiplying the number of faces/vertices). The shape of the cube gets smoothed, making it begin to resemble a sphere. Click Subdivide until the preview/sculpt/render levels in the modifier options reach about 4 or 5. You can always add levels later, so don't add too many for now, as this could cause slow performance.

Figure 3–30. *The Multiresolution panel*

■ **Note** You may have noticed that there are three settings for the resolution of the multiresolution modifier: Preview, Sculpt, and Render (these are on the left of the Multiresolution panel, as shown in Figure 3–30). Essentially, the number in each of these settings is the same thing: the number of times subdivide has been used. The difference is that Preview is for the main 3D view, Sculpt is for when Sculpt mode is being used, and Render is for the amount of multiresolution that will show in the final rendered image. If you push multiresolution too far, Blender may start to slow down. In this case, you can manually change these settings to lower a number. The arrows at each end of these settings buttons allow you to lower and raise the values using mouse clicks (see Figure 3–31).

Figure 3–31. *Multiresolution level control. Using the arrows at either end, you can tweak how smooth the multiresoution levels are.*

Now that the multiresolution modifier is in place, it's time to sculpt.

Starting to Sculpt

The tools needed for sculpting (known as brushes) only show up on the Tool Shelf when you switch to sculpt mode. Currently, you are likely to be in object mode. With the cube selected, switch to sculpt mode using the drop-down menu on the header strip, along the bottom of the 3D window (see Figure 3–32).

Figure 3–32. *Switching to sculpt mode*

The Tool Shelf should now display the sculpting tools. Expand the Symmetry panel near the bottom of the Tool Shelf and check the X box under the Mirror setting, as shown in Figure 3–33. Now, when you sculpt one side of the cube, the sculpting effects will be applied to both sides. This is useful for making faces, which are symmetrical.

Figure 3–33. *Checking the X option*

Types of Brushes

In sculpt mode, you can select different brushes by clicking the image of the brush effect at the top of the Tool Shelf (which will show other brushes). Once a brush is chosen, you then rub the object over the mouse pointer while holding down the LMB. Some brushes have an Add and a Subtract option to give them positive and negative (opposite) effects (e.g., to specify whether the brush etches into the surface or builds areas out).

From this point, you sculpt the mesh simply by drawing on the surface while holding the LMB down. Simply change the brushes and their associated options on the Tool Shelf to achieve different effects. Each brush is different, so you'll need to experiment.

Stop reading now. Experiment with each brush to see what it does. As with many programs, Blender allows you to use Ctrl+Z to undo any actions you are not happy with. Remember that you can maximize the screen by holding down Shift and pressing the spacebar, and you can hide the Properties panel by pressing the N key; doing so will reduce clutter and give you more space to work with.

Table 3–1 gives you a brief summary of what you should find.

Table 3–1. Sculpt brushes

Brush Type	Description
Drawing Brushes	
Sculpt/Draw	This brush pulls the mesh surface under the mouse pointer outward (using the Add option) or inward (using the Subtract option). This is the brush that is the best for drawing lines.
Layer	This brush works similarly to Draw, except that you define a height for the draw lines (the Add option raises the lines and the Subtract option deepens them). If you zig-zag a layer brush over a previous application of layer, it won't build up over the defined height.
Scrape/Peaks	This sinks ravines into or raises mounds on the surface.
Blob	This applies a buffing effect to an area.
Clay	This shrinks areas inward (using the Add option) or expands them (using the Subtract option) against a center point.
Fill/Deepen	This works like Draw, except that Fill targets the hollows in a surface, raising them up to fill them in; and Deepen makes sunken areas of a surface deeper.
Surface-Shifting Brushes	
Nudge	This pushes areas of the mesh along the surface.
Thumb	This generates a subtle rubbing effect. It has more of a digging effect than the Nudge tool.
Grab	This grabs hold of an area and moves it with the brush.
Snake Hook	This is similar to the Grab tool, but allows you to pull areas out in tentacle-like arcs.
Twist	This moves the surface area around in a spiral.
Expansive Brushes	
Inflate/Deflate	Inflate expands an area in a balloonlike manner, whereas Deflate shrinks parts of a mesh.
Pinch/Magnify	Pinch pulls an area into the middle of the brush, and Magnify spreads the surface area outward.
Crease	The Add option pinches the mesh to make a peak, and the Subtract option creases the mesh inward like a valley.

Brush Type	Description
Smoothing Brushes	
Smooth	This smoothes the surface of the mesh by evening out the vertices.
Polish	This smoothes areas of the mesh while trying to maintain the general shape.
Flatten/Contrast	Flatten flattens the area under the mouse pointer, whereas Contrast exaggerates the bumps.

It should be noted that the key to successful sculpting is not in learning a list like Table 3–1. Rather, just experiment and see what each tool does. They have multiple uses, and sculpting is good for experimenting with reshaping large portions of a mesh, as well as refining finer details.

Changing Brush Size and Strength

While you can use the sliders on the Tool Shelf to control brush radius and strength, a quick way to change the radius of your brush on the fly is to press the F key, move your mouse to expand/shrink the brush , and then LMB-click to confirm (or RMB-click to cancel) (see Figure 3–34). Likewise, pressing Shift+F allows you to control the overall strength of the sculpt brush (a denser circle specifies greater strength).

Figure 3–34. Adjusting brush size

Let's look at an example of sculpting from scratch to give you a visual idea of the workflow:

Begin with a cube of multiresolution level 5, as shown in Figure 3–35.

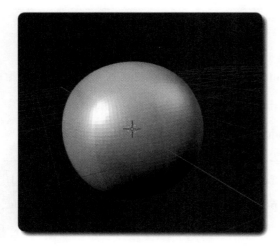

Figure 3–35. The initial multiresolution cube

1. Push in the eyes with the Draw tool, as shown in Figure 3–36.

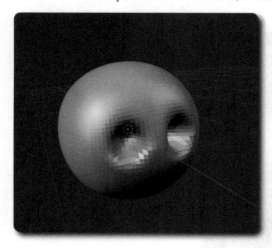

Figure 3–36. The eyes are started.

2. Sculpt in the basic features, as shown in Figure 3–37.

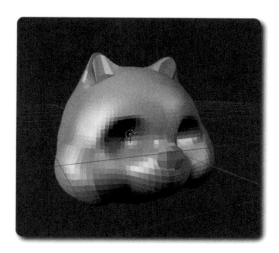

Figure 3–37. Basic features are added

3. Increase the level of the multiresolution modifier (e.g., click the Subdivide button in the Modifiers panel) so that you can sculpt finer details, as shown in Figure 3–38.

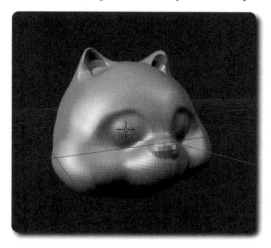

Figure 3–38. Finer details are added

4. Keep raising the multiresolution level in order to suit the level of detail you wish to sculpt, as shown in Figure 3–39.

Figure 3–39. The final head

And there we have it—the sculpted cat's head, which started from the basic cube. This technique can be a lot of fun, and you can learn a lot about the brushes simply by experimenting. For really effective sculpting, you would not normally start with a cube and sculpt it into shape as we have done. This approach typically results in a large number of vertices, as well as an unevenness in the density of the mesh (areas that have been inflated will have fewer vertices than areas that have been condensed through the sculpting process). A better approach is to create the general shape of the mesh using the standard box-modeling techniques, and then apply sculpt mode in order to attain the finer details.

Exercise 1: Monkey Sculpt

Starting with the monkey primitive shape (Shift+A ➤ Add ➤ Mesh ➤ Monkey), sculpt in details to give it a more realistic look. Add warts, wrinkles, and so forth. You might also like to change its facial expression (Figure 3–40).

Figure 3–40. Sculpted monkey

Using Sculpt and Mesh Modeling Together: Retopology

We have looked at sculpting as a means of shaping a model from a simple cube. The method is free-flowing and fun, but it's not ideal for modeling, as this results in a very heavy mesh with thousands of vertices (once you click the Apply button in the Multiresolution panel). Thus, the result slows down rendering and is pretty much useless for animation. There is also no real consideration of edgeflow when using sculpt as the modeling method.

Thankfully, there is a remodeling technique known as *retopology*, where it is possible to mold a new mesh around the sculpted original. This way, you can improve the edgeloops and have a new mesh that is much more suitable for animation, while adopting the shape from the original. Retopology is an advanced technique that combines the strengths of both sculpt and mesh modeling.

With the sculpted model on the screen, make a new plane and shrink it down. Place it in front of the sculpted object so that it is floating a small distance from the surface. In front view, the new mesh should be very small, as in Figure 3–41.

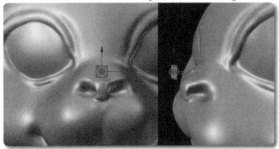

Figure 3–41. Start with a new plane that floats just in front of the surface of your source (reference) model.

In edit mode, click the horseshoe magnet icon under the 3D view. This turns surface snapping (retopology) on. The next button brings up the Snap Element menu, from which you should choose Face (the cube icon). The next button brings up the Snap Target menu, from which you should choose Closest. Finally, you should also ensure that the next button ("Project vertices on the surface of other objects") is active—this is revealed when you hover the mouse over it. (These buttons are shown in Figure 3–42.) With these settings, any moved vertices will drop neatly onto the surface of the mesh behind them, thereby taking its shape.

Figure 3–42. Retopology settings

With the second mesh sticking to the older (sculpted) version like shrink wrap, you can position lines to their edgeflow while maintaining the shape of the original mesh. Press the E key to extrude individual vertices out and around the base mesh, and they should spread along the surface.

Using this method, you can draw topology over your old sculpture by extruding the edges of the newer version, as shown in Figures 3–43 and 3–44.

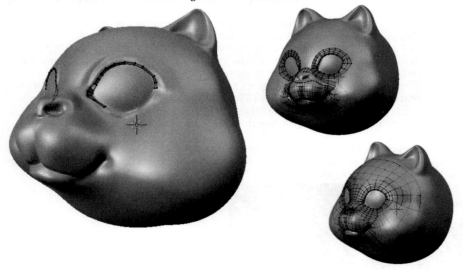

Figure 3–43. Retopology modeling over a sculpted model to recreate a mesh with improved edgelooping

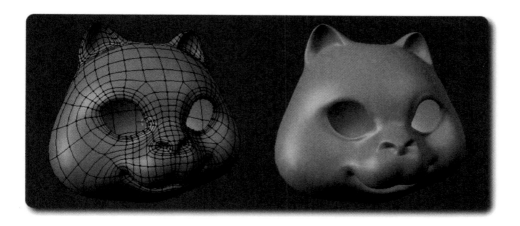

Figure 3–44. The final result: A clean mesh with animation-friendly edgeloops, looking just like the sculpted original

Summary

In Chapter 2, we "created" models by moving simple premade primitive mesh objects around (e.g., we arranged ten cubes to form various shapes). In this chapter, we have gone a step further by editing the individual mesh objects themselves. Mesh objects are formed as a network of vertex points, connected by edges and faces in order to represent a solid-looking physical form.

We looked at the differences between object mode, in which whole mesh objects can be arranged, and edit mode, in which the individual vertices, edges, or faces of the mesh object can be changed to affect the shape of the mesh object itself. There are a variety of commands available in edit mode (e.g., edgeloop commands), and I have only given a few essential ones to get you started. Blender has a lot more tools, and different artists have their favorites, so rather than making a voluminous reference guide for all of them, I've explained a few, and encourage you to experiment further.

In addition to direct mesh editing, this chapter described sculpt mode, which provides for a fun method of modeling that some beginners have reported as being more intuitive. Note, however, that sculpt mode is not a traditionally accepted modeling technique, largely due to its lack of consideration for good edgeflow and the large number of vertices it creates in a mesh once applied.

I ended with showing a method of tying the two techniques together—sculpting to create a desired form, and then using traditional mesh editing with retopology to create a mesh using the sculpted version as a base scaffolding or reference. In practice, you can mix techniques however you like to get the results you need. They are the tools and you are the artist.

CHAPTER 4

■ ■ ■

Lighting and Procedural Textures

Now that you have started modeling, it is important to learn to properly light your scene. If you want to show your amazing creations to others, and you light the scene poorly, the final result will not be impressive, putting all your hard modeling work into disregard.

In this chapter, you will learn about the following:

- Setting up a camera and lights to really show off your work
- How to texture the model and work with procedural material textures

A REMINDER ON TABS

Lighting and rendering require a number of different tabs, which from the default layout can be found in the Properties panel down the right side of the screen, as shown in the following illustration.

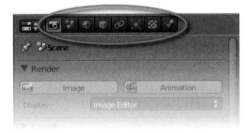

I covered tabs in Chapter 2, but I want to remind you of them here since I use them frequently. When I refer to the Render tab, World tab, or Object Data tab, this is where you should go. Bear in mind that some tabs are contextual. For example, the Object Data tab may have a different appearance depending on what has been selected in the main scene. If in doubt, you can always verify the name of a tab by hovering the mouse over it; after a second or so, the name of the tab should show below the mouse pointer in a floating box.

Setting Up a Basic Scene

We are going to set up a simple scene in order to practice simple lighting. In order for you to easily replicate my examples and workflow, rather than making something like a demo with a really good looking-scene and using models you don't have, I'm going to use the monkey primitive placed on a ground plane as a working example (Figure 4–1). Of course, if you have a model of your own that you wish to render, by all means use that instead.

Adding a Model

Let's start adding the model:

1. Start with the default scene and delete the default cube (RMB-select it and press X).

2. Press Shift+A, and then select Add ➤ Mesh ➤ Monkey to add the monkey primitive to the scene.

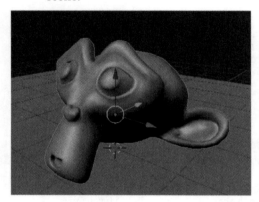

Figure 4–1. *The monkey primitive*

3. The monkey will be facing upward, but we want it to face forward. With the monkey selected, press R and then X, and then type the number **55** followed by Enter to make it face outward to the front view. Note that 90 degrees would make the monkey face straight ahead, but 55 degrees is the angle to correctly position the monkey so that it can sit on a ground plane, as in Figures 4–1 and 4–2.

Adding a Ground Plane

Unless you want the model to appear as though it is airborne, you might also like to add a ground plane:

1. Press Shift+A and select Add ➤ Mesh ➤ Plane.

2. Scale the plane about seven times (press S, type **7**, and then press Enter).

3. Move the monkey upward (in the Z direction) so that it sits comfortably on the plane when looked at from the side view.

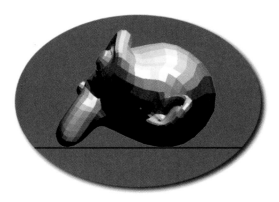

Figure 4–2. Side view of the monkey positioned on the ground plane

Note that pressing numpad 3 will display the side view. Also, pressing numpad 5 toggles between orthographic and perspective view modes, which might also be useful. It is easier to line the monkey up in orthographic view mode because it shows the side view in a very flat manner, which makes it easy to position items on the ground plane.

For the monkey model, I also like to add a subdivision surface modifier to smooth out the octagonal look. With the monkey selected, click the Modifiers tab (wrench icon), click the Add Modifier button, and choose Subdivision Surface modifier. Alternatively, you can select the monkey and press Ctrl+1, which is the keyboard shortcut for creating the modifier.

I also like to set the mesh faces to smooth shading, which makes the square faces of the mesh less obvious (press T to bring up the Tool Shelf and look for Shading: Smooth/Flat, as shown in Figure 4–3).

The monkey should now be positioned so that it is resting on the ground plane, and we are ready to set up lights and render the scene.

Figure 4–3. *Smooth shading from the Tool Shelf*

The Scene Camera

The default scene contains a couple more objects than the cube. If you navigate around the scene you should find two objects. One, a black dot with a couple of dotted circles around it (Figure 4–4), is a lamp to light the scene, and the other, which looks something like a floating pyramid (Figure 4–5), is the scene camera. The square face of the camera is the front end, and is marked with a black triangle to one side, representing which way is up.

Figure 4–4. *The default lamp (point lamp)*

Once a scene has been set up, it is usual to *render* the view. The 3D view within Blender is more of a workbench, preparing a scene for a glorious final render, which is normally taken from the point of view of the camera. We need to know how to line the camera up so that it is looking at the object(s) we want it to see when we generate the all-important final shot.

Figure 4–5. *The camera*

The camera can be moved around like any other object (RMB-select it, and then use the G and R keys to reposition it). However, it is useful to be able to see what the camera is looking at while you are setting it in position for the shot. To do this, split the 3D view into two as described in Chapter 2 (drag the diagonal stripes at the top-right corner of the 3D view into the middle). On the View menu in the header strip of one of the 3D view windows, choose View ➤ Cameras ➤ Active Camera. Now the window you apply this action to will show what the camera can see. You can move the camera around in the other 3D view window while getting instant feedback on how well your shot is lining up.

Aiming the Camera

Even with the aid of a split view to show what the camera sees, lining up the camera can be deceptively difficult. Fortunately there are some techniques for aiming the camera at a given object:

- A very simple way is to navigate in the 3D view to the point of view you would like the camera to have, and then press Ctrl+Alt+numpad 0, which causes the camera to jump to where your view is taken from, and look into the scene from your point of view.

- Another way of lining up your view is to use *fly mode* by pressing Shift+F with the mouse over the 3D view. In this mode, the view pivots around to follow your mouse pointer. Using the W and S keys or rolling the MW causes the view to accelerate in and out of the scene. Clicking the LMB causes the view to halt (but keep the position), whereas clicking the RMB resets the view to the starting position. Using this technique from the camera view moves the camera; alternatively, you can apply it to a non-camera view and then use the previous technique (Ctrl+Alt+numpad 0) when you are happy with the result.

A common and powerful way of aiming the camera accurately is to make it track to another object. The idea is to make the camera automatically face the target object—similar to a strong magnet. Move the object, and the camera will swing around to keep it in view; move the camera, and it will rotate to keep looking in the direction of the target object.

Tracking to an Object

Let's see how to track to an object:

1. RMB-select the camera.

2. Shift-RMB-select the target object so that both the camera and the model are selected.

3. Press Ctrl+T.

4. On the menu that appears, choose Track To Constraint.

Now when you move the camera around, it will always face the target object. You can now position the camera without having to worry about rotating it to line up the shot, because it always faces the object. It is a good idea to split the 3D view into two, and then set one to camera view in order to keep track of what the render camera will look like (this setup is shown in Figure 4–6). Try this, and then move the camera around to see how easy it is to position the camera for a shot.

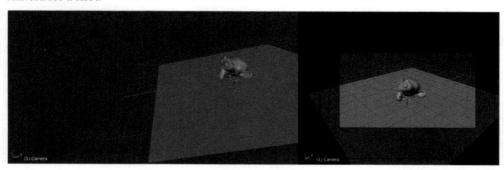

Figure 4–6. Using a split view to show what the camera sees

When tracking to an object, the camera gains a TrackTo constraint in its settings. With the camera selected, go to the Object Constraints tab (the icon for which looks like a couple of links in a chain), and you should see an area where this constraint has been added. This tab allows you to set various options, such as allowing the different axes (X, Y, or Z) of the camera to point to the object (–Z is normally the correct direction for the front of a camera). There is a good chance that the desired options will be set for you by default. Should you want to get rid of the TrackTo constraint, click the big white X at the top right of the TrackTo constraint's panel on this tab. Alternatively, you can press Alt+T when the camera is selected in 3D view, which will give you a couple options: Clear Track, which resets the camera position, and Clear and Keep Transformation (Clear Track), which breaks the TrackTo constraint, but leaves the camera positioned so that it is still pointing to the target object.

Tracking to an Empty Target

The TrackTo method is fine if you want the camera to point straight at an object. However, sometimes you might want the camera to be off center from its target object. Or, in the case of animation, you might not want the camera to keep following the target object around.

One solution is not to track to the target object directly, but instead track to an empty target (as shown in Figure 4–7). This target will not show in the final render, but act as a controller for where the camera is to be pointed. Simply position the empty target at the area of the object you want the camera to focus on.

Figure 4–7. *Tracking to an empty target*

This setup is very easy:

1. First, insert an empty into the scene by pressing Shift+A and then selecting Add ➤ Empty. This will create an empty object, which has no vertices.

2. RMB-select the camera, and then Shift-RMB-select the empty. It is important that the empty is selected last, as Blender knows to make the first selected object point to the last selected item.

3. Press Ctrl+T and choose Track To Constraint.

Now the camera will always look toward the empty. Simply place the empty where you need the camera to look. In this way, you can easily position it to achieve off-center shots when required.

Fixing Up the Camera View

The default camera can tend to give a fish-eye view of models, as though the scene were small and the camera right up close. In order to lessen the perspective distortion, take the following steps:

1. Select the camera and go to the Object Data tab (when the camera is selected, this tab will appear as a camera icon), as shown in Figure 4–8.

2. Go down to the Lens section, and change the angle from 35 to something like 50 (or another setting that you prefer). The scene as viewed through the camera will appear to jump to a bigger size, but pulling the camera back to reestablish the framing of the shot will cause less distortion now, as the camera is further away.

Figure 4–8. *Changing the camera lens*

It is also useful to enable the Passepartout option in the Display panel of the camera's Object Data tab. Using this option causes any 3D view from the camera perspective to visually darken the area falling outside of the immediate camera viewport, making it very clear to see where the edges of a render will fall (see Figure 4–9).

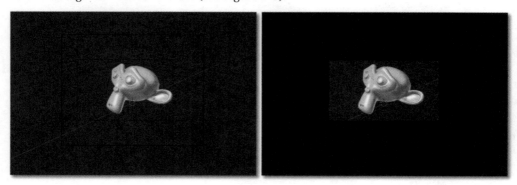

Figure 4–9. *The Passepartout option in the camera settings causes a camera view window to visually define an area for the main camera viewport. This illustration demonstrates both without (left) and with Passepartout (right).*

Once the camera is set up, you can render your view by pressing F12 (or going to the Render tab and clicking the Image button in the Render area). This will generate an image based on what the camera sees, which you can then save by pressing F3.

Lighting Techniques

Since we haven't worked on properly lighting the scene yet, your render may have problems, such as the shadows being too dark, as in Figure 4–10.

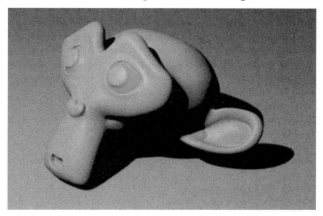

Figure 4–10. A render with a one-point lamp and no lighting enhancements. Notice the very dark shadows.

We are now going to look at a few different ways of lighting the scene better. This section will cover the following:

- The types of lamps available in Blender

- A workflow for positioning the lights

- Some quick-and-dirty tricks to getting a half-decent render

Lamp Types

As demonstrated in the previous render (Figure 4–10), the default point lamp is not the best choice in terms of effective lighting. Blender has several lamps available, including the point lamp, and the sun, spot, hemi, and area lights. The essential differences between these lights are outlined in Table 4–1.

Table 4–1. Different Types of Light

Light Effect	Type	Description
	Point	This light emits in all directions from a single point. With appropriate falloff, it can resemble a candle or a small lightbulb. It is very useful for rim light effects, where parts of an object need to be lit in order to stand out from the background.
	Sun	Otherwise known as a directional light, this is light that floods a scene from a given angle. It gets its name because it is similar to how the sky lights the world: flooding the scene from a given direction, not from a single point. Location does not affect sun lights; it is the rotation that is important. Whichever way a sun light is rotated, the whole scene gets light from that particular angle with parallel light rays.
	Spot	This is similar to a point lamp, but within a restricted V-shape direction. This light works very much like a theater spotlight. It casts a circle on a surface it is aimed at, and has settings to control the softness of the circular edges.
	Hemi	A hemi light produces an ambiance similar to a sun light, except that instead of creating light from a single direction, it acts as though the light is emitted from a sky dome. It is like having a single sun from the dominant direction, accompanied with smaller lights to illuminate the sides of objects in the scene.
	Area	An area light is like having a cluster of lights over an area of a specified size. It is useful for creating light emitted from a surface, such as a TV or the back of a fridge.

There are two ways to introduce any of these lights into your scene:

- By selecting an already existing light, you can change its type through the Lamp area of the Object Data tab. The different types of lights are listed, and by LMB-clicking one, you will accordingly change the type of the selected light.

- Using Shift+A in a 3D view window, you can then choose Add ➤ Lamp, and select whatever type you want to introduce to the scene.

Lamp Settings

The available lights have a lot of options, and it pays to explore them in order to use the lights effectively.

Let's start with an example. In the scene with the monkey, select the lamp and change it to a spot type by going to the Object Data tab and selecting Spot. The lamp in 3D view should now resemble a cone that you can rotate to face the monkey object (much like a stage light). Do this, and press F12 to check that the spotlight is indeed illuminating the monkey object.

Now we are going to examine some of the important options available for the spotlight. There are a lot, so please use Figure 4–11 as a guide while I outline the functionality of some of them.

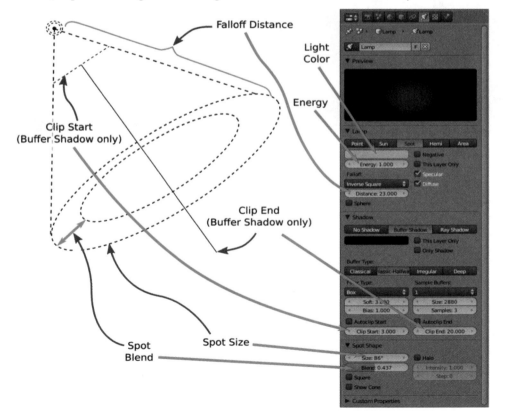

Figure 4–11. *Various options for the spot lamp, and where they can be found on the Object Data tab*

The most important settings are Light Color and Energy. By LMB-clicking the Light Color rectangle, you can set the color generated by the lamp. The Energy setting controls the brightness of the light.

The Falloff Distance setting controls the general reach of the spotlight (and also point lamps), as shown in Figure 4–12. By default, light begins to fade after it has reached the length defined by the falloff distance. However, if you check the Sphere check box under the Falloff Distance setting, then light will fade earlier, reaching zero brightness by the time it reaches the falloff distance.

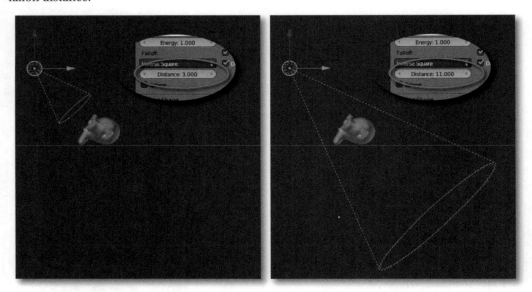

Figure 4–12. Falloff distance

Spot size and spot blend are unique to spotlights. The Spot Size setting controls the size of the circle of light cast by the spotlight. The number in this field directly corresponds to the angle of spread of the spotlight (the V shape of the spotlight as viewed from the side).

The Spot Blend setting defines the thickness of a fuzzy border that is applied to the cast circle of light. With low amounts of spot blend, the circle of light cast by a spotlight has sharply defined edges. As the blend is increased, the edges of the circle fade.

Figure 4–13 shows a sequence of changes made to a spotlight. In the top three images, the spot size is increased, and in the final image, the spot blend is increased to soften the edge of the cast circle of light.

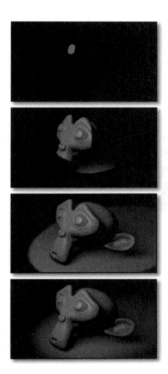

Figure 4–13. Changing the spot size (top three images) and then adding spot blend (bottom image)

In the Shadow area of the panels are Buffer Shadow and Raytraced Shadow options. *Raytraced shadows* provide more physically accurate results, but can be slow to render. *Buffer shadows* are quicker to render, but less accurate. Buffer shadows have Clip Start and Clip End values, which define an area within which the shadows are calculated. Objects should be within the range of these two values if they are to be affected by light and shadows from a lamp casting buffer shadows.

Shadow settings also have a Soft Size value, which works alongside the Samples value to soften the edges of shadows cast by the light. The Soft Size value blurs the shadow to give it a soft look, as shown in Figure 4–14. (The image on the left has a Soft Size value of 0, the middle image has a value of 3, and the right image has a value of 5.)

Figure 4–14. Different Soft Size values applied in the shadow settings of a spotlight

While Soft Size affects the amount of blur on a shadow, the Samples setting influences the quality of the blur, giving the shadow a grainy appearance at low values and a smoother look at higher ones. With low values, grainy dots can be quite visible, as shown in Figure 4–15. In the figure, all of the images use a shadow with a Soft Size setting of 3, but the images from left to right have Samples set to 0, 3, and 5, respectively. Notice the visible graininess of the middle image, which has a low sample size.

Figure 4–15. *Different amounts of shadow samples*

Soft size and samples complement each other. If either of these values is set to the minimum, the other one has nothing to work with. For example, if Soft Size is set to 0, the shadow will simply have very hard edges, and the Samples value will not change the look of it. Inversely, if Samples is set to 1, then no visible blur will be evident, regardless of the Soft Size setting.

Using the Lights Together

The available lights in Blender give you a lot of flexibility for lighting any scene. There is much theory on proper lighting technique. However, at the end of the day, lighting should illuminate the scene and give depth to objects through shading. There should be a range of tones, but areas of absolute black or overblown white should be avoided. Because our eyes adjust, even night scenes should be lit enough to suggest the form of objects. With color and careful consideration of the effects of shadows, lighting can also be used to set mood.

For our purposes, lighting consists of a *key* light, which is the main light source, and as-needed *fill* lights to add ambiance to otherwise unlit areas.

Adding the Key Light

The key to setting up lights is to start simple. Find out where your key light is going to come from. If you are outdoors, it could be the sun. Indoors, it might come from a window or a light.

Delete all lights other than your main key light. As used in scenarios such as lighting the monkey, spotlights generally make good key lights, although different environments will have their own suitable exceptions.

The following are some important considerations when deciding on a key light:

- The key light is usually the strongest light source in the scene.

- In terms of placement, a key light should be strategically positioned so as to define the form of the objects in a scene. Examples would be lighting one side of an object while leaving the other side in shade.

- The key light is the main light, and sometimes even the only light, for casting shadows. (There are always exceptions, though, as scenes can have more than one key light.)

With the light selected, go to the Object Data tab and rename the light **Key**, as shown in Figure 4–16.

Figure 4–16. *Renaming a light*

It is worth taking some time to carefully position your key light, as it's the primary light for your scene. The following subsections describe a couple of simple strategies you can use to help speed up the process.

Tracking Lights to Objects for Easy Positioning

When trying to position ights, it can be useful to have them track to the main object of your scene so that as you move the lights around, you don't end up pointing them in odd directions away from the objects you wish to display. This is done in the same way as tracking a camera to an object:

1. RMB-select the light.

2. Shift-RMB-select the object. It is important that the object is selected last.

3. Press Ctrl+T and choose Track To Constraint from the menu that appears.

Now when you move the key light around, it will always point to the object. It is therefore possible to reposition the key light (e.g., to a window or the sun), and the light will direct to the target object from that point.

Alternatively, you can use the TrackTo constraint so that the light points to an empty target (again, as shown previously with the camera). This allows you to control the angle of your lighting simply by moving the empty around the scene.

Once the light is appropriately positioned, RMB-select it, press Alt+T, and then choose Clear and Keep Transformation from the pop-up menu. This will remove the automatic tracking (TrackTo constraint) so that lights won't react if the object moves around the scene.

GLSL Mode

A computer with a half-decent graphics card should support GLSL real-time lighting in 3D view. GLSL gives you close-to-render-quality lighting as you move your lights around, enabling you to quickly fine-tune lighting adjustments without having to perform a full render for every little change.

To use GLSL, do the following:

4. In the Properties panel, choose GLSL from the Shading drop-down list in the Display area.

5. Select Textured from the Viewport Shading options in the header strip of the 3D window (see Figure 4–17).

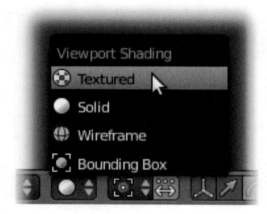

Figure 4–17. Switching to textured viewport mode

Change the color of the key light to suit the environment the lighting is from, depending on the light source. Note that only a slight tint is needed, since key lights are usually nearly white.

Render the image and see the effect your single lighting setup has. Your render should show the object with some pretty strong shadows (which we will soon fix with fill lights). This is the main light though, so again make sure you take time to place the key light in a position that causes the shadows to show off the form of your model (see Figure 4–18).

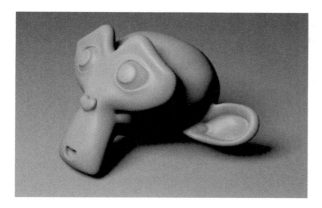

Figure 4–18. Single key light

Adding Fill Lights

In the real world, while the key light source may be at one spot in 3D space, objects tend to be lit from all sides. This is because of ambient light (light that fills a room in general) and bounced light (light that bounces off surfaces in directions that differ from the original source). Because light bounces off things, shadows are never completely black.

To simulate this effect, fill lights are needed. Sun lights are good for this, as they give a constant direction. Unless you want a theatrical effect where a figure has multiple shadows, you should disable the shadows of fill lights. You can do this by clicking the No Shadow button in the Shadow area of the Object Data tab (make sure the light is selected when you do this).

Look for any black areas of your model and position fill lights there. It can be a good idea to use strong, bright colors for fill lights (as in Figure 4–19), in order to isolate their illumination from that of the main key light; however, be sure to recolor them to something sensible when done positioning.

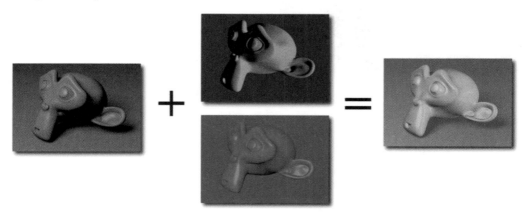

Figure 4–19. Start with a main key light and strategically position fill lights to illuminate the dark areas.

Ultimately, fill lights should not be as bright as the original key light, so turn down their energy. The image should still have a definite sense of key light direction, as in Figure 4–20.

Figure 4–20. Tone down the fill lights.

A scene typically has a key light and two or more fill lights to reduce the darkness at selected areas. Beware of *banding*, which is caused when two sides of an object are lit, leaving a black band in the middle, as shown in Figure 4–21. More light may be needed to deal with such areas.

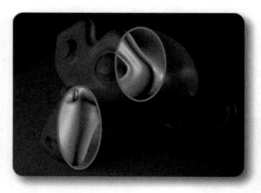

Figure 4–21. Examples of banding caused by a lack of fill lights

Generally, the key light will have a brightness of 1.00 and the fill lights somewhat less. Do not worry too much about altering the scene brightness to perfection (my final version is shown in Figure 4–22). That could take a long time, though a good fix for this is with Nodes, covered in Chapter 9.

Figure 4–22. Match the hues to the environment. The lighting is now fairly balanced.

Changing the World

Besides positioning key and fill lights, there are other global options that can make your renders more effective.

Go to the World tab (shown in Figure 4–23). The first options in the World area allow you to change the default background color of a scene.

Figure 4–23. The World tab

Selecting different combinations of the Paper Sky, Blend Sky, and Real Sky options causes Blender to generate different gradients of sky color. Immediately below this are color squares that allow you to change the horizon color, zenith color, and ambient color. The horizon and zenith colors affect sky colors, whereas the ambient color affects the light that is reflected onto objects in the scene. Basically, these options draw a gradient in the background of your render. Play with these options (and render) to see what each does.

Further down are the options for ambient occlusion. To get an idea of how this works, check the Ambient Occlusion box, and render the scene again by pressing F12. The scene will take longer to render, but a certain element of realism will be added to the shading (see Figure 4–24). Ambient occlusion works by shading in (darkening) areas of scene objects that are close to each other, and where there are tight angles between faces.

Figure 4–24. *The effect of ambient occlusion on the render*

Ambient occlusion is something of a trick, but it can make otherwise plain renders look great.

Also take a look at the Environment Lighting option. This allows the color you chose for the ambient color of the sky to illuminate objects in the scene (see Figure 4–25). Bear in mind that you can change the sky color using the buttons in the World area of the World tab.

Figure 4–25. *Environment lighting has an effect similar to ambient occlusion.*

These methods are given to enhance the scene in a broad sense, yet they also provide a quick way of lighting a scene when you are in a hurry. Once you have positioned a key light, using ambient occlusion can sometimes be sufficient to simulate the lighting effects you would normally assign to fill lights.

Of course, these methods do not beat the effectiveness of well-positioned lighting when you have the time.

Procedural Materials and Textures

In order to play with textures, let's make something worth texturing:

6. Starting with a new scene, delete the default cube, press Shift+A, and choose Add ➤ Text.

7. The word "Text" should now appear (still selected) in the main 3D view, as shown in Figure 4–26. Press Tab to enter edit mode, which will allow you to change the writing.

8. Press backspace four times (to erase the word "Text"), and type in something—perhaps your own name.

Figure 4–26. *A new text object*

9. When done, press Tab to return to object mode, and go the Object Data tab (with the text object selected, the Object Data icon resembles an *F*, as shown at the top of Figure 4–27).

Figure 4–27. Adjusting the settings of the text object

10. In the Geometry area of the Object Data tab (again see Figure 4–27), make the following changes to the settings of the text object to make your name stand out:

- Set Extrude to 0.25 (this makes the letters stand out in 3D).

- Set the bevel depth to 0.02 (this curves the otherwise sharp edges of the lettering). If you like, you can also bump up the Resolution setting to about 3 for a more rounded look.

- Further down, in the Paragraph area, set Align to Center, as shown in Figure 4–28.

Figure 4–28. Center-aligning the text object

11. Move the name you have created onto a plane, stand it upright (e.g., press R, press X, type **90**, and then press Enter), and set up lighting as before so that it looks effective.

We are going to use this new object to experiment with some basic materials.

■ **Note** The object is a text object, meaning that in edit mode, it can be changed by retyping what is written. Should you want to edit the item at the vertex level, from the Object menu on the 3D window header, select Convert ➤ Mesh from Curve/Meta/Surf/Text.

To create a new material for the text, go to the Material tab (see Figure 4–29). It is likely that your object will have no material at all yet. Click the New button, and you should see a whole lot of panels open up, with many settings to play with.

Certainly, with so many new options appearing, it is important to isolate a few of the important ones. I suggest you first look at the following:

- Where to name the material
- Where to set the base color of the material
- Where to change the amount of shininess of the material

Figure 4–29. Creating a new material

I will describe each of these three options here, and I'll point out where they are located in Figure 4–30.

As with new objects, when making a new material, it is a good idea to name it first so that the material can be easily located later, once there are many materials. There is a special name tag at the top of the Material tab where you can type in a unique name for the *material datablock*. The datablock is the base material that all other material properties associated with that material become a part of, so essentially it is the material itself. A sensible name for a material might be Skin, Leather, or Green Plastic. It should describe briefly the type of material you are going to create.

A very important step is to pick the base color (technically known as the *diffuse color* of the material). There is a Diffuse area on the Material tab with a rectangle representing the current material color. LMB-click this rectangle and a dialog will open allowing you to set the color. Aim to have something similar to the material you are trying to achieve. Skin could be light yellow or brown, plastic should be bright, and so forth.

Once you have the base color set, there are numerous options on the Material tab to fine-tune the look of your material. For example, the Specular area of the Material tab controls the *specular highlight*—that is, the shiny dot that appears on a surface when light hits it (seen commonly enough on a billiard ball). By sliding the Intensity bar in this section, you can effectively change the look of a surface from hard and shiny to soft and rubbery (e.g., like skin).

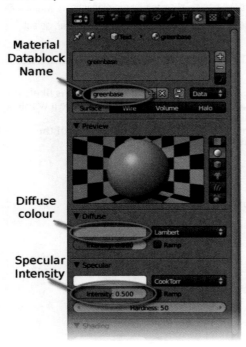

Figure 4–30. Important material settings

There are many settings here. It would be best for you to experiment with each to see what it does. Note that the top of the Material tab shows a sphere preview of what your material should look like when rendered. To the right of this preview are buttons to test the material datablock with different objects.

Of course, it is most rewarding to see your material render on the real object from your 3D view, which should have adopted the material you have created. Then, provided your camera and lighting are well set up, you can use F12 to render the scene (see Figure 4–31).

Figure 4–31. Base color material with green diffuse hue

Using Procedural Textures

Changing the color and a few other properties of a base material is fine, but the real power of procedural materials comes from adding textures. There aren't many things in the real world that are completely flat in color. From the pores in an orange peel to the rough surface of concrete to the grain of wood, most surfaces have some kind of a pattern.

In this section, we are going to take the material we have made and enhance it by adding a textured pattern (Figure 4–32). When this texture is made, we will change the properties so that it does not just affect the color of the material, but also the quality of the surface so that the texture appears to be bumpy (Figure 4–33).

12. Go to the Texture tab.

13. There is a list of texture slots, but it is likely empty because we have not made any textures yet. With the topmost slot selected, click the New button.

14. A cloud texture should immediately be applied to your material. Take a render (press F12), and you should see that the texture has indeed been applied to the material of your model, in a purple color (see Figure 4–32).

Figure 4–32. When first added, textures initially affect the color with a default purple hue.

15. At this point, you can choose a different patterned texture from the Type drop-down list (e.g., another choice might be Marble).

16. Again, render to see the results of any change you make.

17. The purple color probably isn't a good match for your texture. Go to the bottom of the Texture tab, and in the Influence area, LMB-click the purple rectangle to change the color to something more suitable.

18. Alternatively, still in the Influence area, change the material properties the texture affects. For example, activating Geometry ➤ Normal causes the texture to apply bumps to your material surface. There is a slider bar that affects the intensity of these bumps. This should give you results similar to those in Figure 4–33.

Figure 4–33. Material applied as color and as normals (bumps)

Textures can affect bump, transparency, and all manner of surface qualities.

Using Multiple Materials in One Mesh

One of the trickier things to do is mix materials on a single mesh. If you give the mesh a material (e.g., yellow), enter edit mode and select a few faces, and then add a red material, the entire mesh will change to red—not just the faces you've chosen. Any time you select faces and change the material, the whole mesh changes.

The reason is that for a mesh to have separate materials, it must first be divided into separate islands of material slots, each of which can then be assigned its own separate material as needed. Once these material slots are so assigned, then it is possible to assign them to separate faces.

19. Start with default cube.

20. Go to the Material tab.

21. Make a new material (or use an existing one).

22. Make the material yellow, name it `yellow`, and change its diffuse color to match.

23. Notice that the material slots at the top displays the material, as shown in Figure 4–34.

24. Click the small + sign to the right of the material list to create the new material slot (or duplicate the selected one). There should now be two slots, both showing that they are sharing the same yellow material. If you change the material qualities for one slot, it will inadvertently change the material used by the other, because they are actually using the same material.

25. Now go down to the material datablocks. There should be a 2 next to the yellow material, meaning that there are two slots sharing the material datablock. Click the 2 to make the materials *single-user*. This effectively clones the material so that there are two copies, yellow and yellow.001. Now making changes to one will no longer affect the other.

26. With the material slot using yellow.001 selected, rename the material to red, and likewise change the diffuse color to red.

27. At the moment, the whole object is using the first material slot with the yellow color. Now go into edit mode and select a few faces.

28. Make sure the material slot with the red material is selected, and click the Assign button. The selected faces should now bear the red material.

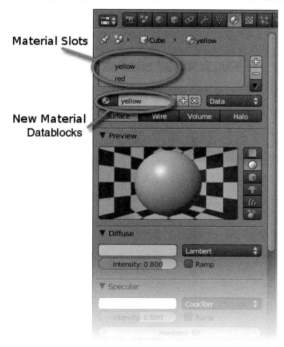

Figure 4–34. Material slots

By adding new material slots, adding new materials to these slots, and then assigning them to different faces of your object, you can have separate procedural materials for different areas of your mesh.

Exercise: Applying Textures

To put what you have learned into practice, model something simple such as a cup, duplicate it several times using Shift+D, and apply different procedural textures to each copy. Take a final render showing them all (see the example in Figure 4–35).

Figure 4–35. Same cup, different textures

Summary

This chapter examined how to set up cameras and lights for creating renders that will do justice to your work. It covered what Blender has to offer in terms of the available lights, and it explored how particular lamp settings can change the appearance of a scene. We also took a brief look at lighting theory, with an emphasis on the importance of setting up key lights and fill lights to illuminate a scene.

Finally, we had a look at the steps involved in applying a simple procedural texture to a mesh. We examined how such textures are capable of affecting not only the color of an object, but other surface qualities such as bumpiness.

Lighting and texturing are very in-depth subjects, and these examples have only scratched the surface. I encourage you to experiment with the settings to create your own lighting and texturing effects. To further your understanding of lighting, in Chapter 9 I will cover composite nodes, which allow you to fine-tune your renders in terms of brightness and contrast.

In the next chapter, we will examine how to hand-paint on a mesh to create textures that are more realistic than ever.

CHAPTER 5

■■■

UV Mapping

UV mapping is a process of applying textures to an object by hand. With the procedural textures of last chapter, you made a material and changed its properties to create the look of a surface texture you wished to emulate. However, there are limitations to how much a procedural map can do. If, for example, you want your company logo on the side of your model, procedurals aren't going to do; you need the accuracy of manually painting your texture onto the surface. Table 5–1 compares the two techniques.

Table 5–1. *Procedural and UV-Mapped Textures Compared*

Procedural Textures	UV-Mapped Textures
No texture files needed	Very accurate
Very flexible with regard to experimentation and fine-tuning	Paint applied to textures directly in 3D or through an external 2D paint program (e.g., Gimp/Photoshop)

UV mapping works by having texture(s) in the form of a 2D image transferred onto the surface of the mesh (see Figure 5–1).

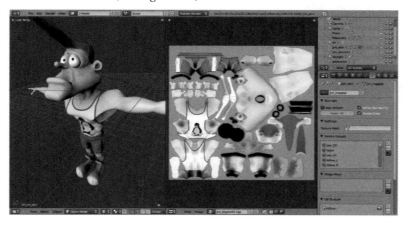

Figure 5–1. *Blender model textured through a UV map*

■ **Note** *u* and *v* refer to the axes of the 2D plane, as opposed to the x, y, and z of the 3D space.

Creating a UV Map

The first stage of UV mapping is to create the UV map layout itself. This is like the paper pattern for making clothes. The basic process involves deciding where to make the cuts (as shown in Figure 5–2) so that the unfolded plan appears ready to texture in the UV editor, as shown in Figure 5–3. For the cutting process, selected edges of the model are marked as *seams*. From these seams, the final unwrapped pattern is able to unfold—not literally in the 3D view, but in a different window type, known as the *UV editor*.

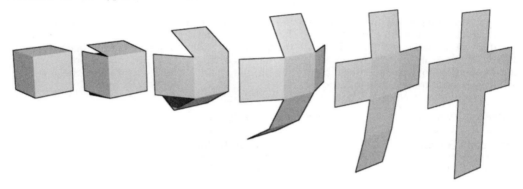

Figure 5–2. *Theoretical image of the unwrapping process*

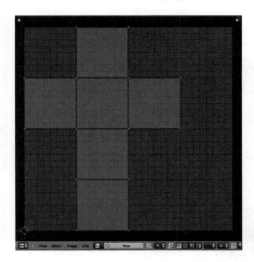

Figure 5–3. *The completed unwrap as it appears in the UV editor*

To get an idea of the process, perform the following steps:

1. Start with a simple mesh, such as a sphere or cube.

2. Split the screen into two views, and change one of them to UV/image editor, using the editor icon in the header strip.

3. Enter edit mode and choose edge select mode, as shown in Figure 5–4.

Figure 5–4. Edit mode with edge select

4. Select the edges (Shift-RMB) that will be seams. Try to select areas that when cut will result in the mesh being able to unfold into a flat pattern. Press Ctrl+E and choose Mark Seam from the pop-up menu. If you make the mistake of marking incorrect seams, you can undo them with Ctrl+E ➤ Clear Seam, which is found just below Mark Seam in the Edges menu (see Figure 5–5).

Figure 5–5. Choose Mark Seam from the pop-up menu.

5. When you think you have achieved well-placed seams, press A to select the full mesh, then press U, and then select Unwrap from the pop-up menu. Blender will attempt to flat-unwrap your mesh in the UV editor window. At this point, errors in seam positioning may become apparent (see some of the examples in Figure 5–6). If necessary, fix the seams as needed and simply unwrap again.

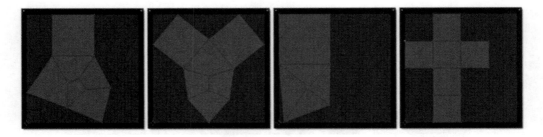

Figure 5–6. Various attempts at unwrapping cubes. Only the last example has seams in sensible places.

The unwrapped pattern in the UV editor window is Blender's best guess at how the pattern should be arranged. You can rearrange the layout if you wish. Simply select the vertices in the UV layout and move them around using the G,S, and R keys, just as you would arrange vertices of a model in 3D view.

SELECTING VERTEX GROUPS

There are faster ways of selecting groups of vertices than using Shift-RMB each in turn. You can use block select (the B key) to select a rectangle-shaped area; just drag your mouse diagonally while holding down the LMB. If you select only a few vertices (or even just one), then pressing Ctrl+L selects all connected vertices.

Once you are happy with the UV layout, save it. This can be done via UVs ➤ Export UV Layout, at the bottom of the UV editor.

When working with UV maps, you should always use dimensions that are powers of two for the UV image canvas (i.e., 16×16, 32×32, 64×64, 128×128, 256×256, 1024×1024, 2048×2048, etc.—each doubling the width and height of the last). The reason for this is that graphics cards find these the easiest sizes to work with.

Open the saved UV layout with a 2D paint program such as Photoshop or Gimp. Paint the surface (something like that shown in Figure 5–7 will suffice) and resave the image in PNG format (or any of the others that can be applied as a texture from within Blender).

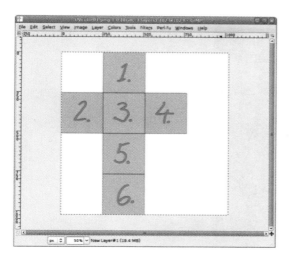

Figure 5–7. *UV layout being edited in Gimp*

Once the UV map is painted and resaved, you can then load it as a texture onto the mesh. To allow the texture to show when rendering (e.g., via the F12 key), add the texture to the material as follows:

1. Go to the Textures tab in the main Properties panel.

2. There is probably already a texture called Tex. If not, click the New button to generate a new texture.

3. From the type selector, choose Image or Movie. This will change a number of the remaining panels, including revealing a new Image area further down the tab.

4. In the Image area, click the Open button and direct Blender to your texture.

5. On the mesh will now render with the texture (e.g. with the F12 key) but the image won't be correctly aligned around the cube object. This is because the texture is being placed onto the model without consideration for the UV map layout. To fix this, go down to the Mapping section and select UV from the Coordinates drop-down list (most likely, Generated will be the current selection). The mesh should now render with the texture correctly positioned.

If you have a computer with a GLSL-capable graphics card, you can set the 3D view to Textured and the Display ➤ Shading attribute on the Properties panel to GLSL to enable the texture to show in 3D view (see Figure 5–8).

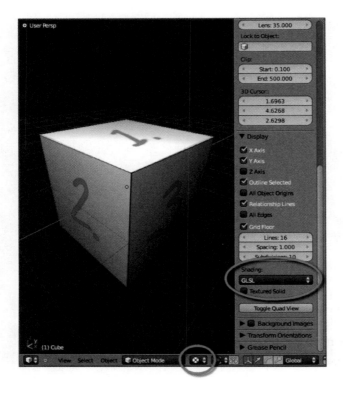

Figure 5–8. *Textured material in 3D view on a GLSL-capable computer*

Using UV maps in conjunction with a 2D paint program, you have the power to create highly detailed and accurate textures. One problem, though, is that it can be difficult to align the textures of separated edges (where they have been split apart on the UV map layout) so that they line up with each other without an obvious seam around the edge of the model.

Wouldn't it be great if textures could be painted on using the 3D view? Fortunately, they can.

Texture Painting

Once your object is unwrapped and a texture is applied to its material through UV coordinates, it is possible to paint directly onto the mesh within Blender itself (painting onto the mesh literally applies changes to the UV-mapped texture). This is a powerful technique because it allows you to paint directly against the surface of your model without having to visualize (in your head) what the results would be like were you to paint the unwrapped UV map texture. Texture painting is heavily reliant on the UV layout, so you should load the texture into the UV editor window.

Go into edit mode and press A to select every vertex of the model. While all vertices are selected, check the UV editor to ensure the model is satisfactorily unwrapped. If not, you need to unwrap the model as described earlier in this chapter.

The UV layout may show that the model geometry is unwrapped, but to enable texture painting you need a texture behind the layout on which the painting will be created. Either load a previously saved image or create a new one.

- If an image is already loaded into Blender (e.g., you might have added the texture previously), then clicking the picture icon to the right of the Image menu at the bottom of the UV editor window should give a list of textures Blender has loaded so far. Choose the texture you want and it will be applied as the UV layout.

- To load an image, in the UV editor go to Image ➤ Open. Remember that images with dimensions of powers of two are best (16×16, 32×32, 64×64, etc.).

- To make a new image, follow the UV editor menu through Image ➤ New and specify the size.

An asterisk next to the Image menu (e.g., Image*) means the current texture is not saved. You can save it by choosing Image ➤ Save As in the UV editor window.

■ **Note** If the texture on the model is different from that shown in the UV editor, you can fix the conflict by going to the Textures tab and selecting the correct texture from the drop-down list under Image.

Now that the UV mapping is all set up, here is how you do the actual texture painting:

1. Go into texture paint mode, using the mode selection drop-down.

2. Press T to bring up the Tool Shelf, which should now display brush options similar to those found in a paint program like Photoshop or Gimp. By default, the chosen brush (which can be changed by LMB-clicking the big image) should be set to TexDraw.

3. To ensure the brush paints a strong line, move the Strength slider to the right, to a value of 1.000.

4. Choose a color from the palette circle above.

5. Draw on the model using the LMB. The texture in the UV window should immediately update to reflect your work in the 3D view, as shown in Figure 5–9. Note that when the "Enable image painting mode" button is enabled (this button is shown in Figure 5–10 and is located in the header strip of the UV/Image editor view), then you can also paint with the mouse directly onto the UV/Image editor view (the unwrapped image).

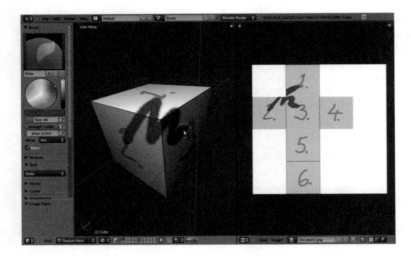

Figure 5–9. Texture painting

Figure 5–10. The "Enable image painting mode" button

Brushes

Once you are in texture paint mode, the Tool Shelf (use the T key to show/hide) is filled with Brush options. While individual properties such as size and strength can be changed, the basic toolset is as follows:

- **Draw**: This is your basic paintbrush. Use it to draw lines.

- **Soften**: This creates a blur effect. Note that Soften only seems to work properly when used with the UV editor window, but it works like Draw (it paints color) when used in the 3D view. This is most likely a bug to be fixed in a future release of Blender.

- **Clone**: Place the 3D cursor in one area (in texture paint mode, Ctrl-LMB-click to reposition the cursor) and paint in another using the LMB. The texture from the location of the 3D cursor duplicates at the second painting area. You should keep the LMB held down while painting or else the paint will reset itself to the position of the cursor.

- **Smear**: This is a smudge tool allowing colors to mix, as when working with charcoal or chalk pastel.

Saving the Texture

The texture is separate from the Blender file, so you will lose it if you don't make an effort to save the image from the UV editor. In the UV/Image editor, you can see the resulting image of your texture painting, and there is an Image menu in the header strip, possibly followed by an asterisk symbol. As stated earlier, an asterisk next to the Image menu indicates that the current texture has not been saved. Follow the menu through Image ➤ Save to do this.

Exercise 1: Cube Painting

Take a couple of cubes and give them some character by using texture paint to give them some personality (see Figure 5–11).

You may like to include editing the textures with your favorite paint program, as multiple programs are often used in production pipelines.

Figure 5–11. *Cube characters*

Projection Painting

Projection painting takes texture painting one step further. Instead of painting with colors, the settings are changed in order to paint with photographic textures taken directly from reference photos. UV mapping can have several layers, which projection painting makes good use of.

In this section, we'll first create separate UV layers for the views (front, side, back, etc., depending on the reference available), and then use these as a basis from which to paint onto the master, or base UV layout.

For this task, we want to texture a head model based on reference photos of the front, side, and back views (see Figure 5–12). The process of projection painting will result in the model being painted over with textures taken from our reference photos.

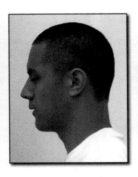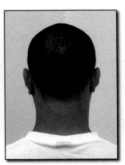

Figure 5–12. Reference photos to be used for texturing our 3D model. Note that the images do not have to line up perfectly with each other because each texture alignment will be corrected in the UV layout window.

Step 1: Unwrapping the Base Mesh

Let's start by unwrapping the base mesh.

1. First of all, unwrap your mesh (I have made a head of my friend in Figure 5–13) and arrange the UV layout to make the most of the available space.

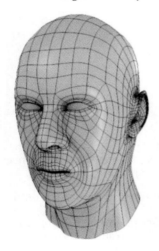

Figure 5–13. A mesh model based on the character from my photo reference images

2. As shown in Figure 5–14, in the UV Texture area on the Object Data tab, rename the UV layout base.

3. Make sure you are in edit mode, and press A to select all vertices. This ensures that you will assign the UV texture to the current mesh for the base layout when you carry out the steps in the next section.

4. In the UV editor window, create a new image (Image ➤ New). Save the image with a name like `base.tga` or `skin.tga`. The image is shown in Figure 5–15.

Figure 5–14. *Renaming a UV layer*

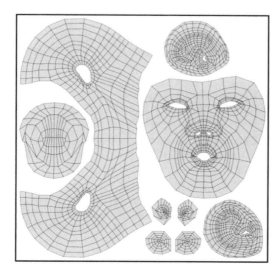

Figure 5–15. *Base head UV layout*

Step 2: Loading in a Reference Image

Once the model is unwrapped, you need to make new UV layers for each of the reference images (front, back, and sides). Ultimately, you are going to clone paint these onto the base mesh.

1. On the Object Data tab, the UV Texture area shows the base material. Click the + button to the right to add another UV layer. At the bottom of the UV Texture area is the Name field. Select the new layer and use this field to call it front, as shown in Figure 5–16.

Figure 5–16. Add and name a new UV layer.

2. With the front layer active, go into edit mode and select the whole mesh with the A key.

3. When we unwrap (which we will do next), we will want a front-on, flat projection without perspective distortion. In a 3D view window, change the view angle to a front orthographic view (use numpad 1 for front view and then numpad 5 to switch between perspective and orthographic modes).

4. Press U for unwrapping options and choose Project From View from the pop-up list. In the UV editor you should see that a new UV layout has appeared, resembling the front-on shape of your model. This is how Project From View differs from plain unwrapping—it unwraps as-is from the view window instead of auto-unwrapping to a best fit.

5. Still in the UV editor, use the Image menu to load in the front view reference. (Image ➤ Open). As long as the 3D view of the mesh is in edit mode and all vertices are selected, you should see the full mesh in the UV layout.

6. Reposition and resize the mesh within the UV editor so that it matches the reference image, as shown in Figure 5–17. It is fine to move individual vertex points in the UV editor to adjust to shape. At this stage, you should find that the 3D view shows a front-on projection on the model going right through the mesh so the face appears on the back of the head, as depicted in Figure 5–18.

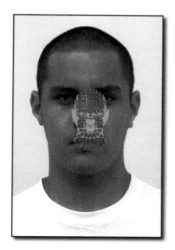
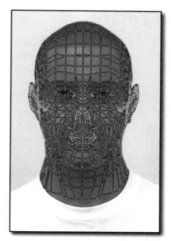

Figure 5–17. Reshaping the vertices to fit in the UV editor window

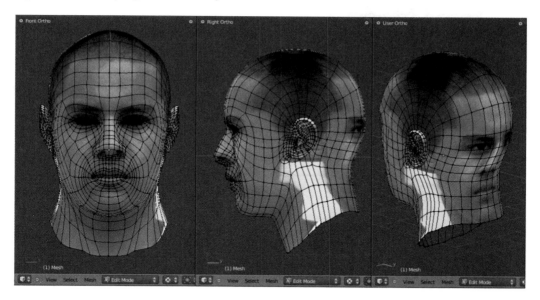

Figure 5–18. Frontal projection going straight through the mesh

7. Repeat the preceding actions to make UV layers for side, back, and any other views you have. When clicking the UV texture area by name on the Object Data tab, the UV editor window should change to show the selected map over its appropriate reference image. Once the different layers are mapped out, you are ready for the final texture painting.

Step 3: Painting the Textures

Once working, texture painting looks like magic. The mouse paints over the mesh, and surface textures appear all in the right place (see Figure 5–19). Of course, in order to paint the textures, certain settings need to be in place. Make sure you can see the textures in 3D view. This means that as you click through the different UV layers on the Object Data tab, different textures appear on the main mesh. The following are some things to watch for here:

- You should be in "Textured" Viewport Shading mode , although you can use "Solid" Viewport Shading mode when the Textured Solid option is checked under the Shading heading of the Display area in the 3D window's Properties panel (shown in Figure 5–20).

- You should also be able to use GLSL and multitexture modes (in the Display properties of the Properties panel), although multitexture is sometimes easiest, because in GLSL mode, the 3D view can be quite dark. You may have to experiment to find the best settings for any model. Results may vary depending on the graphics hardware of your computer, as well.

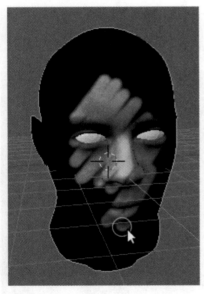

Figure 5–19. Projection painting in progress

Figure 5-20. The Textured Solid option

Let's paint:

1. On the Object Data tab, choose base as the current UV map and texture. This will become the current mesh texture, and is the one we will be painting onto.

2. Switch to texture paint mode, as you did with texture painting earlier on.

3. Under Brush, choose Clone.

4. Set the strength of the brush to the maximum: 1.000.

5. Make sure Project Paint is on.

6. Still within the Project Paint area, make sure Layer is checked.

7. To the right of Layer is the name of one of the UV layers. Select it and choose front.

If all is going well, you should be able to paint on the front of your model (hold down the LMB and rub over the model with your mouse) and paint on the front texture.

When moving around the sides, the front texture will becomes unsuitable, and you'll want your brush to paint textures from the side reference. To do this, simply click the front slot at the bottom of the Project Paint section of the Tool Shelf. A drop-down list like the one in Figure 5–21 will appear, allowing you to choose the side UV layout as your new brush texture.

Sometimes there will be a color variation making a visible seam where front runs into side. In order to blend smoothly, decrease the strength of the brush to allow for some overlap.

Figure 5–21. *Changing the source texture*

With this technique, you should be able to zip around your model very quickly, resulting in a filled-in base UV map, and of course a textured head mesh, as in Figure 5–22. The accuracy is achieved by carefully lining up the vertices in the individual UV layers. Don't forget that you can also touch up the result by other means (ordinary texture paint or your favorite 2D paint program) to really push the quality of the final result.

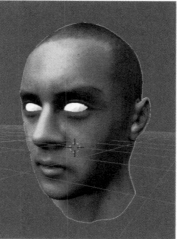

Figure 5–22. Projection painting works by coloring the UV map.

Step 4: Save, Save, Save (Can I Say It Enough?)

Don't forget to save the final UV layer. It is separate from the Blender file.

Exercise 2: Painting a Boxlike Model

For this exercise, take front, side, and back view photos of something boxlike and easy to model, such as a car (Figure 5–23), oven, or fridge. Use these as background images to model over, and then use projection paint techniques to texture your model.

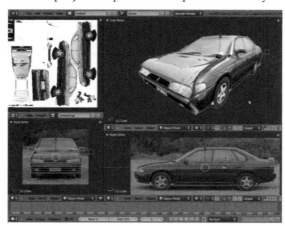

Figure 5–23. Simple car model with texture

Normal Maps and Bump Maps

Both normal maps and bump maps add detail to the surface texture of a model in the form of bumps and dents, making the surface geometry appear a lot more detailed than it actually is. In most cases, where a professionally made 3D character has large amounts of detail down to the wrinkles, skin flakes, and warts, these details are not modeled but are achieved through texture mapping techniques (see the example in Figure 5–24). The render engine treats normal and bump textures as though they are really sticking out, and if done right, the illusion can be very convincing.

The main differences between normal maps and bumps maps are as follows:

- Bump maps are grayscale height maps, with the lighter shades representing added height to the surface at any point. Being grayscale, this is the easiest of the two methods to use if you want to touch up the result in a 2D paint program like Photoshop or Gimp.

- Normal maps are tricolor (based on red, green, and blue). Instead of height data, the color of each pixel in a normal map represents the angle that the area is slanted. One way to think of this is to imagine that the surface is illuminated by three different-colored spotlights from different angles (although the overall tone of a normal map usually has a bluish tinge). Because the lighting is simulated from three angles (as opposed to the single-angled top-down grayscale bump map method), normal maps are the more physically accurate of the two.

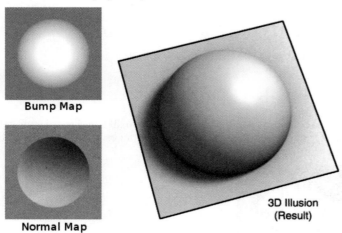

Figure 5–24. *Both the bump map and the normal map can produce the 3D texture effect shown on the right. They are technically different ways to achieve similar ends. Normal maps generally have more accurate results.*

To further illustrate how normal maps work, I created my own by taking three photographs of a coin with lighting from different angles. I colored each image: one red (lighting from the bottom right), one green (lighting from above), and one blue (lighting from the bottom left), so that it looked like each had been lit from its respective colored light before being combined together to form a normal map image. When this image was applied to a single plane as a normal map texture (I'll describe how to do this shortly), the result did indeed produce a 3D-looking coin from the otherwise flat surface, as shown in Figure 5–25.

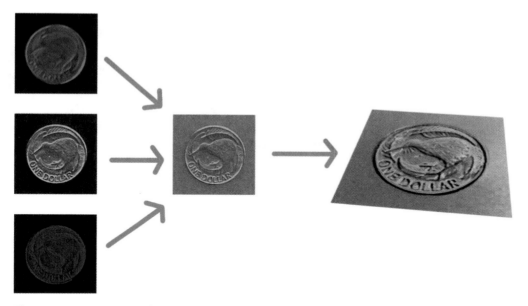

Figure 5–25. *A coin was photographed with lighting from three different angles. When these shots were combined with the correct color for each angle, they produced a working normal map for use in Blender.*

Making a Normal Map

We are going to use the normal map method to add detail to a low-poly mesh, as shown in Figure 5–26. A *low-poly* (or low-resolution) mesh is made from few vertices and can therefore only form a simple shape; on the other hand, a *high-poly* (high-resolution) mesh can be created with thousands of vertices, allowing for fine details such as facial wrinkles). To add the detail to the low-poly mesh, we need two versions of the same model: one low-resolution model, and one high-resolution model with lots of detail. We are going to make a normal map texture based on the details of the high-poly model and apply these to the low-poly model. The important thing is that both models are the same shape.

An overview of our workflow is as follows:

1. Start with the two models—a low-poly version and a high-poly version.

2. Unwrap a UV map of the low-poly version.

3. Bake the high-poly model against the low-poly model to generate a normal map.

4. Apply the normal map as a texture to the low-poly version with the right settings to make it produce bumps instead of color.

Figure 5–26. A low-detail model with a normal map added can look high-detail.

The end result is that the low-poly version will adopt all the detail of the high-poly mesh when the texture is applied, only this low-poly imitation won't be as intensive on rendering as the actual high-poly version, making it the preferable choice for games and other animations for which the render time needs to be reduced.

To obtain the two models, do either of the following:

- Use a low-poly mesh, duplicate it (Shift+D), add layers of multiresolution to make it high-poly, and then sculpt in some details to make the high-poly version.

- Start with a high-poly mesh and use the retopology editing tools to create a low-res version.

Both of these methods were discussed in Chapter 3.

In the properties box, name the versions highres and lowres so you don't mix them up if using the Outliner, as shown in Figure 5–27.

■ **Note** The Outliner is by default positioned above your main panels. It is very useful for selecting an object if the screen is cluttered or if your object is off the screen.

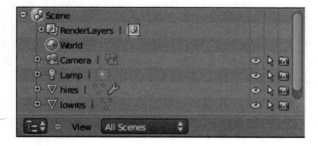

Figure 5–27. The Outliner

The high-poly mesh may look good, but it has far too many vertices to be of practical use for animation (see Figure 5–28). We are now going to map it against the low-poly mesh shown in Figure 5–29 to generate a normal map, based on their geometric surface differences.

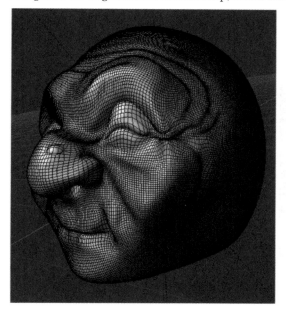

Figure 5–28. *Once applied, a sculpted mesh has a very high vertex count.*

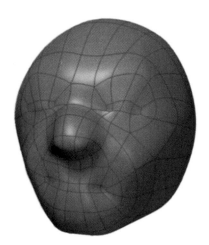

Figure 5–29. *The low-poly mesh has much less detail than the high-poly version, but retains the same shape.*

Step 1: Preparing and Unwrapping Your Low-Poly Model

Let's get started:

1. As described earlier, unwrap the low-poly model. (The high-poly version does not need to be unwrapped. Blender will map the physical space differences of the two models onto the UV map of the low-poly version.) A good normal map depends on a quality (well-spread-out) UV layout, so make sure the map makes good use of the UV area, as in Figure 5–30.

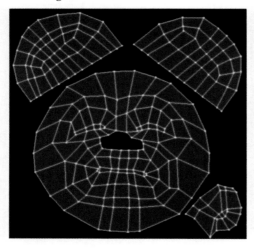

***Figure 5–30.** Low-poly mesh unwrapped*

2. Because we are going to bake a normal map to the low-poly mesh, the low-poly model needs to be assigned a texture in the UV editor. In the UV editor, create a new texture. Save it with the name `normalmap.tga` or similar. Of course, it won't really be a normal map yet (that will happen in the "Step 3: Baking the Normal Map" section).

■ **Note** It is an advantage to have the surface of both models set to Smooth; otherwise, hard edges may taint your results. This can be done in the Shading section of the Tool Shelf when in object mode.

Step 2: Selecting Both Models

The important thing here is to select the low-poly mesh—which will ultimately have the UV texture baked to it—last. This can be tricky when they are both in the same place. Following are a couple of techniques you can use to achieve this:

- If you place each model onto a different layer, you will be able to turn the low-poly layer off, select the high-poly mesh, reenable the low-poly layer, and then Shift-RMB-select the low-poly mesh. It is important that you select the low-poly mesh *after* the high-poly mesh, because it's the UV map of the last item selected that will receive the normal map data in the process you are about to follow.

- Alternatively, if the models are appropriately named, it is easy to Shift-LMB-select them in the right order through the Outliner window—though again, make sure the low-poly mesh is selected last.

■ **Note** When baking one mesh against the other, it is important for the models to be in the same xyz position, as Blender creates the normal map by comparing the surfaces. Having the models apart will give you incorrect results.

Save your work now, even though you're not done, in case Blender crashes during the CPU-intensive baking stage.

Step 3: Baking the Normal Map

With the `normalmap` texture loaded into the UV/image editor and both models selected, you are nearly ready to bake the normal map. There are just a few settings to take care of first:

1. On the Render tab (camera icon) in the Bake area (see Figure 5–31), set the options as follows:

    - Set Bake Mode to Normals.

    - Set Normal Space to Tangent.

    - Check the Selected to Active box.

Figure 5–31. Baking options

119

2. Finally, click the Bake button at the top. If all goes well, there may be a pause, and then your normal map, resembling Figure 5–32, should be generated in the UV editor window.

3. When done, make sure you save the image using the Image menu at the bottom of the UV/Image editor window.

Figure 5–32. Normal map

POSSIBLE ERRORS

If you get the report "No image to bake to," it means you have failed to assign an image to either to the model (as a texture) or the UV window. There are several additional possible problems you might encounter, including artifacts ranging from odd colors to some faces rendering as black. If you're confronted with any of these, you can try the following:

1) Reset the normals of your mesh by going into edit mode, selecting all faces of the model, and then following the menu through Mesh ➤ Normals ➤ Recalculate Outside (Ctrl+N). Also check that your mesh does not have any twisted faces in terms of which way is inside and which is out.

2) There are also some options you can experiment with, such as Margin, Distance, and Bias, in order to remedy odd artifacts. Which are needed may vary depending on the model.

At the risk of repeating myself, save the map through the UV editor when you are done.

Step 4: Applying the Normal Map to the Low-Poly Mesh

The normal map is made, but we now need to apply it to our low-poly model. The low-poly model has already been UV-unwrapped, which is important because it is this unwrap that will align it to the normal map we've saved; they are of identical UV layout. This means that when we add the UV map texture file, it will be prealigned with the mesh surface. You should understand that if you were to use a different model, or even unwrap this one, the texture map layout would be in disarray.

Let's load in the map: Note that the texture is already loaded into the current Blender file. On the texture tab you only need to select the normalmap texture for this part. However, if you need to load a new texture file, here are the steps:

1. On the Texture tab, add a new texture—or, in this case, you can actually select the normals texture because it is still in this particular Blender file. You should add a new texture for the cases in which you want to import the normal map to another model.

2. If not already named, at the top of the Texture tab, rename the selected texture normal.

3. Set the texture type to Image or Movie.

4. Click the file button to load a new image.

Now that the texture is loaded in, set it up as follows:

5. Under Mapping, make sure the coordinates are set to UV. This causes Blender to use the UV layers to line up the textures.

6. Because the map is meant to influence normals (bumps), not color, in the Influence area, disable Color and enable Normal. This prevents the texture from affecting the diffuse color of the surface, and instead allows it to affect the bumping caused by a normal map (which is what we are doing).

7. In the Image Sampling area, check the Normal Map box and choose Tangent. These settings are important for telling Blender what kind of normal map is being used, as there are variations. Tangent maps are good for models as they allow the object to rotate. Other types do exist, with some of the older ones (like those originally made for the walls of games) not allowing for real-time rotation of the object.

Perform a render of your model (e.g., by pressing F12), and you should see the results. However, we still need to show them in 3D view. Provided you are using a computer with a GLSL-compatible graphics card, try the following:

1. Press N to bring up the Properties panel in 3D view, and then go to the Display area and change the shading: type to GLSL.

2. Change the viewport shading of your 3D view to Textured, as shown in Figure 5–33.

Figure 5–33. Changing the viewport shading of a 3D view

Figure 5–34 shows the final result.

Figure 5–34. *The final result (left) looks highly detailed, but the mesh is is actually low resolution (right, showing wire).*

So that's it. Now you can use normal mapping to give your low-resolution meshes some high-resolution punch, without compromising heavily on animation render times.

Summary

We have moved on from the procedural textures of the last chapter to more accurate UV-mapping and texture-painting methods. It is possible to use procedurals as a starting point for UV mapping via the bake functions.

We looked at projection painting: a fast method of texturing from a photographic reference, as well as how you can use normal maps to add a good amount of detail to otherwise flat surfaces.

UV mapping differs from procedural textures in that it gives you the power to hand paint a lot of fine detail on a surface with accuracy.

■ ■ ■

CHAPTER 6

Curves and NURBS

In this chapter we are going to explore some advanced modeling techniques, mostly suited for curved or wirelike structures that would prove tricky to model as a straight polygon mesh. The techniques covered in Chapter 3 are good for modeling most items, but there are times when a specialist tool makes the job easier. Specifically, we are going to examine

- *Metaballs/meta objects*: Useful for modeling liquid objects like mud

- *Curves*: Useful for modeling wire, especially of the bendable variety

- *Spin editing*: Useful for modeling circular forms

- *NURBS (nonuniform rational basis spline)*: Useful for accurate modeling of curved surfaces

Learning these techniques will expand your modeling capabilities in a variety of areas.

Metaballs

Metaballs (aka meta objects) are like ordinary primitives, but with a special ability to act like mud—squishing into each other in order to make new shapes.

Let's see how to use them now:

1. Start with a new scene, select the default cube, and press X to delete it.

2. Add the metaball via Shift+A ➤ Metaball ➤ Meta Ball.

3. The new sphere looks ordinary enough so far, except that it has an extra ring around it. While you are in object mode, duplicate the metaball with Shift+D.

4. Drag the new metaball away from the first. As you do, notice how they meld together, as shown in Figure 6–1.

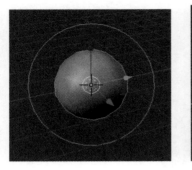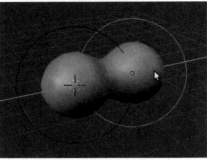

Figure 6–1. Duplicating and pulling apart metaballs

■ **Note** As with polygon objects, if you are in edit mode when adding or duplicating items, they become part of the object you are editing. You should be in object mode when adding new items to ensure they really are separate objects.

---

5. Experiment with how the meta objects interact with each other, including the other available types: Meta Tube, Meta Plane, Meta Cube, and Meta Ellipsoid (see Figure 6–2). Be sure to transform (scale, rotate, and move) the shapes in order to observe the effects.

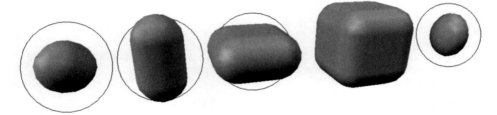

Figure 6–2. From left to right, Meta Ball, Meta Tube, Meta Plane, Meta Cube, and Meta Ellipsoid objects

How Meta Objects Work

If you observe a meta object in edit mode, you will notice it has a field of two circles: one red and one green. While in edit mode, you can RMB-select either of these circles and resize them using the S key (conversely, in object mode, resizing the meta object has the same effect as resizing the outer red circle).

The outer red circle is known as the selection circle. Selecting this circle is the same as selecting the meta object itself, as though in object mode. The perimeter of the selection circle marks the maximum possible size of the inner green circle.

The inner green circle marks the stiffness of the meta object, which in addition to being resized via the S key, can also be changed manually through the Stiffness value in the Active

Element area of the Object Data tab when the meta object is selected in edit mode (see Figure 6–3). The larger the Stiffness value, the larger the green circle gets.

Figure 6–3. *The Stiffness setting*

The size of the 3D metaball is typically slightly smaller than the green stiffness circle. This circle can be resized from a stiffness of 0 (where it is so small as to render as nonexistent) to a stiffness of 10 (where it becomes almost as big as the selection circle).

Where the green circles of two meta objects overlap, the resulting 3D meta objects they influence begin to merge in a gravity-like manner, as shown in Figure 6–4.

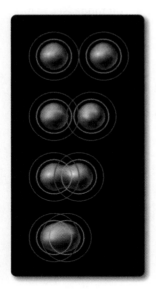

Figure 6–4. *How meta objects merge*

Exercise 1: Mud Monster

For this exercise, try to use meta objects to form a mud monster like the one in Figure 6–5. You might want to utilize non-metaball polygon spheres for the eyeballs so they don't mix with the other meta objects.

Figure 6–5. *Making a mud monster*

Meta Object Properties

Meta objects have a few special properties that can be accessed through the Object Data tab. The following subsections give a breakdown of the options.

Standard Options

Following are the standard options on the Object Data tab for meta objects (see Figure 6–6):

- *Resolution*: This affects the smoothness of the meta object. Note that there are different resolution settings for the 3D view and for what shows up in a render. This is because with large scenes and/or slow computers, higher resolutions may slow performance. You can set a low resolution for the main 3D view so the computer works very fast, while enabling a high resolution for a very smooth result on the final render.

- *Threshold*: This affects the overall influence of the meta object. To understand how this works, realize that meta objects are created as though they are a liquid volume inside a force field that pulls them to their finished shape (the area of this field is represented by the circle you see around the meta object in the 3D view). If the threshold is set to 0 or exceeds the area of the force field, the meta object becomes void and so will not be visible.

Figure 6–6. *Meta object options*

Edit Mode Options

The following meta object options are only available in edit mode:

- *Type*: Meta objects are interchangeable. If you chose a Meta Ball but really want a Meta Cube, the Type option allows you to change it.

- *Stiffness*: This setting affects the size of the meta object, as discussed previously. This setting defines the size of the green circle, and the end 3D meta object is usually just smaller than the green circle.

- *Negative*: Whereas meta objects are normally solid shapes that merge together in a liquidlike way, activating the Negative property transforms the meta object into a void, making them empty spaces that forms holes in other meta objects they come into contact with.

- *Hide*: This setting makes meta objects invisible, and causes them to lose their influence on other meta objects.

- *Size*: This option does not apply to the Meta Ball shape, but applies to all the other meta objects; it allows them to be stretched in different directions.

Curves

You can add curves by pressing Shift+A and accessing the Curve menu. There are three types of curves, as follows:

- Bezier (curve and circle)

- NURBS (curve and circle)

- Path

They can produce some awesome organic-looking effects, such as growing vines or the tentacles shown in Figure 6–7. At first these curves look very similar, but there are distinct differences in how they work. When you enter edit mode, their differences become apparent.

Figure 6–7. *Proog gets a case of curve phobia in Elephants Dream.*

Bezier (Curve and Circle)

Circles and Bezier curves are controlled in a similar way to the paths in vector art programs such as Inkscape and Adobe Illustrator. The control points are like seesaw lines that can be moved, rotated, or scaled to influence the positioning and curvature of the curve, as shown in Figure 6–8.

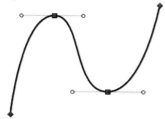

Figure 6–8. *Bezier curve*

Figure 6–9 gives an example of the type of complexity that can be created with a Bezier curve.

Figure 6–9. *This cord is made with a Bezier curve.*

NURBS (Curve and Circle)

NURBS curves and NURBS circles are similar to the circles and Bezier curves of the last section, except that the control handles act more like magnetic corners of a cage around the curve object, as opposed to actual points on the object itself. As mentioned, *NURBS* stands for *nonuniform rational basis spline*, which is a technical description basically stating that the NURBS points control the shape of curves or surfaces in a gravity-like manner. A friend of mine put it simply by saying that NURBS modeling is "like modeling with magnets." The effect is easier to see with NURBS surfaces than on single curves (we will be exploring NURBS surfaces in more detail later in this chapter). With NURBS, the location of the control points is what affects the shape (pulling the surface); scaling or rotating individual control points of a NURBS curve makes no difference to the final shape of the curve.

Path

For a path, the controllers are joined as a line, with the path object flowing through the curve of the line; the object's positioning is affected as an average of the values of the control points.

By changing certain settings (e.g., the Endpoint: U option, which defines whether the curve should stretch to the end control points), you can make the default path object look very much like the default NURBS curve.

Modifying a Curve

Remember that in edit mode, it is possible to simply move control points around to change the shape of a curve. Bezier control points have handles (as shown in Figure 6–8), allowing them to be rotated or scaled (once a point is selected, the R and S keys will work to rotate or scale the area), unlike the control points of NURBS shapes. There are also three methods to add new points to an existing curve:

- With the first or last control point selected, you can extrude the curve and make it longer by pressing E.

- You can select adjacent control points, press W, and then choose Subdivide to add control points between the selected ones.

- To delete selected control points, you can press X and then choose Selected from the pop-up menu that appears.

Path Editing

Understanding how NURBS and Bezier curves differ is one thing, but of course you still need to see firsthand how you can edit them:

Add a Bezier curve to the scene by pressing Shift+A and choosing Add ➤ Curve ➤ Bezier.

1. Select the new Bezier curve and switch to edit mode.

2. Click the endpoint. Note that every controller point on a Bezier curve is in fact a pink line connecting three points; the main controller point is in the middle, and two handles extend out either side. For now, it is important that you select the main (middle) controller.

3. Click E to extrude a new point from the controller. Move the mouse pointer to pull the newly extruded section to a different position, and then LMB-click (or press Enter) to drop the point into place.

4. Use the E key to extrude a few more times until you have a reasonable path.

Adding Points

So far, you know that you can use the E key to extrude the ends of a path outward. This only works with the very endpoints of a curve. A path is supposed to be a single line, so you can't fork branches out from the middle (although this can be faked by using SHIFT-D to duplicate selected areas of a path). It is possible to add new control points in between other points along the path. To do this, Shift-RMB-select two control points that are next to each other. Then press the W key and choose Subdivide from the menu that appears. Blender will add new control points between any adjacent pairs you have selected. This works even with selecting multiple selections of the path at the same time.

Deleting Points

To delete points, RMB-select them (you can Shift-RMB-click to select multiple points) and press X. When the menu appears asking what you would like to delete, choose Select to delete the chosen points. This will cause the selected points to disappear.

You can also break a path (tearing it into two) by selecting two adjacent points, pressing X, and choosing Segment from the pop-up menu. At the time of writing, you cannot delete multiple segments at once—only one at a time.

After a segment is deleted from the middle of a path, you normally end up with a gap. You can bridge any such gaps by selecting the end control points of the paths and using the F key to fill them. Note that this only works with separate parts of the same path (e.g., the path cannot be two different paths when in object mode). Indeed, if you want to combine separate paths into one, Shift-RMB-select them both in object mode, and then press Ctrl+J to join them. Back in edit mode, if you have separated segments of a path that you wish to literally split into separate objects, select the control points of one section and use the P key to break it off as a separate object.

Controller Handle Types

You can change the type of controller handle depending on whether you want a section of a curve to meet the controller in a smooth curve or as a sharp corner. When selecting points along a Bezier curve, the Handles section of the Tool Shelf offers four varieties to choose from (see Figure 6–10), as summarized in Table 6–1.

Table 6–1. Different Types of Handles

Handle Effect	Type	Description
	Align	This kind of handle is very useful for defining curves. It works by always keeping the handles for any control point on a straight line between them, so that the resulting path passes through as a smooth curve. You can still move the handles, rotating them to change the angle of the curve or scaling them (move them in and out from the main control point) to widen or narrow the curvature. This is the default handle type for Bezier curves.
	Auto	This is like the Align option in that it creates curves by having the handles at the opposite sides of a straight line between them. The difference is that the rotation of handles switches to automatic mode, and the length and angle of the handles is automatically adjusted to create the smoothest curve for their control points. This means that you no longer manipulate the control point yourself. The moment you do so, the handles will switch to align mode. This handle type is the default handle for Bezier circles.
	Free	With this option, each handle of a control point becomes independent of the other. You can still create curves by manually placing the handles on opposite sides of the main control point, but generally this type is useful because of its ability to create sharp corners.
	Vector	Like the auto handle type, the vector handle is also automatic. Instead of making smooth curves, however, vector handles create sharp point-to-point paths by having handles because they point toward the next adjacent controller in the path. Like auto handles, if you try to move the handles yourself, they switch to free mode.

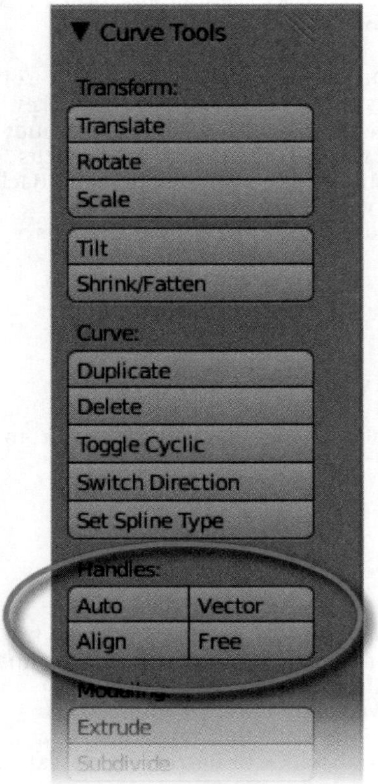

Figure 6–10. Tool Shelf options for changing the type of selected handles

At this point, you should experiment with making a path so that you get comfortable with moving the points around. The G,S, and R keys work when repositioning control points and handles, although you should also take care to notice the subtle differences between repositioning the control points and repositioning their handles (e.g., moving handles around with the G key has the effect of rotating the control point). Note that you can't directly rotate control points of the automatic types (auto and vector). To do so, you need to move the handles manually (using the align or free types).

Making a Circle

It's also important to know how to make a curve cyclic, in which the curve completes itself, connecting the last point to the first in a large loop. You can do this either by clicking the Toggle Cyclic button in the Tool Shelf, or by means of the shortcut Alt+C.

2D and 3D Curves

Regardless of whether curves are Bezier or NURBS, they have a very important setting that divides them into two groups: whether they are 2D or 3D. This setting can be changed through the Shape area of the Object Data tab, as shown in Figure 6–11. The main difference is that a 3D curve can have its control points positioned anywhere in the 3D space, whereas 2D curves are always flat on a 2D plane.

Figure 6–11. Interchanging 2D and 3D curves

We will next look at how to implement 2D and 3D curves.

Modeling with a 2D Curve

In order to familiarize you with the process of modeling with 2D curves, I am going to give some step-by-step instructions for path modeling a simple ring (the kind you would wear on your finger).

> Start with a blank scene (delete the default cube).

1. Add a Bezier circle (click Shift+A, and then select Add ➤ Curve ➤ Circle).

2. Add a second Bezier circle and shrink it down a little inside the first so the two circles form the outside and inside of the ring.

3. In object mode, Shift-RMB-select both circles.

4. Press Ctrl+J, and the two circles will become one object, looking something like Figure 6–12.

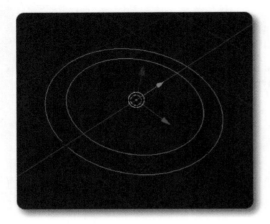

Figure 6–12. Two Bezier circles joined

5. Go to the Object Data tab. By default, the curve type is probably set to 3D. Set it instead to 2D, and the space between the two circles will be filled in, as in Figure 6–13. This is because 2D paths form flat surfaces, filled in where possible.

Figure 6–13. When made 2D, the closed path is filled in.

6. A little further down the Object Data tab, in the Modification section, slide the Extrude value up to something like 0.2. This Extrude controller works much like pressing the E key to extrude polygon surfaces. When you increase the Extrude value, the circle is raised, forming a solid ring shape, as shown in Figure 6–14.

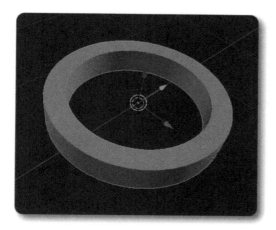

Figure 6–14. The ring extruded

It is worth noting at this stage that if you don't want the front or back face of the ring to be filled in, you can uncheck the Front or Back Caps options found in the Shape area of the Object Data tab, as these directly control the visibility of each end of the extruded design (as shown in Figure 6–15). Note that the bevel depth can interfere with the look of this, so set Extrude Depth to 0 in order to ensure seeing the expected result. The Caps options only work for 2D curves that have been extruded. (With 3D curves, which we will look at soon, they control the side of the curve on which a specified bevel depth is applied.)

Figure 6–15. The flat edges of the ring (made with 2D curves) are filled via the Caps options.

You can use the Width controller to adjust the thickness of the ring. Beware of setting the Width value too low, however, which will cause the inner wall to become the outer wall and the outer wall to become the inner wall. This effectively turns the ring inside out, and can create odd shading effects known as reversed normals. Put simply, the normal direction for an outside wall is to be facing the outside. When you invert shapes, the outer wall is really the inside wall from the inside.

The ring is a rough shape at the moment. You can increase the bevel depth to make the edges sharp, and then bump up the bevel resolution to make the bevel rounder (see Figures

6–16 and 6–17). This can greatly increase the amount of vertices used in the final shape, so don't push it further than what you visually need.

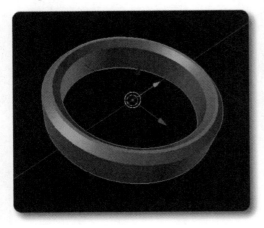

Figures 6–16. *Bevel without bevel resolution*

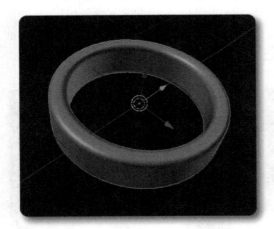

Figure 6–17. *Bevel with bevel resolution*

And there you have it; a simple example of what is needed to model from a 2D path. Of course, using the path-editing tools we looked at previously, you can create more sophisticated shapes than this ring. Perhaps you could apply the same technique to make a 3D company logo (see Figure 6–18 for an example). Bear in mind that I'm only messing around with the idea here. Blender is open source, but its logo is copyright protected, so if you're going to use it, please first read www.blender.org/blenderorg/blender-foundation/logo for the official terms of use.

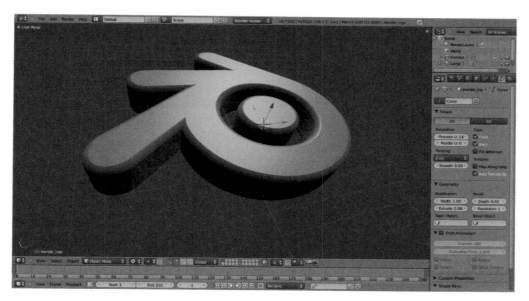

Figure 6–18. *The Blender logo, produced using a 2D path*

Even after extruding the path into a ring shape, you can still go into edit mode and freely manipulate the control points and/or their handles. What you cannot do with a 2D path is pull one of the control points up into the air (i.e., if the ring were lying flat on the ground), as this would make it a 3D path. Even though extrusion makes objects look 3D, the 2D path itself is always flat.

Modification and Bevel Parameters

At this point, I'd like to give a brief summary of the parameters found in the Geometry area of the Object Data tab for curve objects.

Width

Width is a modification parameter that causes the curve to act as though the control points are either closer together or further apart along the curve. This gives the effect of offsetting the position of the curve against the literal position of the control points. In the case of our ring, the resulting effect made the ring appear to have a different thickness, so "width" was indeed a sensible name for the influence. The Width setting can range from 0 to 2, and the default value is 1. In most cases, you would want to use the default setting.

Extrude

Extrude is a modification parameter that stretches the curve shape in a direction perpendicular to its natural flat shape (technically, the local z direction of the curve), so as to give the otherwise flat shape a 3D appearance. As an example, if a 2D curve were drawn on the ground, the local z direction would be upward into the air.

Depth

Perhaps the most important bevel setting, this produces a chiseled bevel of a width directly specified by the Depth value. A Depth value of 0 causes no bevel, whereas higher values result in a wider bevel around the otherwise sharp-edged corners of the extruded curve shape.

Resolution

By itself, the Depth parameter creates a straight, angular bevel. Increasing the Resolution parameter allows the bevel to become curved. Bear in mind that this increases the internal geometry of the resulting 3D form—you can see this by going into wireframe view mode (via the Z key). In other words, the internal construction of the shape becomes more complicated.

Modeling with a 3D Curve

Now that you've seen how 2D curves work, we'll take a look at 3D curves. As stated earlier, 3D curves have the advantage over 2D curves that their controller points don't have to lie in a single plane; they can be placed anywhere in terms of xyz location.

Select the ring made from the 2D curve.

1. In the Shape area of the Object Data tab, click the 3D button (refer back to Figure 6–11). Notice that the caps of the ring will instantly disappear—they are not supported with the 3D version of curves. Now, if you use the Front and Back caps options in the Shape area of the Object Data tab, they will control whether the corresponding side has a bevel enabled.

2. Go into edit mode so you can manipulate the controller points.

3. Select a couple of controller points and move them upward (the Z direction) from their previously flat position.

Unlike the points in a 2D curve, the points can move anywhere, and you should be able to warp the ring as in Figure 6–19, making it look like an old, soft tire.

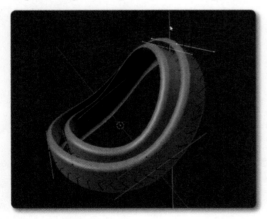

Figure 6–19. *In a 3D curve, the controllers can be moved from the flat surface to which they were restricted in 2D curves.*

One more difference you will see with 3D curves is that the inner curve has what looks something like fins along its length. Unlike 2D curves, 3D curves can be twisted, and these lines are displayed to give you a better sense of the direction of curve flow. Any beveled edges of a 3D curve will lean toward the inside of the shape. Note that you can select all control points along a curve and then click the Toggle Cyclic button on the Tool Shelf to reverse the direction of the curve, thus inverting the inside and outside and reversing any bevels.

Now, you may be wondering why the 3D curves don't allow for filled-in caps like the 2D curves do. In truth, they probably could, but with the amount of freedom that users have with 3D curves, it would be too easy to create shapes that would be difficult for Blender to fill in as end caps. If the cap edges have different heights, for example, Blender may not be able to easily work out the direction that the caps surface should go especially if the path were made to twist. Such would be the case if a user created a curve that overlaps or spirals over itself, as in Figure 6–20. However, although this is a difficult task for the developers to work out and isn't supported in Blender currently, it might yet be possible in a future Blender version.

Figure 6–20. *If paths have areas of overlap, it could potentially be difficult for Blender to work out where the caps should go.*

Another way of modeling with curves is to add properties to make the curve appear as though it is a pipe. This works with 3D curves and 2D curves, although if you want the pipes to rotate in multiple xyz directions (as opposed to lying flat along a plane), then a 3D curve would be the obvious choice.

Start with a simple curve like a Bezier (press Shift+A, and then select Add ➤ Curve ➤ Bezier). You can extrude the endpoint in edit mode if you like.

1. In the Shape area of the Object Data tab, make sure that both the Front and Back options for caps are off (uncheck them).

2. In the Geometry area of the Object Data tab, increase the Extrude value of the curve. You should see the curve stretch upward, resembling something like a piece of tape.

3. Now increase the Bevel Depth value. The tape should grow in width so that it resembles a hexagonal pipe.

4. Increase the Bevel Resolution setting if you want a curved bevel instead of a hexagonal one.

At this point, I should make a special note of how the caps work for this kind of pipe. You'll only get a full round pipe if the Front and Back Caps options are unchecked. Once you activate either front or back caps, half the pipe will disappear, and the Front and Back values will become controllers for whether the front (top side) or back (bottom side) bevels should be shown. These results are a little confusing at first, but easily understood if you examine the options shown in Figure 6–21.

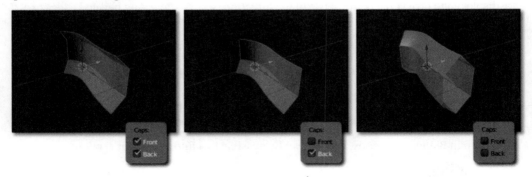

Figure 6–21. *The effect of Caps settings on a pipe made from a curve*

As you can see, the results are a little weird in terms of the Caps options indicating whether the front (top) side has a bevel or the back (bottom) side has a bevel.

Using Other Objects to Define a Custom Curve

There is another interesting method for creating curves that doesn't involve using the extrude or bevel functions, but instead allows you to borrow the shape of a curve-based pipe from another object. This may sound complicated, but it's actually quite straightforward and gives you a lot more power in shaping your 3D curve–based tentacles once you get the idea. However, this technique only works when using other curve shapes. The following exercise shows you how to use it:

Start with a path that you want to make into a pipe.

1. Off to one side of the path, create a new NURBS circle (press Shift+A, and then click Curve ➤ Nurbs Circle; make sure you are in object mode when you do this).

2. With the NURBS circle selected, go to the Object Data tab in the Properties panel. The very top of this panel contains a text box where you can rename the NURBS curve object. The NURBS curve will be called Curve by default; rename it something like Bevel Object.

3. Select the original path again. On the Object Data tab in the Geometry area, enter the name of the NURBS circle into the Bevel Object field. The path will now transform into a pipe, as in Figure 6–22.

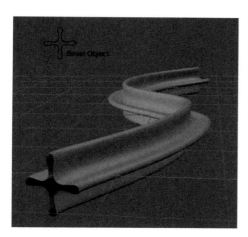

Figure 6–22. The path getting its shape from a bevel object

4. Edit the shape of the Bezier circle, and you will see that the original path adopts the same shape along the length of the pipe.

5. Add a new curve and enter its name into the Taper Object field for your main curve. Doing so will create a shape with which to define the thickness of the pipe from one end to the other. Taper objects always go the full length of a curve, giving results similar to those shown in Figure 6–23.

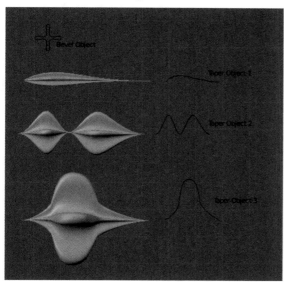

Figure 6–23. The effect of differently shaped curves used as taper objects

Hooks

Paths are great for modeling long, bendable shapes like cords and wire. Going into edit mode and changing the control points will get you the shape you need, but the editing route is not always the best. The edited path is fixed, and does not allow for animation of the path (e.g., if it were to represent a wavy hose or a moving snake).

For this, you would use hooks. Simply put, you can hook control points of a curve onto other objects so that moving that object has the same effect as if you were moving the control point itself, but without the need for returning to edit mode. (Incidentally, points of a standard mesh can also be hooked to external objects, though we are focusing on curves for now). The following exercise describes how to use hooks:

Start with a curve (it does not matter whether you use a Bezier curve, NURBS curve, or standard path).

1. In edit mode, select one of the control points (note that you can Shift-select others as a group, but choose just one control point for now).

2. Use Ctrl+H to create a new hook. When the menu pops up, choose Hook to New Object. This will cause Blender to create an empty target right over the selected control point.

3. Go into object mode and move the empty. The control points of the curve will also be moved. If the curve type is Bezier, you will also be able to use resizing and rotation.

The Ctrl+H menu also has a Hook to Selected Object option, making it possible to use another object in place of the empty Blender created in the preceding method. To use this, take the following steps:

Start in object mode.

1. RMB-select the object you would like to use as the controller.

2. Shift-RMB-select the curve to be influenced (the last selected curve will be the active object).

3. With both selected, go into edit mode.

4. Select a control point of the curve.

5. Press Ctrl+H and choose Hook to Selected Object.

You can use this to connect two objects to each other by a wire, perhaps with midpoint controllers influencing the positioning of the line between.

Note that hooks also work with selected vertices of a mesh object.

Exercise 2: Curve Bugs

Now that we have lookedat the properties of curves, practice modeling with them by making an insect or an alien life form using curves as the primary modeling technique. Check out the amazing picture in Figure 6–24 by Ugis Brekis for some inspiration.

Figure 6–24. Wasp: Curve-based modeling by Ugis Brekis (aka Duffy of the BlenderArtists forums)

Of course, I wouldn't expect that amount of detail from someone just learning curves for the first time—curves can be very difficult to control! Try making simpler versions like the examples in Figure 6–25, or perhaps try a stick person if you want something easier.

Figure 6–25. Example wire bugs

Spin

The Spin tool takes selected vertices of a model (in edit mode) and spins them around the 3D cursor to create either tubelike forms or a ring of repeating objects (the Dupli option determines whether the spin results in a ring or repeating objects in a circle—see Figure 6–26).

It is an unusual tool in that it depends on the angle from which you are looking at the object (e.g., the position of your 3D window view) as well as its use of the Blender cursor, which acts as the center of rotation for the spin function.

To see how spin works, start with some object in the view selected. The default cube is fine. LMB-click somewhere off to the side to place the 3D cursor at that point.

1. Switch to top view (numpad 7) and position the main view window so you have a clear view of both the object and the 3D cursor.

2. Go into edit mode for the object and select all vertices (press A).

3. Press T to bring up the Tool Shelf if it is not there already.

4. In the Mesh Tools section, click the Spin button under Add.

Figure 6–26. Spin options in the toolbar

You should see a trail of cubes spinning clockwise around the 3D cursor. The default spin is unlikely to have the settings you are after, though (e.g., you might want a different number of cloned objects).

Spin Properties

At the bottom of the Tool Shelf, as shown in Figure 6–27, some new items appear for tweaking the outcome. The really useful ones are as follows:

- *Steps*: This is the number of extra objects created.

- *Degrees*: This option specifies how far around the circle the last object of the spin trail will be around the circle, in degrees. If you choose 360, the final object will fall back onto the first, due to the nature of how spin works—anything that spins 360 degrees ends where it starts.

- *Dupli*: If this option is on, your spin will create a ring of separate shapes, and if it's off, the spin will be filled in around the edge to form a tube (very useful for making round shapes like bottles). The difference is illustrated in Figure 6–28.

Figure 6–27. Spin options

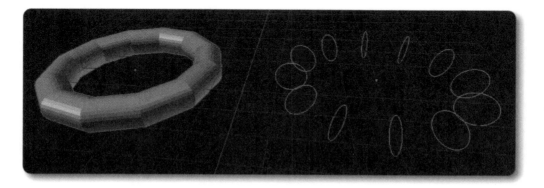

Figure 6–28. The result of performing a spin with Dupli off (left) and on (right)

Calculating the Spin Angle

If you want to have an object spin in a full circle, leaving a trail of clones like the cubes in Figure 6–29 (e.g., a ring of 12 objects to mark positions for the hours of a clock), you will need to calculate the number of jumps (or steps) and the angle the spin needs to travel. Working out the correct angles and distances takes a small amount of mathematics.

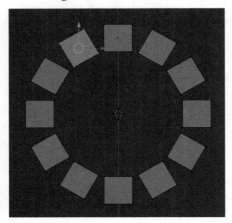

Figure 6–29. *Cubes dupliverted by the spin function*

To make a full circle of cubes, choose the following settings for the spin:

- Activate Dupli.
- Make the number of steps one fewer than the number of final objects wanted (in this case, 11).
- For the angle in degrees, divide 360 by the final number of objects wanted, and multiply the result by the number of steps.

In this case, the actual math would be as follows:

- Steps = 12 − 1 = 11
- Degrees = (360 / 12) × 11 = 330

Note that the formulas for calculating the spin angle apply only to solid sections, such as cubes, and Dupli must be on to produce a ring of clones. Alternatively, you can make tubular forms from a single line by spinning it 360 degrees without Dupli enabled. With this method, the final vertices will end up rotating over the first, creating a shape that is doubled over itself. You can apply the math to work out exactly how far the object needs to spin so that it does not duplicate; alternatively, you can fix this by selecting the full mesh in edit mode and selecting Mesh ➤ Vertices ➤ Remove Doubles.

Using Spin

Now that you understand how spin works, you can see how it can also be used to make circular models such as a wheel. It can take a bit of trial and error to make sure the vertices match and the shape closes nicely after a spin. Sometimes the best way is to spin, adjust the vertices so they meet evenly, delete objects of the first spin, and then spin again.

The example in Figure 6–30 models a bottle. Let's see how to do it:

1. First, place an image of the bottle behind the 3D view, using the Background Images area of the Properties panel.

2. Check the box indicating that you want a background image, and then click the Add Image button.

3. Next, click the expandable triangle before the Not Set option, and click the Open button to locate the bottle image on your hard drive. For background images to work, the 3D view needs to be a front or side view and set to orthographic mode.

Figure 6–30. *Tracing and extruding a single vertex to outline half a bottle for spinning*

4. Once the bottle is loaded, create a new object (using Shift+A to add a plane), and in edit mode delete all but one of the vertices. You should snap the vertex to the cursor (by pressing Shift+S and choosing Selection to Cursor) and then use the E key in vertex selection mode to extrude the single vertex point so that it is traced around the edge of one side of the bottle, as in Figure 6–30.

5. Once you have traced around half the bottle, with the cursor in the middle (the center point of rotation), switch to top view. Still in edit mode, select all vertices by pressing the A key, click the Spin button on the Tool Shelf, and then set Steps to 12 and Degrees to 360, as shown in Figure 6–31.

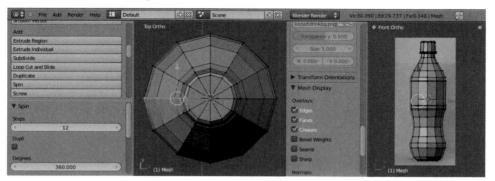

Figure 6–31. *The spin in action*

6. As a final step, select all the vertices again and follow the menu through Mesh ➤ Vertices ➤ Remove Doubles. Once complete, the bottle should look like the one in Figure 6–32.

Figure 6–32. The final result

Having spin is useful, but there are some situations in which it's inefficient. Spin is fine for modeling something like a gear wheel, a chandelier, or the spokes of a bike wheel because of the obvious circular repetition in the shape. However, because spin works with polygon geometry, the end result risks looking octagonal like the bottle just shown, or, at the other extreme, ends up having a very high vertex count in order to make smooth-looking curves. Fortunately, for smooth objects, there are more efficient ways to achieve a similar result, such as NURBS surfaces.

NURBS

In Chapter 3 we looked at modeling polygon objects, which are basic meshes made by connecting straight lines to form the object faces. NURBS surfaces are similar, but curve based. They are highly accurate when modeling large curved areas like a bathtub, the keel of a boat, or the curved surfaces on a modern car, although they lack the control that polygon modeling offers at the individual vertex level.

Controlling the Points

The best way to learn about NURBS surfaces is by using them. We'll make a bottle, as shown in Figure 6–33.

1. In an empty Blender scene, add some NURBS surfaces of various kinds (press Shift+A, select Surface, and choose the NURBS type (e.g., NURBS tube).

2. At first glance, NURBS surfaces look like standard primitives; however, if you select one and go into edit mode, instead of seeing a mesh of vertices you will notice a frame of control points.

3. Move these points to pull the shape within.

Figure 6–33. This NURBS version of the bottle is smoother than the polygon spin version made earlier, and it contains about a third of the points.

■ **Note** The NURBS control points always unfold to a flat rectangular (or square) grid. You can add extra loops through subdivision (as explained following), but you can't extrude selected areas as you can with polygon modeling.

NURBS modeling can be tricky. While polygon models have vertices directly touching the surface, NURBS surfaces have their control points floating around the object. Moving these points pulls the surface around as if you were dragging the shape with magnets. There are a number of unique methods for editing NURBS surfaces, so I suggest you try the following in order to get used to how they work:

- Using the NURBS shape you added before, and while in edit mode, RMB-select one of the control points.

- Use Shift+R to select the entire edgeloop.

- Use Shift+R repeatedly to switch the direction of the selected edgeloop. (Note that NURBS edge directions are u and v, referring to the surface/texture area of a mesh, just as u and v are the 2D directions in UV mapping, as opposed to the x, y, and z coordinates, which refer to object positioning in 3D world space).

- Select one edgeloop, use Shift-RMB-select to select a control point of the next row, and then press Shift+R to select the whole row so that two edgeloops are selected, side by side. Now when you press W you will be given options. Choose Subdivide to add a new loop.

- Press X when a loop is selected to erase the selected points. (Note that this only works where the control points form a grid.)

You can combine NURBS shapes in object mode by selecting them as a group and pressing Ctrl+J. You'll see an example of this next.

NURBS Modeling Example: A Simple Shark

Let's go through a NURBS modeling example:

1. Load a shark into side orthographic view using the Background Images area of the Properties panel.

2. Add a series of NURBS circles to form the head-to-tail frame of the shark, as shown in Figure 6–34. Aim to have the minimum number to form the shape of the body.

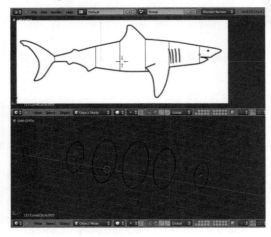

Figure 6–34. Placing NURBS circles in position to define the shark body

3. Select all the circles and use Ctrl+J to combine them into one NURBS object.

4. Enter edit mode for the combined NURBS shape. You should see the control points around the circles. Make sure all are selected and then press F to fill the frame with NURBS skin. The result should be a solid-looking surface, as shown in Figure 6–35.

■ **Note** We could have also used a NURBS tube as the starting point for the shark, but given that each loop should be precisely positioned, and that it is useful to know how to make a skinned NURBS form from scratch, we are taking the single-circle approach.

---

5. By default, skin does not stretch to the end circles of the shape. To fix this, check the Endpoint option in the Active Spline section of the Object Data tab.

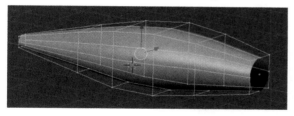

Figure 6–35. The NURBS cage forming the body of the shark

■ **Note** If the shading looks odd, toggle the Switch Direction button on the Tool Shelf. It could be that the normals are inverted, making the shading appear in reverse.

---

6. Select the end vertices around the neck. Use E to extrude them out to more points. Reshape these to form the nose and mouth (see Figure 6–36).

7. Don't add too many points when modeling with NURBS because they cause the object to become difficult to reshape if there are too many. Curves shape well with minimal control points. Add a few, reshape, and then add more.

8. Don't forget to model both sides in unison. Selecting opposite points and then scaling allows you to draw the points together or further apart without breaking symmetry.

Figure 6–36. Shaping the nose and mouth

9. To add the fins, you will need to create new loops in the NURBS cage. Select parallel loops on either side of where you want the new loop to appear. You can select a loop by picking one control point and then using Shift+R to select the entire loop. If the selection goes the wrong direction, simply press Shift+R a second time. These fins are shown in Figure 6–37.

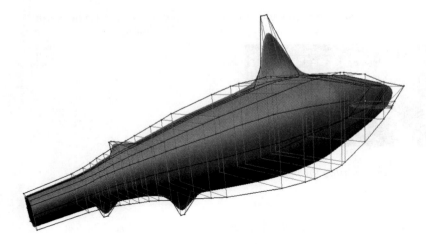

Figure 6–37. Subdivision is used to add loops for shaping into fins.

Remember that a NURBS cage is designed to create a single smooth shape. It is sometimes best to create extra details like the side fins as new NURBS objects, rather than attempting to extrude them from the main body, as shown in Figure 6–38.

Figure 6–38. Creating a separate NURBS model for the side fins

The finished version of the shark is shown in Figure 6–39.

Figure 6–39. The finished shark. Note that the eyes are separate objects.

NURBS surfaces are very fast for modeling curves, but they are slow to render. You can convert a selected NURBS model to a polygon model in object mode by selecting Object ➤ Convert ➤ Mesh from Curve/Meta/Surf/Text.

Summary

To be honest, NURBS modeling is not one of Blender's strong points. NURBS surfaces can be difficult to shape, and adding loops by subdividing seems something of a step backward when compared with the much easier options available with Blender's polygon modeling. Nevertheless, NURBS modeling is still a fast and useful tool for curved models. Blender NURBS modeling is under heavy development and could well have changed considerably by the time this book is published.

The techniques explained in this chapter are advanced methods suited to specific situations. They should provide you a good amount of flexibility when deciding how to approach different modeling projects.

CHAPTER 7

■■■

Basic Rigging and Animation

Now that you are comfortable with modeling techniques, I am going to reveal how you can prepare your models for animation and really bring them to life! There is a lot involved, so we are going to start with looking at moving simple objects before progressing onto rigging characters. Toward the end of this chapter you'll get a walkthrough of using the techniques to rig a simple character.

This chapter is the first of two on rigging and animation techniques. It provides an essential foundation needed before moving on to the more advanced techniques of the next chapter.

A REMINDER ON GLOBAL VS. LOCAL COORDINATES

When objects are animated, they move about—their location changes, and their rotation often changes as well. By default, the green, red, and blue xyz manipulator arrows that display on a selected object follow global coordinates, not local coordinates. This means the arrows always face the same direction, regardless of the direction the object is facing. Likewise, when you move an object by pressing G and then X, and then typing the distance, the specified x, y, or z direction defaults to the global direction. Some people find the global direction confusing because they prefer the coordinate directions to remain local to the model even after an object has changed direction.

To make the manipulator arrows reflect local coordinates, use the Transform Orientation menu in the header of the 3D view, as shown in the image in this sidebar. Once you have done this, specifying a direction with the X, Y, or Z keys will still apply to global coordinates (e.g., press R, press X, type 90, and press Enter), but if you press the X, Y, or Z keys twice, Blender will revert to using local coordinates (e.g., press R, press X, press X, again, type 90, and then press Enter).

Keyframing with the Timeline

The first principle in animation is learning to keyframe. In the old days of flipbook animation, animators had to draw every single frame of the scene. However, as computers are here to make life easier, we can simplify the process by marking out only the main keyframes and leave the computer to work out the in-between frames, as in Figure 7–1. These processes are aptly called *keyframing* (on the part of the animator) and *inbetweening* (on the part of the computer).

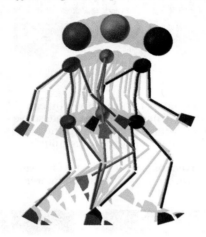

Figure 7–1. In this keyframing example, the animator posed three positions, and Blender filled in the in-between frames.

Let's work our own example.

1. Start with a default scene, delete the cube, and add a monkey.

2. Rotate it 90 degrees along the x axis so that it is sitting upright (press R, press X, type **90**, and press Enter).

3. On the default scene, there is a timeline window below the main 3D view, looking like Figure 7–2. A vertical green line is in position for frame 1, at the far left. Use the LMB to drag this line to different positions along the timeline. You should be able to simply drop the line onto any frame you like.

Figure 7–2. The timeline

4. Notice that there are Start, End, and current frame text boxes below the timeline itself, as shown in Figure 7–3. To bring the green timeline bar back to the starting position, simply type **1** into the current frame slot. You should always start animations at frame 1.

Figure 7–3. *Start, End, and current frame slots*

5. Once the timeline is back at the start position, with the monkey selected, hover the mouse over the 3D view and press the I key (that's an *i*, not an *L*) to insert a keyframe. At this point, a list of options will appear, with the main choices being Location, Rotation, Scaling, LocRot, and LocRotScale. As demonstrated in Figure 7–4, choose LocRot to key both the current location of the object (Loc) and the rotational direction it is facing (Rot).

Figure 7–4. *Selecting which properties to keyframe*

■ **Note** Blender is asking whether you want to keyframe where the object is (location), the direction it is facing (rotation), or its current size (scale). By choosing LocRot, you specify that you want to keyframe both the location and rotation properties.

---

6. Now that you've keyed the LocRot properties of the monkey object on the first frame, you want the monkey to move. Move the slider bar along the timeline—say, to frame 50. Animations in Blender have a default setting of 25 frames per second (fps), so frame 50 would be 2 seconds into the movie.

7. Once on frame 50, move the monkey forward in the direction the monkey is facing.

8. Then press the I key again and insert another LocRot keyframe.

Each keyframe you set is marked on the timeline with a new yellow line. Now when you LMB-slide between the keyframes (this manual dragging of a timeline is known as *scrubbing*), you will see the effects of inbetweening on the animation.

You can also autoplay the animation with Alt+A. The animation will play repeatedly in a loop until you cancel with the Esc key. Pressing Esc resets the animation to where it was when you pressed Alt+A to start it playing. If you press Alt+A a second time (while the animation is running), the animation will stop right where it is (as if paused) instead of resetting to the start position.

Note that the length of the animation is determined by the start and end frames specified below the timeline (these effectively change the limits of the scene, so even the frames rendered as final animation footage are affected by these values). Often the timeline is zoomed in, showing only a portion of the frames. Placing the mouse pointer over the timeline and pressing the Home key resizes the timeline length to the best fit for the length of the timeline window.

Automatic Keyframing

Underneath the timeline is a red circle that looks like a record button on a music player (see Figure 7–5). By pressing this button you enter automatic keyframing mode. This means that any movements you make are automatically keyframed so you no longer have to press I to insert new keyframes. When using this, make sure you move the timeline bar to a different frame and then move the model being animated, because the keyframe is recorded to the current keyframe the instant an object is moved.

Figure 7–5. *The Automatic Keyframe button*

Exercise 1: Flying Monkey

See if you can make the monkey fly in a loop like the one in Figure 7–6. This will require you to keyframe both the location and the rotation of the object. Alternatively, you could make an obstacle course for the monkey to fly through. Could you make a chase scene with two or more animated objects?

Figure 7–6. *A flying monkey!*

The Dopesheet

The default timeline is good for showing keyframes, but it does not offer much real editing power. You can't delete keyframes or slide them along the default timeline. However, there is an alternative known as a dopesheet (see Figure 7–7) that makes this level of editing possible. On the dopesheet, the keyframes are displayed as diamonds and can be selected with the same basic controls that you would use on an object in the 3D scene:

- You can RMB-select the key points on the dopesheet.

- You can press B to use block select (diagonally drag the mouse to lasso-select a rectangular area).

- You can press A to toggle-select all/none of the keyframes.

- You can press G to move the selected keyframes along.

- You can press X to delete selected keyframes.

- As with the standard timeline, you can press the Home key to zoom the dopesheet to fit the screen.

Note that the diamonds show as yellow when they are selected and white when they are not.

Figure 7–7. The dopesheet

There are some unique controls for a dopesheet:

- By clicking the triangular arrow to the left of mesh, you can expand the dopesheet to manipulate location, rotation, and size individually.

- Clicking the eye icon turns a particular channel off so that it has no effect on the 3D view/animation.

- Clicking the padlock icon secures a channel so it cannot be edited accidentally.

■ **Note** While the dopesheet-editing options are indeed powerful, to change the start and end frames of the animation, you still need to go back to the timeline.

Parenting

Parenting is the technique of joining one object to another so that when the "parent" object is moved, it pulls any "children" objects along with it. Parenting is an important principle with many applications. Even if you are not strictly animating, objects are often connected to each other in some sort of parental hierarchy; doors are parented to walls, a car door is parented to the car body, and so on.

To demonstrate the principle of parenting, we'll add a propeller to our moving monkey:

1. Go to frame 1 of the timeline.

2. Make a propeller for the monkey, something like the one shown in Figure 7–8. A simple resized cube is fine, and it does not matter if you prefer a front-on propeller (as on an airplane) or an overhead one (as on a helicopter). To make it easier to spot in the graph editor later on, name the propeller.

3. Position the propeller with the monkey.

4. Select the propeller first, and then Shift-RMB-select the monkey.

5. Press Ctrl+P and choose Set Parent To ➤ Object from the menu that appears.

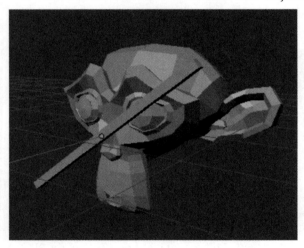

Figure 7–8. *Monkey aircraft with propeller*

Now when you run the animation, the propeller will be attached to the monkey. We now have to make the propeller spin. Make sure only the propeller is selected (RMB-selecting the propeller should deselect other objects), and then do the following:

6. Go back to frame 1 again.

7. Press the I key, and when asked, choose to keyframe the rotation of the propeller.

8. Slide to the final frame of the animation.

9. Spin the propeller a dozen times (you may need to specify x, y, or z to keep the movement straight).

10. Keyframe the final propeller position (use the I key).

Now when you scrub the animation (or run it with Alt+A), the propeller while still attached to the monkey will have its own spinning animation.

Parenting works as a hierarchy. If you parent another object to the propeller, it will also spin. You cannot make an object the parent of something that is its parent further up the parenting hierarchy (trying this results in a *loop-in-parents* error). If you want to drop the parent relationship of an object, select the child object (e.g., the propeller) and press Alt+P. From the menu that appears, choose Clear Parent to completely reset the parent relationship (this will cause the propeller to reset its location to where it began as an object before the parenting), or choose Clear Parent and Keep Transform if you want the child object to break from the parental relationship while remaining in its current location.

Graph Editor

While the dopesheet gives more editing power than the timeline, there is another animation editor, the Graph editor, that offers another level of control again. The Graph editor, as with other window types in Blender, can be accessed through the leftmost button of a window's header strip, as shown in Figure 7–9.

Figure 7–9. *Opening the Graph editor*

In this Graph editor interface (shown in Figure 7–10), the keyframes are displayed as Bezier curves. Not only can they be moved around, but they can also be scaled and rotated to give precise control over the speed of specific parts of a movement. For example, a bouncing ball hits the ground hard and fast on each bounce, but then slows down as it rises, and begins speeding up when it starts falling again. With the Graph editor, it becomes possible to alter the curves of movement so that the change in vertical direction (usually z) is sharp on the actual bounces, yet smooth on the high points when the ball is in the air.

Figure 7–10. The Graph editor

By default, Blender shows all curves of an object's movement in the Graph editor, but you can narrow down which you are viewing by toggling the colored check boxes to the left of the curve names. When you have the curves narrowed down, press the Home key with your mouse over the Graph editor window to autozoom in on the selected curve.

If doing this with the monkey example, you may notice that the propeller starts its spin slowly, speeds up, and then slows down again at the end of the movement. If you select the spin curve (either Y or X Euler Rotation, depending on which axis you are rotating around), press Shift+T, and select Linear from the pop-up menu, the movement curves will change to straight lines so that Blender won't ease in and out of movements, and will instead make the spin constant.

■ **Note** An *Euler rotation* is simply the angle around the xyz axis that something has been rotated. Blender also understands another type of rotation, called quaternion rotation, but this is quite a bit more difficult to understand than straight Euler-based axis rotation.

Pressing Shift+E and choosing Constant Extrapolation makes the graph curve continue indefinitely, so that the propeller spins forever.

Pivot Point: The Center of Rotation

Once you know how parenting works, the pivot point becomes very important. This point is shown as a small orange dot for any selected object, as shown in the bottom-left corner of Figure 7–11. It marks the real location of the object. The mesh is simply a cluster of connected vertices, which are, in their own way, parented to this pivot point. Move the pivot point, and this in turn moves the connected mesh. When you select an object in object mode, it's not really the mesh you're selecting, but rather the pivot point. It's when you go into edit mode that you are able to move the vertices of the mesh shape.

Figure 7–11. *Rotation around a pivot point*

By default, when you rotate a single object, it is the object's pivot point that marks the center of rotation. The main exception to this rule is when the Pivot Point menu is set to 3D Cursor (look at Figure 7–12 to see how to do this), in which case the scaling and rotational movements are treated as though the 3D cursor is the center point. In real life, not all objects rotate from the center. For example, your forearm rotates from the elbow, the bicep from the shoulder, the lower leg from the knee, and so on. If you were to make a person from shapes, it would help to set the pivot point to the actual rotational centers of the limbs. There are a couple of ways to do this, as I'll describe following.

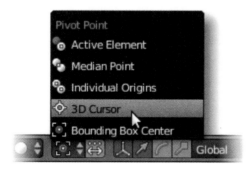

Figure 7–12. *The main exception to pivot point rotation is 3D cursor rotation, in which the 3D cursor takes over as the default center of rotation.*

First, in edit mode, you can simply select all vertices (with the A key) and reposition them away from the pivot point. Second, you can also use the cursor to specify a new position for the pivot point.

- In object mode, choose Object ➤ Transform ➤ Origin to 3D Cursor. This repositions the pivot point to the location of the 3D cursor.

- Alternatively, when you are in object mode with an object selected, you can click the Origin button in the Transform area of the Tool Shelf (see Figure 7–13), which offers the same options as the Transform menu.

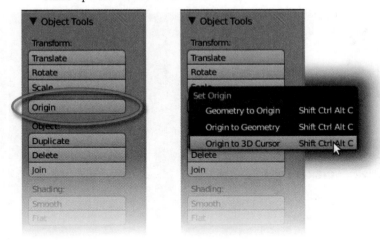

Figure 7–13. *The Origin button on the Tool Shelf*

Of course, you can LMB-click to move the cursor around, and there are ways to snap the cursor to precise positions. For example, switching to edit mode, selecting a vertex point, pressing Shift+S, and then selecting Cursor to Selected causes the cursor to snap to your selected point. Doing the same with more than one vertex selected causes the cursor to snap to the center of the selected group. Selecting two opposite vertices in a circle results in snapping the cursor to the midpoint of that circle.

Restricting the Movement

There are times when you will want to restrict the movement of an object. For example, you might want to make a hinge, which rotates only in one direction. Two ways you can implement such restrictions are with *transform locks* and *constraints*.

Transform Locks

To restrict movement through Transform Locks, use the padlock buttons found in the Transform Locks area of the Object tab (cube icon), as shown in Figure 7–14. Alternatively, you can find the padlock buttons in the Transform area of the Properties panel (see Figure 7–15).

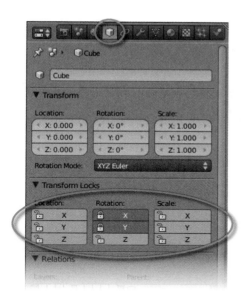

Figure 7–14. Transform lock buttons on the Object tab

By clicking the appropriate padlock buttons, you lock the respective movement type (location, rotation, or scale for x, y, or z) into place. In Figures 7–14 and 7–15, the rotation is locked for both the x and y axes, resulting in the selected object only being able to rotate around the z axis.

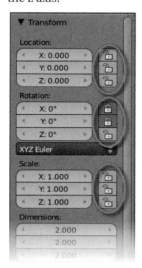

Figure 7–15. Transform lock buttons in the Properties panel

There are a couple of important considerations you should understand about the transform lock method of restricting an object's movement:

- The restriction is applied to the global (as opposed to local) x, y, or z axis, so it locks direction along the world-space axis.

- Even though transform lock direction is global, parental relationships can offset the end result. For example, if a cube had location movement transform locks so that it could only move along the x axis, and the cube were parented to another object, such as a sphere, then if that sphere rotated 45 degrees, the transform lock would thereafter work in a diagonal direction.

Constraints

In the main Properties panel is the Object Constraints tab, bearing the icon of a couple of chain links. We use this panel to add all manner of constraints to a selected object. The following exercise will show you how to use constraints:

1. Start with the default scene and the cube.

2. RMB-select the cube.

3. Make sure the Properties panel is visible, allowing you to see the x, y, and z rotation parameters of the selected cube, as shown in Figure 7–16.

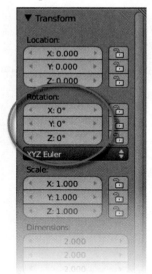

Figure 7–16. Rotation parameters

4. Navigate to the Object Constraints tab and click the Add Constraint button. This will open a whole list of choices, sorted into three columns headed Transform, Tracking, and Relationship.

5. For this exercise, we wish to restrict the rotation of the cube, so in the Transform section, choose Limit Rotation, as shown in Figure 7–17.

Figure 7–17. *Adding a limit rotation constraint*

6. Immediately, a new area will appear in the panels. In this area, check the For Transform box for under the Limit options (see Figure 7–18) (the For Transform option is explained in more detail after this exercise).

7. Notice the columns for Limit X, Limit Y, and Limit Z; check the box for Limit X (see Figure 7–18).

Figure 7–18. *The Limit X and For Transfrom options*

8. Now try to rotate the cube in different direction; the cube should be able to rotate around the y and z axes, but not x.

9. Underneath the panel where you activated the Limit X option are two values—Min and Max—both currently set to 0 degrees. Change these numbers to something else (e.g., leave Min at 0 and set Max to 45), as shown in Figure 7–19.

Figure 7–19. Setting Min and Max values for the constraint

10. Examine how the cube is able to rotate. You should find that the cube can once again rotate around the x axis, but only within the range of degrees that your input specifies.

So now that you have seen the constraint in action, what is the For Transform option in step 6 all about? If you look at the rotation data for the cube in the Properties panel, notice that as you rotate the cube, the X value never goes outside of its specified range (from 0 to 45 degrees). This is only possible when the For Transformation option is active. If you deselect the For Transform option, the object will be able to move outside of the range of the x value; however, the object will *appear* in the 3D view to halt at the specified Min and Max constraint values. In effect, you could rotate the cube 90 degrees around the x axis, but it would look like the cube rotated only to the Max value you'd specified (45 degrees). Then, on deleting the constraint (this can be done by clicking the white X at the top-right corner of the Limit Constraint panel area), the cube would jump to the full 90 degree rotation, revealing how far it had actually been rotated. In short, the For Transform option ensures that objects don't move beyond their constraint limits without your knowing it, and I recommend always using this option.

Constraints are more powerful than transform locks. Not only can you specify a restriction for a specific range of movement, but you can also choose whether the constraint should evaluate against world or local space through the drop-down list near the bottom of the Limit Rotation constraint panel, as shown in Figure 7–20.

Figure 7–20. The Limit Rotation constraint has the option to use local space.

Exercise 2: Making a Robot

Make a robot from parts (you can use primitives or model pieces individually, as I've done in Figure 7–21). Set the pivot points of each piece to their correct rotational positions. Parent the pieces together. Finally, create a short animation. Start at frame 1, press A to select all objects, and keyframe the starting position. Then move through the different frames to key some actions for an animation.

Figure 7–21. Robot made from parented shapes

Basic Tracking: Eyes That Follow

While it is possible to simply key the rotational properties of eyes, it is sometimes easier to have a target object that the eyes always navigate to, and then move that object around to where you want your character to look. Figure 7–22 shows an eyeball following around an empty target. The following short exercise will show you how to make this happen.

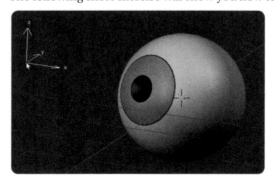

Figure 7–22. Eyeball tracking an empty

1. Create a new empty scene, deleting the default cube.

2. Press Shift+A, and select Add ➤ Mesh ➤ UVSphere.

3. This sphere is going to be the eyeball. Usually, the y axis is the front-to-back axis, so go into edit mode, press A to select all vertices, and rotate them 90 degrees around the x axis (press R, press X, enter **90**, and press Enter). Then enter object mode again.

4. Press Shift+A, select Add ➤ Empty, and name the empty `target`. You can use any object you like for the empty. Place the target shape in front of the eyeball.

5. RMB-select the eyeball.

6. Shift-RMB-select the `target` empty.

7. Press Ctrl+T and select TrackTo Constraint from the list. Now, whenever you move the target around, the eyeball will follow it.

8. Press Shift+D to duplicate the eyeball. The copy will already be set up to follow the target object. Should you wish to break the connection (you might like to assign a different target for each eye), select the eyeball and press Alt+T.

Parenting the eyeballs onto another mesh (i.e., for the head) is an easy way of making puppet rigs, as in Figure 7–23.

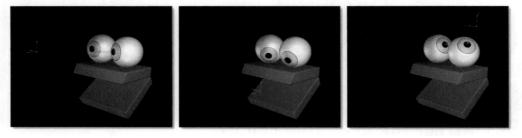

Figure 7–23. Tracking eyes in action

Rigging with Bones

Unlike the robots we have made, which are surface objects, character animation usually involves making limbs that can bend. To do this, we model the body shape, and then place bones inside that warp the mesh as they bend. This process is what most CGI artists refer to as *rigging*.

Adding bones is similar to adding any other object:

1. Press Shift+A and select Add ➤ Armature ➤ Single Bone.

2. With this bone selected, go into edit mode (press Tab). Notice that there are three distinct areas of the bone: a long body of the bone itself, and two balls at either end, known as the *root* and the *tip* of the bone (in Figure 7–24, the root is at the bottom end, and the tip is at the top). These three parts can be RMB-selected individually.

Figure 7–24. A single bone

3. Select the tip and press E to extrude. Now, as you pull your mouse away from the bone, a new branch will be extruded. As with moving objects, the X, Y, and Z keys can be pressed to specify a specific axis direction, so use Z if you want to grow the new branch straight up.

Subdividing also works with bones. Selecting the body of a bone and pressing W divides the bone into two.

On the Tool Shelf is an X-Axis Mirror option (shown at the bottom of Figure 7–25). When this option is checked, extruding new bones with Shift+E causes Blender to try for a symmetrical pair of new bones. This only really works well from the center of the scene. Blender uses individual bone names to keep track of which bones are opposite partners. As a rule, any bones ending in _R or _L are opposites (e.g., bone_L and bone_R for a left-and-right pair).

Figure 7–25. The X-Axis Mirror option

Because they are easy to createi, it is tempting to add lots of bones without taking the time to name them. Bone names are very important, though, as they help when using bone constraints (covered in Chapter 8), and also because some functions, like the aforementioned x-axis mirror, rely heavily on the bone names. The name of an individual selected bone is stored at the top of the Bone tab (this tab shows a bone icon when a bone is selected), as shown in Figure 7–26. By default, Blender calls the main skeleton Armature, and the bones bone, bone.001, bone.002, bone.003, and so forth. It is good practice to name bones as you make them before the sheer number creates a nightmare renaming job later on.

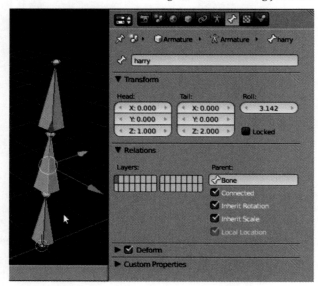

Figure 7–26. *Naming the selected bone*

The Display area of the Object Data tab (which now displays an icon of a small figure) has two useful options, as shown in Figure 7–27:

- A Names option, which displays bone names in the 3D view

- An X-Ray (Object) option, which makes the bones show through other objects so you can see them at all times, even when they are inside or behind a solid mesh object

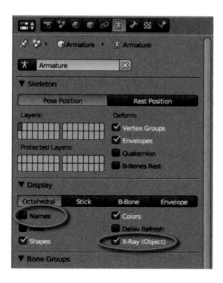

Figure 7–27. The Names and X-Ray options are designed to make working with bones easier.

Types of Bones

For the sake of completeness, it may be worth mentioning that there are four bone types in Blender: there are octahedrons (the default bone type); thin sticks (very handy for weight painting. These are described later in the chapter, as they are small in size and don't get in the way); B-bones, which are able to bend (we'll look at these near the end of this chapter); and envelope bones. Figure 7–28 gives an example of all the types. Each of them has its own advantages. However, in this book, until we specifically need those extra functions, we'll use the standard octahedron bone type.

Should you need to change the bone type, simply select the armature (the bones) and go into the Object Data tab (being contextual, the Object Data tab will have a small figure icon when bones are selected). Look down the panels to the Display area and you should see buttons allowing you to specify the type of bone you want to use.

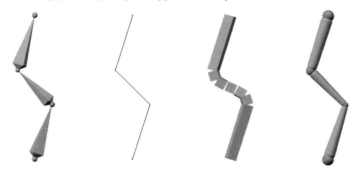

Figure 7–28. Different display types for bones (from left to right, octahedron, stick, B-bone, and envelope)

Making Bones Work with a Mesh

Now that you can make bones, you're ready to learn to apply them so they affect a mesh.

1. Start with a new scene and delete the default cube.

2. Press Shift+A and select Armature ➤ Single Bone.

3. Enter edit mode (press the Tab key) and extrude the tip end of the bone upward in the z direction. Do this twice to make a total of three bones. You can do the extrusions by selecting the tip of the bone and keying in the following sequence twice: E, Z, 1, Enter.

4. Go into object mode (press Tab again)

5. Press Shift+A and select Add ➤ Mesh ➤ Tube.

6. Scale and reposition the tube so that it contains the three bones. Make it fairly thin, scaling it up again in the z direction to match the shape, as shown in Figure 7–29. It helps to be in side or front view with the previously mentioned X-ray mode enabled for the armature/bones.

Figure 7–29. *Size the tube around the bones to fit like this.*

7. Switch to edit mode for the tube, position the mouse over the side edges, and press Ctrl+R to add edgeloops. While the line is pink, roll the MW to add about a dozen loops up the tube, as shown in Figure 7–30. These lines will be necessary for allowing an edgeflow so that the tube can bend.

Figure 7–30. Adding a dozen edgeloops to the mesh

We will now link the armature with the tube mesh. Make sure you know the name of the armature skeleton (by default, Blender will have called it Armature if you haven't renamed it).

1. RMB-select the tube in object mode.

2. On the Modifiers tab (the tab with a wrench icon), add a new armature modifier.

3. In the new panel that appears, enter the name of the armature skeleton into the Object box. Notice that on clicking the box to enter the name, Blender will show a list of possible items for you to enter, so you don't really have to type anything!

4. RMB-select the armature bones.

5. Switch from object mode to pose mode, as in Figure 7–31.

6. Move the bones around (RMB-select and then rotate a bone).

Figure 7–31. Entering pose mode

Hopefully, when you move the bones in pose mode, the tube will bend to match the bones. This is the mode that bone-based animation is normally keyframed in. This mesh deformation would not happen if you were to move the bones in edit mode. Make sure you understand the difference between the modes:

- Object mode is for moving whole objects around.

- Edit mode is for changing the internal shape or properties of an object, whether it is a mesh or an armature.

- Pose mode is for moving bones of an armature around as part of an animation.

In pose mode, you should find that the mesh deforms with the bones, although some areas of the mesh might not deform quite as expected (look at how the mesh is scrunching up in Figure 7–32), and you may need to tidy up the rig. There are two methods of tidying up the results: using bone envelopes and direct weight painting, both of which will be described in the following sections.

Figure 7–32. *A first attempt at making the mesh follow the bone in pose mode*

Before using either of these methodst, I recommend resetting the pose to the resting position. That is, if the bones are now bent over, put them back where they started. The efficient way of resetting them is as follows:

1. Make sure you are still in pose mode.

2. Press A to select all bones.

3. From the Pose menu, select Clear Transform ➤ Rotation (or press Alt+R).

4. Choose Clear Pose Rotation from the list that appears.

This should reset the rotation of all bones that may have been previously bent into a pose. Now you are ready to work with Envelope bones.

■ **Note** As things can and do go wrong with rigging, I would also like to remind you to save your work regularly before attempting each technique.

Using Bone Envelopes

The idea with this method is to resize certain fields of influence around each bone to encompass the area of the mesh which the active bone is meant to affect. It is a very fast method for setting up a rig, although it is not as accurate as the weight painting method (described next).

1. Select the armature skeleton. For this technique, you may be in either edit mode or object mode.

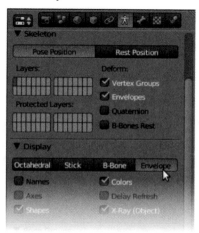

Figure 7–33. Selecting the bone type

2. On the Object Data tab, in the Display panel, there are options to choose between Octahedral, Stick, B-Bone, and Envelope. Choose Envelope, as shown in Figure 7–33. The bones will change to cylinder shapes, and a white field will surround the selected bone, as shown in Figure 7–34.

3. Enter edit mode.

4. Place your mouse near the active bone and press Ctrl+Alt+S. This works like scaling, but instead of changing the bone size, it changes the size of the surrounding influence field.

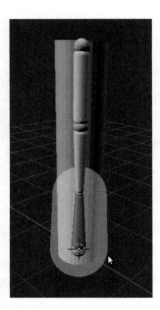

Figure 7–34. Envelope bones with fields

5. You can also affect the shape of the fields by resizing the bones and the ball ends (root and tip) by pressing the S key. However, you need to be in edit mode in order to select the root or tip, as pose mode only allows you to select the main body of a bone. Resizing the top and root ends allows for more variation of shape to the bones and their surrounding influence fields.

Weight Painting

With this technique, you literally paint the amount of influence of the bones directly onto the mesh surface.

1. Just to be safe, reset the current modes for the bones and the mesh by selecting each in turn and choosing object mode. This step is not normally needed—it is a precaution to lessen the likelihood that you will be in an odd mode (e.g., edit, sculpt, etc.) for either the bones or the mesh.

2. Select the armature, enter pose mode, and RMB-select one of the bones.

3. Shift-RMB-select the mesh. This will put you back into object mode.

4. Now, enter weight paint mode via the Mode menu in the header strip of the 3D view (the same one that allows you to switch between edit mode, object mode, sculpt mode, etc.). If all works to plan, the mesh should turn a dark blue while the bone is still selected.

At first glance, weight paint mode may seem like pose mode in that when you LMB-select and rotate different bones, they deform the mesh (this works with both modes). However, weight paint mode allows for one more function: when you LMB-drag over parts of a mesh, they begin to look "hotter" (i.e., changing from blue, to green, to yellow, to red, as shown in Figure 7–35). In weight paint mode, the hot colors represent those parts of the mesh that are set to deform with the currently selected bone. If you rotate a bone, any part of the mesh painted in red will turn with the bone. You can use this to touch up parts of your mesh that have deformation problems.

While painting, the Tool Shelf offers different brush options to fine-tune the painting. You might start out using the Add and Subtract brushes, and move on to Blur and some of the others to make the bends smooth.

When weight painting, you can toggle the Envelopes option off (on the Object Data tab) to nullify the effects of the default envelope fields. Usually, though, it is fine to leave this on.

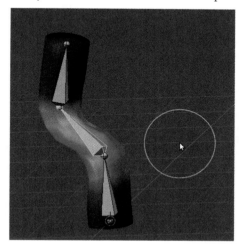

Figure 7–35. Weight painting

Dividing the Two Techniques

We have looked at two different techniques—using bone envelopes and weight painting—for doing what is essentially the same thing: specifying which parts of the mesh are supposed to deform with which bones. But what happens if a part of the mesh is contained in the influence field of a certain bone, but not influenced by the weight paint of that bone (or vice versa)?

To resolve such issues, you can turn either of the two methods off. With the mesh selected, go to the Modifiers tab (the wrench icon), where you originally added the armature modifier. In the Bind area there are some options for both vertex groups and bone envelopes (weight painting influences the mesh through vertex groups, so the vertex groups options govern weight painting). Simply uncheck the option you do not wish to use. For example, if you only want the rig to use weight painting (but ignore the influence of bone envelopes), then uncheck the Bone Envelopes option.

I can imagine some readers might react to this knowledge exclaiming, "Why didn't you tell me that before I started weight painting?" In truth, it's often fine to have both options enabled, with bone envelopes controlling the bulk of the mesh and weight painting being used to touch up the finer deformation or parts that did not work well with the envelopes.

Rigging a Simple Character

It's one thing to study a few bones, but you're more likely get the gist of rigging with a practical example. The following is a walkthrough of setting up simple rig for a character. You can use any figure you like, although the best models usually follow a few simple rules:

- Characters are usually best rigged in T-pose, with the legs straight up and down and the arms stretched wide (see Figure 7–36). It is harder to bend objects smoothly than to unbend them, so this pose, which has the fewest bends possible, is the least likely to have problems.

- Any limb that has a bend, such as knees, elbows, and finger joints, should have three edgeloops around the bending area. This allows for a smoother shape when the joint is used.

- Subdivision surface modifiers are deadly to being able to efficiently pose a rig. When subdivision is enabled, Blender has to recalculate the smoothness of all the vertices of your mesh every moment while you try to fix a pose. This causes a huge lag in the performance of your computer and may cause everything to seize up. If you want to use the subdivision surface modifier, then use the eye icon to disable its effect in 3D view. Alternatively, you could simply apply the subdivision surface modifier, which will make the smooth vertices real, and may lead to more accurate weight painting.

Figure 7–36. Simple character model in T-pose

Let's start the walkthrough:

1. Start by modeling the spine. You will want to activate the X-Ray option (on the Object Data tab) so you can see the bones through your mesh. The spine should grow upward starting about the halfway point between the belly button and the bottom of the body, and in the horizontal center of the body.

2. For now, an extrusion of two bones are all that you'll need for the spine. Extrude again for the neck, and finally for the head. Your armature should now look something like the one shown in Figure 7–37.

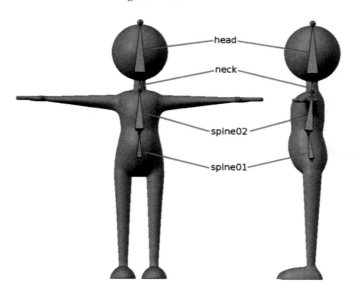

Figure 7–37. Spine, neck, and head bones

3. Take care to name the bones. From the base up, sensible names would be spine01, spine02, neck, and head.

4. We are about to extrude arm and leg areas, so make sure the X-Axis Mirror option (in the Tool Shelf, under Armature Options when the armature is in edit mode) is enabled.

5. Select the ball root end of the neck bone. Using Shift+E so that both left and right arms are made at the same time, extrude new bones outward to the armpits. Select one of the new bones and press W to subdivide it so that the bone, going from neck to shoulder becomes two bones: the clavicle (collarbone) and the shoulder bone (see Figure 7–38).

___

■ **Note** For a very simple character where only the arms move, one bone is often all that is needed to link the neck to the shoulder. if you want realistic shoulder roll/shrug actions, it is good to have two bones to make the shoulder area.

___

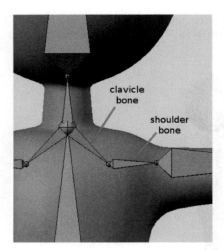

Figure 7–38. Double-boned shoulder area

6.   It is usually best to make arms fairly straight, pulling the elbow back just a little to define the direction they will later bend in (this will be looked at more closely in the next chapter). For now, make the arms straight by extruding along the x axis (by pressing E to extrude and then X as you pull the new bone out).

7.   To ensure the arm is really straight, rather than extruding twice (from shoulder to elbow and then a second time from elbow to wrist), you might get better results from extruding all the way from shoulder to wrist as one bone, and then subdividing the bone (press W) to create the elbow socket.

8.   Pull the elbow socket back just enough to bend a little, as shown in Figure 7–39.

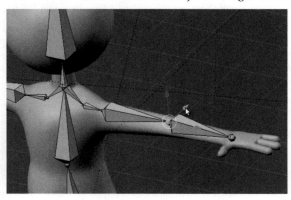

Figure 7–39. Making the arm bones and giving the elbow a little bend

9. You have now extruded four bones for each arm, totaling eight in all. Now would be an excellent opportunity to name them. From the neck outward, name the right arm bones clavicle_R, shoulder_R, bicep_R, and forearm_R. Name the left arm the same but with an _L suffix, making them clavicle_L, shoulder_L, bicep_L, and forearm_L. It is important that you name the opposites appropriately, as X-Axis Mirror relies on the names to work, and further extrusions into the hands will not mirror if the naming is not consistent.

10. Go into top view to extrude the hands. You will need a hand bone, and then extrude from here to each of the fingers, which normally have two joints (or three bones) for each finger.

11. You will want the fingers to be reasonably straight, although if you extrude them and move the joints into place, chances are they will zig-zag a little. How can you prevent this? One technique is to do the following:

    a. Make the finger one finger-length bone.

    b. Select the base socket of the finger and make the 3D cursor go to this point by pressing Shift+S and choosing Cursor to Selected.

    c. Change the pivot mode to 3D cursor.

    d. Create a joint in the finger by selecting the long bone and pressing W to subdivide the bone.

    e. RMB-select the new joint socket, and instead of moving it into position, use scale (S key) to slide the joint into place (see Figure 7–40).

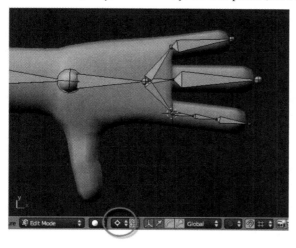

Figure 7–40. With pivot mode set to 3D cursor (circled) and the cursor positioned at the base of a finger, selected joints will move toward the base in a straight line when scale is used.

12. Use the same technique to create the other finger joint.

13. In the same way that arms should have a slight bend (especially with some of the inverse kinematics [IK] techniques discussed in the next chapter), so should the fingers. Select the middle bone of each finger and pull it upward slightly.

14. The thumb should simply be extrudedout like another finger. Note that you should make this extrusion from the tip end of the hand bone, not the base, so that it is parented to the hand and moves when the hand moves.

15. The bones from the hand bone tip to the root of the fingers and thumb can be deleted (select them and use the X key), as shown in Figure 7–41. This will leave the digits floating but still parented to the hand bone, so they will still be attached to the hand when it is moved around in pose mode.

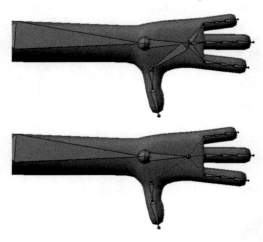

Figure7–41. *Delete the bones from hand to finger base. Dotted lines indicate that the finger bones are still parented to the hand bone.*

16. You now have a lot more bones to rename. Appropriate names for the index finger bones on the right hand might be index01_R, index02_R, and index03_R. Use this convention to name the bones in other fingers as well. (Note that my character has only three fingers.)

17. To make the hips, use Shift+E to extrude from the base socket of the spine. Legs should be straight up and down in a properly T-posed model. Give the knees a very slight bend. Extrude the feet forward to the toes. If you want the foot to bend, it should be made from two bones.

18. Name the leg bones hip_R, thigh_R, shin_R, foot_R, and toe_R. Rename their opposites with _L versions. The bones in your rig are pretty much complete now (see Figure 7–42), except we want to add a root bone as the most senior parent, which will be useful for moving the entire character around as a whole.

Figure 7–42. The full set of bones

19. In edit mode for the armature, RMB-select the socket at the base of the spine. From side view, press E and extrude out of the back. From the tip of this bone, press E again to make a new bone in an upward direction, as in Figure 7–43. Name this new bone root and unparent it from the first by erasing the entry in the Parent field on the Bone tab. Delete the bone you made that was going out to it.

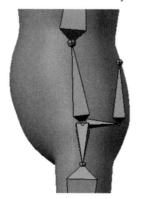 

Figure 7–43. Making the root bone

20. Enter root into the Parent field for spine01, hip_L, and hip_R. Take care to ensure that the Connected box is not checked just prior to doing this, or you might find that the bones jump out of their current position in order to join to the root (not good). Be sure to save your work regularly so as to prevent a lot of rebuilding in case such things happen!

21. If you have performed the last step correctly, then moving the root bone around in pose mode will move the entire rig.

22. Some bones are not supposed to deform the character. For each of the following, turn off the Deform option on the Bone tab (see Figure 7–44). If you remember to do this, there will be fewer bones to worry about when you get to the weight painting stage. The only bones you'll have to deal with are the following:

   - root
   - hip_L
   - hip_R
   - clavicle_L
   - clavicle_R

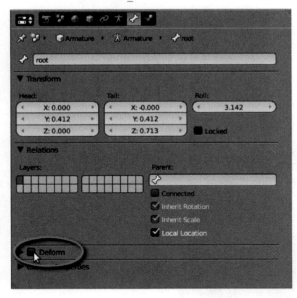

Figure 7–44. Turn off Deform for bones that will not directly influence the mesh.

Once the bones are in place, it's time to link them to the mesh and get ready for animation. You'll kickstart this with the previously discussed bone envelope and weight painting methods.

Applying the Bone Envelopes

Now it's time to apply the bone envelopes:

1. On the Object Data tab, and while in edit mode, change the bone display type to Envelope.

2. Select the bones and use Ctrl+Alt+S to adjust the size of the surrounding white influence fields to fit just around the surrounding flesh, as in Figure 7–45. Don't forget you can also resize the bones and the ball sockets with the S key to adjust the overall shape of the bones.

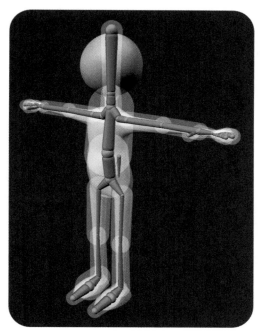

Figure 7–45. *Envelope bones and their influence fields*

Notice that bones that are marked as not needing to deform will not have the white influence fields around them. Also, if X-Axis Mirror is on, what you do on one side will equally affect the other.

Adding Weight Painting

After adjusting the envelope bone field sizes, you may notice that the results are not as perfect as you'd like. We'll remedy that with some weight painting:

1. Select a bone of the armature in pose mode, Shift-select the mesh, and enter weight paint mode.

2. Use the techniques outlined earlier in this chapter to paint the limbs so they deform properly. Unpainting areas (with the Subtraction brush) is sometimes as important as painting the weight. Blurring is good for smoothing out jagged curves. You can bend bones while you are painting for quick feedback on the results of your work, as shown in Figure 4-46.

Take care on each and every joint, right down to the fingers. Bend each as you go, making sure it folds nicely. This can take considerable time, but when it is complete, your rig will be done . . . almost.

Figure 7–46. Weight painting the character

B-Bone Body

The current body has a spine of only two bones, which is fairly angular. If you want a smoother bend, take the following steps:

1. On the Object Data tab, choose the B-Bone option in the Display area.

2. In pose mode with the bone selected, go to the Bone tab and give the bone several segments (the entry for segments is found in the Deform section).

3. Do this for the two spine bones to make them bend (in pose mode) with more of a curve (see Figure 7–47).

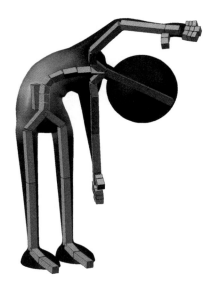

Figure 7–47. B-bones make a smoother curve in the spine.

Animating the Figure

Now that the character is finally set up to work with the armature bones, simply go into pose mode, move the bones into position, and press I (insert keyframe) to key selected bones at their physical positions for the current frame of the timeline. Some animators like to press A to select all bones when keying in order to get a true pose-to-pose sequence of key poses. (If you only key a few joints at a time, inbetweening can alter previously good poses). All animation features in this chapter work with armature bones in pose mode, including autokeying and the dopesheet.

Your animation can be viewed n the 3D view by pressing Alt+A. You can also render out your work as a movie, although you may need to keyframe the camera if the character walks off the side of camera view (you switch to camera view via numpad 0). Making movies from animation will be discussed more in depth in Chapter 9.

Summary

In this chapter, we looked at keyframe-based animation. You can apply the principles to either solid objects or parts of rigged characters. There are subtle differences in rigs, ranging from rigged parented objects, objects linked by constraints, and weight-painted models driven by armature skeletons.

Certainly, there is a lot to study in animation, and what you have seen in this chapter is merely an introduction. Aside from animation, rigging itself is full-time work for someone in the computer graphics industry. Like modeling, rigging and animation are arts in themselves.

Over the next chapter, we will be venturing beyond the simple forward kinematic rigs described in this chapter and on to more sophisticated inverse kinematic versions. We will also look at advanced techniques for shaping mouths to animate characters talking.

CHAPTER 8

■■■

Advanced Rigging

We finished off the last chapter by making a simple character, which was rigged with bones. While there was a bit to learn in terms of weight painting the bones to the mesh, the rig was a relatively simple setup. In this chapter we are going to examine some more advanced tricks you can use to make your rigs move better. While initially harder to set up, they should be a lot easier for an animator to use.

Beyond this point, we are starting to look at some pretty advanced rigging techniques. Don't worry if you don't fully understand everything at first. That said, different animators all have their favorite setups, and no one method is definitely more correct than another. There are many ways to crack a nut, and the techniques outlined in this chapter are simply ones that I have found to be useful for my own purposes.

Forward Kinematics vs. Inverse Kinetics

The rig in Chapter 7 was purely a forward kinematics (FK) setup. This means that each bone is parented to another, forming a hierarchical chain. So, for example, if you want to move a hand to a specific location, you need to bend the arm at the shoulder and then at the elbow so the hand meets the desired position. It's very much like moving a character made of stiff wire. It's fine for many situations, but it can be awkward to line up the shoulder and elbow if all you want is to make the character's hand reach out for a door handle. Wouldn't it be easier if you could grab the hand and just place it directly where we wanted?

An inverse kinematics (IK) setup is the opposite of FK. Here, the hand is free floating in that it does not move when you move the shoulder or elbow. Instead, when you move the hand around, the arm bends naturally at the elbow to match the position. This kind of setup is similar to using a cloth puppet with floppy arms, whose hands are moved around on the ends of sticks. To make a character reach out for a door handle, all you need to do is grab the hand and position it, and the arm will automatically follow.

Making an IK Arm

Start off with a basic FK arm rig. This can be on your character, or you can set up an arm specially. You should have a minimum of bones for shoulder, bicep, forearm, and hand, as shown in Figure 8–1.

Figure 8–1. *FK arm bones*

■ **Tip** Blender has some premade parts, so if you are in a hurry and need a quick arm rig, use Shift+A and follow the menu through Add ➤ Armature ➤ Meta-Rig ➤ "Arm biped." Don't assume they are model examples just because they come with the program. For example, the leg models would be more ideal if they were vertically straight when viewed from the front view.

Because we are soon going to add constraints to various bones, which requires linking them to each other by name, it is important to name bones appropriately. forearm_L and bicep_L (for the left arm) are better names than bone1 or bone2. Also, you should know the name of the whole rig as an object (the default name is usually Armature, though you can of course rename the rig). You can call the bones what you like, although you should take care to pair left and right opposites as, for example, thisbone_L and thisbone_R.

1.   An IK setup should never be exactly straight, as this can make it difficult for Blender to pull out slightly, as in Figure 8–2, in the direction the elbow naturally bends. Make sure the ball at the elbow is pulled back to bend the arm just a little.

Figure 8–2. *Bend the arm slightly (note that this is take from the top-down view).*

2.   In an IK setup, you move the hand around freely while the arm follows it around. However, as long as the hand remains parented to the forearm bone, it can't be moved independently because it maintains an FK relationship, which makes it dependent on the movement of the arm it is anchored to. Therefore, unparent the hand from the forearm, like this:

a.   Select the hand bone in edit mode.

b.   On the Bone tab, look for the Relations area. You will see that the hand is parented to the forearm (shown in Figure 8–3). Delete this entry in order to make the hand free floating (nonparented). Alternatively, you could press Alt+P and choose Clear Parent from the resulting pop-up list.

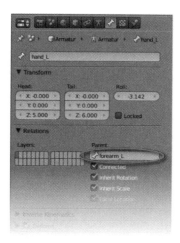

Figure 8–3. *Delete this entry to clear the parent of the hand.*

3. Select the forearm bone and make sure you are in pose mode. Add an IK constraint to the bone by going through the Bone Constraints tab. Be careful to select the correct tab—this is not the Object Constraints tab that has a chain link. Rather, the Bone Constraints tab is the one with a chain link next to a bone. Look at the top tabs in Figure 8–4 to see the correct tab to choose.

4. With the forearm bone still selected, go to the Add Constraint menu and choose to add an IK constraint. At the moment, the bone should turn an orange color, signifying that the constraint has been added, but the settings are not yet in place to get it working.

Figure 8–4. *Constraint settings for the forearm*

5. First, we need to give the arm a target. This is an object or bone at the extreme end (at the wrist), which the forearm bone will always try to join itself to. It can actually be any object in the scene, but in this case we want to use the hand bone. With the forearm bone selected, click the Target box and choose the name of the rig (most likely this will be `Armature`, `meta_arm_biped`, or whatever else you named the main rig). The instant you do this, a new box will appear asking you to identify the specific bone from that rig. Click this box and choose the hand bone from the list that appears. The forearm bone should now turn yellow, indicating that the settings are now active, *but don't move any bones yet.*

6. Notice that, when the forearm bone that has the constraint is selected, a dotted line will appear, running from the tip of the forearm bone (e.g., the wrist end) to whichever bone is highest in the parental hierarchy (in this case, the shoulder bone—though in a full rig it could well be down to the base of the spine). At the moment, the IK constraint causes all bones in the rig to this point to move when the hand is repositioned, which is not ideal; you don't want nearly the entire figure to bend whenever you move the hand! To fix this, change the Chain Length value from 0 (which means all bones) to 2, meaning that the length of the IK chain causes two bones, the forearm and the bicep only, to adjust when the hand is repositioned. This is represented by the dotted line only going as far back along the bone chain to the base of the bicep.

    Now, when you move the hand bone around in pose mode, you can see the arm automatically adjust for the new position, as in Figure 8–5. The action is just like a cloth puppet—pretty neat! The hand is still free floating, and can be pulled away from the rest of the arm; however, most animators know about this and simply take care not to overstretch things when working on movement.

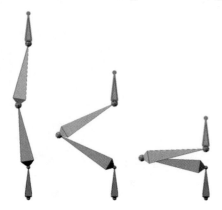

Figure 8–5. Once set up, an IK constraint causes the arm to bend when the hand (shown in red) is moved.

The problem with our setup now is that while the elbow bends automatically, we have no control over the direction of the bend. We sometimes might want to specify that the elbow points to the ground (e.g., holding a cup of water), and other times up toward the air (e.g., when the character performs push-up-type movements). To do this, we add a target for the elbow to point to (commonly referred to as a *pole target*). This can be any object, although for pose mode and keyframing purposes it is an advantage to create a new bone.

7. In edit mode of the bones, and from top view, select the ball between the elbow and the bicep.

8. Press E to extrude and pull the new bone outward in the direction the light bend of the elbow is pointing. It is a good idea at this point to use the X, Y, or Z keys (which one of these you use depends on which way up your rig is) to tell Blender to pull bones out at a straight angle. LMB-click once (or press Enter to finalize this bone).

9. Press E a second time and pull a small bone out, LMB-clicking (or pressing Enter) to finalize the move. This bone will soon be assigned the job of becoming the pole target for the elbow.

10. Select the first of the two bones you made and delete it (X key), leaving the second bone free floating. Why didn't we just add the second bone the conventional way using Shift+A? Because by extruding if from the joint of the elbow, we know everything lines up nice and straight, especially when you use the X, Y, or Z keys when you pull the new bones into place.

11. Name the remaining bone elbow_pole_L or something else appropriate (the _L or _R is commonly used to distinguish whether limbs are on the left or right side of a character. Blender understands this when performing various mirror functions, such as inverting a pose or when adding bones symmetrically).

12. The new pole target bone is still parented to the arm it was extruded from. With the pole target bone selected, enter the Bone tab, and unparent it by deleting the listed parent from the slot in the Relations panel. Another way would be to press Alt+P and choose Clear Parent from the pop-up list. The dotted line going from the elbow to this elbow pole should disappear, and the pole should be freely moveable when in pose mode.

13. In pose mode, select the forearm bone and go to the Bone Constraints tab, as shown in Figure 8–6. You want to specify that the elbow is to point in the direction of the elbow_pole_L bone you just made. First, In the Pole Target field, enter the name of your rig, and in the new Bone field that appears, choose the elbow_pole_L bone.

Figure 8–6. Setting up a pole target

14. If the elbow points directly to the target, you are lucky, though this is not usually the case. Usually the elbow will flip out in some seemingly random direction. In the Pole Angle field of the IK constraint, you need to enter a pole angle offset (in degrees) so that the IK constraint correctly aligns toward the pole target bone. More often than not, the correct value is 90 or –90, although this can vary. Experiment with different values until you get an angle that results in the elbow pointing directly to the pole target bone when the target bone is moved around in pose mode (Figure 8–7).

Figure 8–7. *Fully working IK arm with pole bone to control elbow direction*

Now you have made an arm that automatically bends when the hand is moved, along with a target bone which can be used to fine-tune the direction of the bent elbow. Congratulations, your IK arm is complete.

Setting a Custom Bone Shape

Looking at professionally made rigs, you might notice that you don't see much in the way of bones. Instead, what you see are controller shapes that are easy to grab. How do they do this? The secret is that these shapes are still bones that are linked to other hidden mesh objects from which they copy their appearance.

For example, in order to make a custom-shaped hand bone as in Figure 8–8, do the following:

1. In object mode, make a new mesh and name it (e.g., handshape).

2. With the hand bone selected in pose mode, look on the Bone tab, and find the option for Custom Shape in the Display area of the Properties panel. Change this Custom Shape field to handshape (or whatever mesh object you otherwise wish).

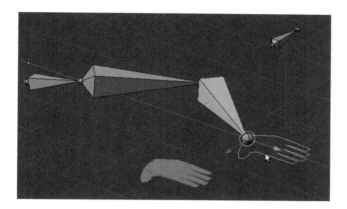

Figure 8–8. Hand bone taking its shape from a polygon mesh (placed in front)

On first assigning a shape to a bone, the result will be an incorrect size and poor alignment. To fix this, go into edit mode for the mesh object (in this case, handshape), select all vertices (the A key), and resize/move them around so that they are aligned when applied as a bone shape. This can take some trial and error, and it is useful to know that the origin point of the mesh will be located at the original base of the bone using its shape. Hide the mesh object when done, by moving it to another layer (in object mode, use the M key).

Exercise: Creating an IK Leg

Now that you have made an IK arm, apply the same steps to create an IK leg like the one shown in Figure 8–9. The goal is to make a leg where moving a foot into the air causes the knee to bend automatically. Don't forget to unparent the foot from the shin bone. Once the basic IK is working, you should also make pole target bones for the knees to point to. This will make taking steps much easier than if you had to rotate from the thigh bones in FK.

Figure 8–9. IK leg

There are some basic differences you should expect between an FK and an IK leg setup. Normally, in an FK setup, the order of bones is as follows: hip bone, thigh bone, shin bone, foot bone, and finally toe bone (depending on whether you want the foot to bend). An IK setup changes things a little. You need a knee pole for the knee to point at (and of course, the knee should be slightly bent to start with). You also need to completely break the foot off at the ankle so that it can float around freely; otherwise, the IK constraint in the shin bone causes the ankle to have a double movement, and the leg flails around wildly because the foot movements are trying to control the ankle and shin movements.

Once you have these things in place, you should be able to get your IK leg working with an IK constraint applied to the shin bone, target set to the foot bone, pole target as the floating knee_target bone, and chain length of 2 (the IK is to affect the shin and thigh movement).

Reverse Foot Rig

The IK rig is fine, but the control is not as powerful as you might like in your rigs. For example, it is easy enough to tap the foot up and down from the ankle end (lifting the toes), but what if it's the toe end you want to keep in place on the floor, and instead lift the heel? You could do clever things like rotating around the cursor, but that's a lot of work to go to every time you want to make your character take steps and peel his or her feet off the ground. The simple IK leg rig can't bend or peel off the floor like a professional animator would expect.

I like a foot that is easy to use, but also capable of the following movements, as shown in Figure 8–10:

- The foot should be able to move as a whole, with the knee automatically bending (basic IK setup).

- The foot should be able to pivot from the heel (heel roll/pivot).

- Opposite to this, the foot should be able to pivot from the toe tip (toe pivot).

- The toes should be able to peel up or bend down from the ball of the foot (toe roll/wiggle).

- The foot should be able to peel from the floor, lifting the heel while keeping the toes flat to the ground (ball roll).

These extra movements are where the *reverse foot* rig comes into play. A reverse foot rig is a way of setting up foot bones so that you can easily control each of those movements using separate bones within the foot of an IK leg. It is called "reverse foot" because it reverses the order of bones in the foot. Instead of going from ankle to midfoot (ball of the foot) to toe tip, the bones go in reverse order.

Let's have a go at making the Reverse Foot rig. To start building the reverse foot from scratch, create bones as shown in the progression of Figure 8–11. Here, we start with a leg bone that has been extruded vertically from a hip bone. This leg is then subdivided into two bones (the thigh and shin), bent slightly at the knee, and then a knee pole target is created for the knee to point to.

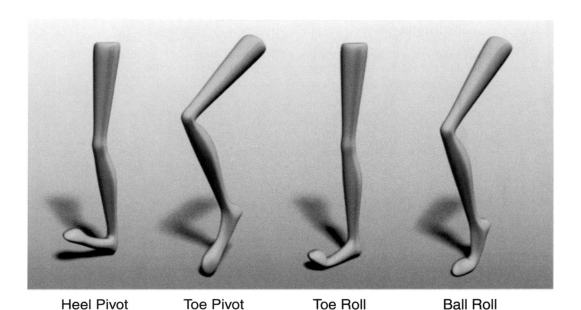

| Heel Pivot | Toe Pivot | Toe Roll | Ball Roll |

Figure 8–10. Desirable foot movements

Figure 8–11. The making of the leg bones

On following Figure 8–11, please consider these points:

- Have the leg bone going straight down from the hip to the ankle (extrude it from the hip down in the direction of the z axis).

- Create a knee by subdividing the leg bone and pull the knee joint slightly forward so there is a very slight bend (forward to the character).

- Extrude the knee forward some distance, and then upward to make the knee pole bone.

- Delete the bone leading out to the knee pole and unparent the pole from the main leg.

Note that in these instructions, I am coloring the bones different hues in order to show parental groups (here the knee pole becomes purple now that it is no longer parented to the leg).

It's good to label the bones as you go. See Figure 8–12 for guidelines on sensible bone names. Note that as I am making a left leg, every bone label has the suffix _L.

Figure 8–12. Names for the leg bones

We will now begin to make the foot bones, which are IK (the animator can grab them as a handle to move them around freely), and therefore will not be parented to the leg.

1. To position the heel directly under the base of the leg, take the bottom tip of the leg and extrude it downward, along the z axis, as shown in Figure 8–13.

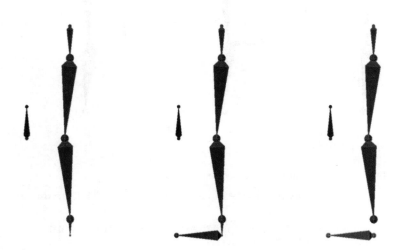

Figure 8–13. Positioning the foot bone

2. From this heel position, extrude a new bone to where the toe tip resides.

3. Delete the first of these two bones.

4. Unparent the remaining foot bone from the rest of the leg and name it foot_L (see Figure 8–14).

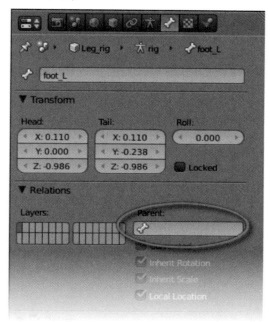

Figure 8–14. Make sure the the foot bone is not parented to the shin

5. Extrude from the toe tip end of the foot_L bone. Use your cursor to snap the end of the new bone to the very end tip of the leg bones.

6. Extrude it horizontally out the back of the foot. This new bone won't actually do anything except to serve as an IK target for the leg to attach to as the foot moves. Call this bone ankle_L.

7. Select the middle bone of the three (the one going from the toe tip end of foot_L and up to ankle_L), and press W to subdivide the bone into two. Lower the newly made joint so that it is positioned where the foot bends as the foot peels in a step. For these two bones, name the toe end bone toepivot_L and the other ballroll_L. The progression of what you have just done should look like the example in Figure 8–15.

Figure 8–15. *Creating the main bones of the feet*

8. There is one last bone to make, which is the one used to lift the toes into the air. Select the joint between the last two bones (`toepivot_L` and `ballroll_L`) and extrude it outward, as shown in Figure 8–16. Name this new bone `toewiggle_L` and snap its end tip to the toe end of `foot_L`.

Figure 8–16. *Extruding out toewiggle_L and laying it flat down to the toe tip*

In Figure 8–17, I have provided a visual guide for how the bones have been labeled. Bear in mind that I have broken the foot off at the shin to show that it is a separate piece from the leg, and I have pulled up `toewiggle_L` so that it can be clearly seen.

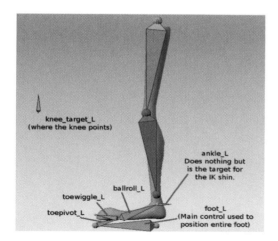

Figure 8–17. *Inner workings of the Reverse Foot rig*

Note that just for this figure, I have separated the foot from the tip of the shin bone, and I have also lifted the toe wiggle bone, which would normally be resting flat. (The foot bone would also lie along the sole of the foot.) Figure 8–17 serves to show which bones are where.

■ **Caution** There is a good chance that some bones may have done something like a barrel roll during the building process. If this is the case, select the bone that is not straight and follow the menu through Armature ➤ Bone Roll ➤ Clear Roll (Z-Axis Up). This tidies up the bones so that they lie as flat as possible. If you use this, it must be applied before any bone constraints or it could throw them off center.

All bones are now in place, and you need to change the deform properties of each bone so that Blender will know which ones are meant to have weight paint influence on the mesh.

While there are a few bones in the foot, only two of them, the toe wiggle and ball roll bones, will be needed for weight painting the foot to. So, for each of the following—knee pole, foot, toe pivot, and ankle—go to the Bone tab and uncheck Deform. These are mainly controller bones.

To really put the icing on the cake, use bone shapes to make the bones easy to access. The foot bone is the primary controller and usually takes the shape of a shoe step or a scoop. The toe pivot needs only to be small and at the toe tip. I usually shape the toe wiggle and ball roll bones so that they look like a hinge that the foot can bend from. I normally hide the ankle and leg bones. I give the knee_target_L bone the shape of a *K*. To see these shapes, look at Figure 8–18.

Remember that for a full figure, you need both left (*bonename_L*) and right (*bonename_R*) sets of legs.

Figure 8–18. Shape the bones you want as controllers and hide the others.

Single-Bone Finger Control

Fingers can be difficult to animate because of the total number of bones involved when taking all fingers into consideration. Each basic finger has three bones, resulting in two *joi nts* where it bends (this excludes the thumb, which has two bones where the other digits have three. I am not counting the thumb palm bone here, as it is too different in structure and function to be considered the same as any of the finger bones). The result is that the positioning each joint of every finger into place over the course of an animation is a very time-consuming and tedious process if we are going to use basic IK bone structure.

Here is a way you can rig a finger to work from a single bone. The setup is basically IK, so the bending of the finger becomes largely automated, with the animator only controlling a single bone instead of having to manipulate three separate bones for each finger. With this method, a controller bone extends from the base of the finger right up to the tip, and it controls both the direction the finger is pointing (through rotation) as well as the amount the finger is bent (through scaling).

Figure 8–19 shows the end product, in which rotating the controller bone allows you to change the direction of the finger, and scaling the controller bone causes the finger to bend.

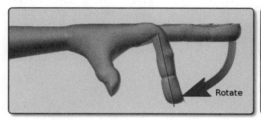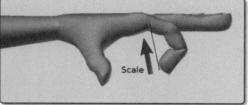

Figure 8–19. A single bone (in red) can be rotated to point the finger, or scaled to bend the finger.

Here are the basic steps behind setting up such a finger control:

1. The finger should be rigged with three bones just as though they were plain FK, and these should be appropriately named. For example, if rigging the index finger of the left hand, sensible names would be index1_L, index2_L, and index3_L. In the same way that IK legs and arms should not be straight, the finger should also have a slight bend. This can be done by slightly raising the middle bone, as indicated by the purple arrow in Figure 8–20. At this point, I take some time and weight paint the finger bones, which is why for the rest of the illustrations you will notice that the hand mesh bends with the bones.

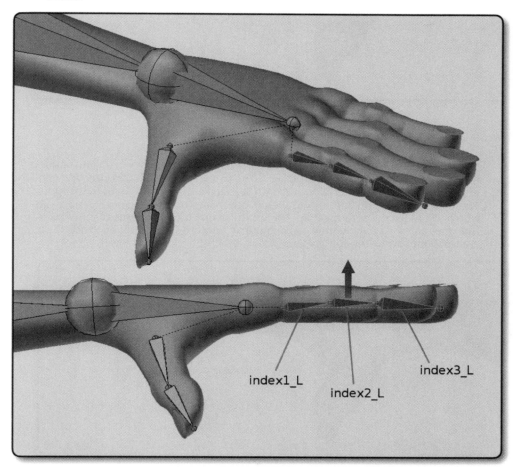

Figure 8–20. The main finger bones

2. To make the controller bone that the animator will use to control the entire finger, select the root of the base finger bone, and press the E key to extrude it out, as shown in Figure 8–21. Don't worry about the bone color in these diagrams; I am only doing that to clarify the illustrations.

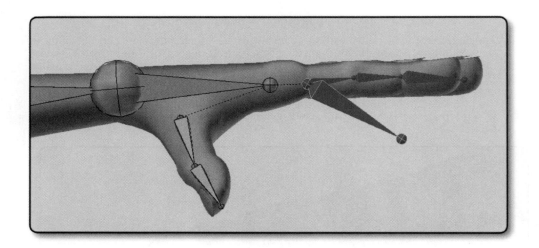

Figure 8–21. Extruding out the control bone

3. Snap the tip end of the controller bone so that it is positioned at the tip end of the very last finger bone, as shown in Figure 8–22. You can do this by selecting the tip end of the finger, and then using Shift+S ➤ Cursor to Selected to move the cursor to that point. Then select the end tip of the controller and use Shift+S ➤ Selected to Cursor again, which will make the ends meet up. Do not worry that the main bones cannot be seen (the ones colored green in previous diagrams); they are simply hidden inside the large control bone. Name the control bone index_control_L.

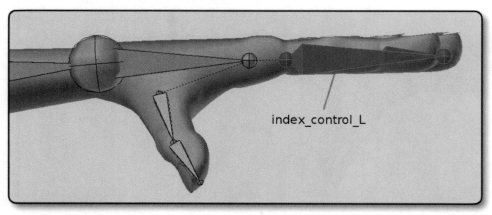

Figure 8–22. Snapping the the tip of the index_control_L bone into position

4.   The end tip of the controller bone is going to be extruded twice, as shown in Figure 8–23: once for the IK target, and another time in the process of making the pole. I will now explain each of these separately. Note that you would not normally be able to see the main finger bones (shown here in green) because they would be concealed inside the controller bone. I have added them to the illustration for clarity when positioning the index_pole_L bone. You can use wireframe mode (the Z key) to see the all bones if you need to, or simply hide bones that might be getting in the way (select them, press H to hide them, and then later press Alt+H to bring them back when needed).

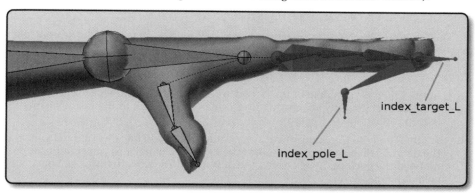

Figure 8–23. Extra extruded bones from the tip of the finger

c.   To make the IK target, simply extrude the end tip of the controller bone. Call it index_target_L.

d.   From the tip of the controller bone, extrude a second time, but lead the new end so as to position it directly below the middle of the three finger bones. From here, extrude a new bone and call it index_pole_L. Delete the first bone that leads up to it, but unlike the elbow and knee pole targets, don't unparent the newly made pole target, because we want it to adjust its position when the animator shrinks the controller bone to bend the finger. The result should look something like Figure 8–24.

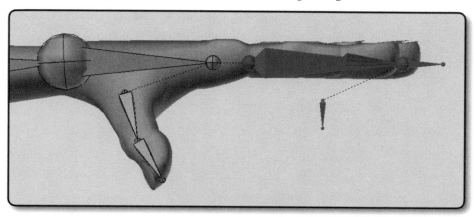

Figure 8–24. The bone leading up to index_pole_L is deleted.

5. Only the three main fingers bones will actually deform the mesh in terms of weight painting. For index_control_L, index_target_L, and index_pole_L, turn off the Deform option on the Bone tab. This will ensure that the wrong bones won't have influence on the hand mesh.

6. For tidiness, you may find that some bones have rolled during the positioning, and you might like to straighten them up. Select the finger bones (all at the same time) in Edit mode. Follow the 3D view header menu through Armature ➤ Bone Roll ➤ Recalculate with Z-Axis Up, which should straighten any leaning bones. Be aware that results for bone roll operations can vary from rig to rig.

7. With all the bones in place, it's now time to set up the finger to work with the controller. In pose mode, select the end main finger bone (index3_L), and on the Bone Constraints tab, add an IK constraint. Add properties as outlined following, and shown in Figure 8–25:

    a. In the Chain Length field of the IK constraint, enter the number 3. This ensures that the IK chain only affects the three bones of the finger and nothing further (e.g., not the hand or the arm).

    b. Set the Target to the name of your rig/armature. (If you have not named your rig, the default will be Armature). Look at the top of the panel and you should see the name of the current rig just under the tabs, next to a cube. In my case, I have called the rig arm_rig).

    c. In the new Bone entry field that appears under the Target entry, enter index_tip_L (this should be included in a drop-down list when you LMB-click in the field, although you can type it in).

    d. Set the Pole Target to the name of your rig/armature.

    e. In the new Bone entry field that appears under the Pole Target entry, enter index_pole_L.

    f. On setting the Pole Target entry, the main finger bones will likely spin around at an odd angle. With the index3_L bone still selected, change the pole angle to a number (in degrees) that best causes the finger to line itself up straight. This can vary from rig to rig, although the most common numbers are 90 degrees and –90 degrees.

Figure 8–25. *Properties of the IK constraint*

8. As demonstrated in Figure 8–26, the finger is now working. If you scale the controller bone while in pose mode, the three main finger bones bend as a finger does, and if you rotate the controller bone, the finger likewise points in different directions. It is a bad idea for the animator to grab the controller bone and change its location, though, so in pose mode, at the top of the Properties panel, click the padlocks next to the X, Y, and Z location parameters, as shown in Figure 8–27. This will lock the property in place so the user cannot change it by dragging the controller to other locations.

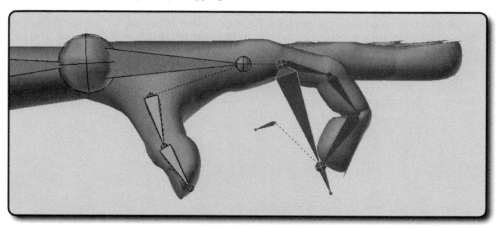

Figure 8–26. *The finger now works when rotating or scaling the controller bone (the large red one in this illustration).*

Figure 8–27. Locking the location of the controller bone

9. Finally it is a good idea to hide all finger bones except the controller bone, which is needed. Select bones to hide, and either press H to hide them (in this case, Alt+H will unhide them, which is easy to do by mistake, so it is not my preferred method) or press M to send them to another bone layer. Note that when moving bones to different layers, bone layers are not quite the same as the usual layers that are represented at the bottom of the 3D view; to switch between bone layers, you should use the Layers section of the Skeleton area of the Object Data tab. This only works when bones are selected, and the Object Data tab icon resembles a stick figure. On the same Object Data tab, in the Display area are options to shape the bones on a per-armature basis (Octahedral, Stick, B-Bone, and Envelope). If you're not using custom bone shapes, a good choice is Stick (see Figure 8–28), resulting in thin bones that don't get in the way of other objects, as shown back in Figure 8–19.

Figure 8–28. *Choosing Stick as the bone display type*

Now you only need to do the other fingers! Setting up all the fingers with this technique is tedious, although it makes animating the hand poses a lot easier, so is worth the effort in the long run.

Blender 2.5 Rigs

Designing and rigging your own character can take some time, and a good amount of experience is needed before you can rig a character so that is efficient for animation use. If you want something really sophisticated and polished, you might also consider downloading some of the rigs that experienced users have already put hours into on your behalf.

Rigging is an art, and different artists go about things in different ways, so how one rig works may not be the same for another. When faced with a new rig, you should try to clear up certain things:

- Make sure you are in pose mode. This might sound obvious, but occasionally riggers forget to enter pose mode just before saving their work, which means it could be in object or even edit mode when you open the file. The last thing you want is to move things around and then find you're pulling apart the model.

- Find out how the arms and legs move. Are they IK or FK? Is there an IK/FK switch somewhere allowing you to select which type of movement you want in the arms?

- Examine the facial controls. How are the eyes rotated? Is there a floating target they track? What control is used to open the mouth? How do the facial controls for smiling/frowning and making different mouth shapes work? How about controlling the eyebrows?

- Not all the Blender rigs you find will work with the latest version of Blender, as some are for older versions and Blender has been undergoing a lot of changes.

- Look for root or master bones (see the "Root and Master Bones" sidebar).

With these things in mind, the following sections describe a few rigs I have found on the Internet that are compatible with Blender 2.5.

ROOT AND MASTER BONES

A root bone is usually located around the hip or spine, and when it is moved, it grabs the entire body area including the spine, the head, and so on, except that it does not grab the IK foot or hand controls. The idea is that you can use this controller to move the bulk of the body into position while leaving the feet planted firmly where they are on the ground.

A master bone is usually positioned on the ground, and when it is moved, the entire rig goes with it, including IK arms and legs. It is good for moving the character to a suitable starting position; or with some rigs it can be scaled in order to resize a character to fit a scene (not every rig can be resized, though).

Unfortunately, not all riggers stick to the words "root" and "master." Indeed, I have seen a lot of Blender rigs where the master is called "root" and the root is called "torso." The main thing is that you should see whether there are primary bones for performing large body movement.

Unofficial Mancandy 2.5

The original Mancandy character was designed by Bassam Kurdali and is available from `http://freefac.org/mancandy/mancandy_2.48.blend`.
However, this is an old version of the rig and has bugs when used in Blender 2.5, and it may have been taken down recently as I have not been able to download the file of late. Bassam is said to be developing a new version, but in the meantime, Wayne Dixon has made an unofficial version that can be used in Blender 2.5, which you can download from `http://vimeo.com/12313617` or `www.waynedixon.com.au/ManCandy/mancandy.2.5.2.blend`.
Mancandy, shown in Figure 8–29, is an iconic rig that was used as the basis for the characters in the making of the Open Movie *Elephants Dream*.

Figure 8–29. Mancandy

As always, make sure you are in pose mode when animating the rig (the rig is in object mode when opening). At the bottom of the Properties panel is a Rig Layers area containing buttons for turning the various controls on and off. On selecting a hand or arm bone, a slider for IK Arm appears at the very bottom, allowing you to switch to whether the arm acts as FK (slide left) or IK (slide right) controls.

Ludwig

Ludwig, shown in Figure 8–30, created by Jason Pierce, is an older rig for Blender that works well in Blender 2.5. You can download Ludwig from `http://jasonpierce.animadillo.com/resource/ludwig/ludwig.html` or from the direct link at `http://jasonpierce.animadillo.com/resource/ludwig/ludwig.blend`.

On opening Ludwig, you'll find that the usual Properties panel controls have been replaced with a note to the user explaining the controls in a good amount of detail. You can use the leftmost button in the header to change the window type from Text Editor back to Properties, which will bring back the more familiar tabs. The tabs will appear along the bottom, though if you then RMB-click them and choose Flip to Top from the resulting menu, the layout will become more familiar.

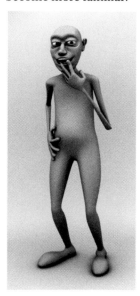

Figure 8–30. Ludwig

By default, Ludwig's bones are not in X-ray mode, which I recommend activating in order to make his controller bones easily accessible. To do this, select one of the bones (you should be in pose mode, although the mode does not actually matter when activating X-ray mode) and then check the X-Ray option, which is located in the Display area of the Object tab.

Ludwig has a master controller bone named `Root` underneath the entire rig. He has `Torso` and `Upper body` bones protruding out of his back for large body movements, as well as `Foot_Root.L` and `Foot_Root.R` bones sticking vertically out of the bottom of each heel; these are used for IK leg movement. Facial expressions can be altered by moving around the cubes above Ludwig's head.

For more information on the specifics of Ludwig's movements, read through the notes on display in the right side of the layout when you initially open the file.

KM

KM (shown in Figure 8–31), by Kalev Mölder (aka Artkalev) is a relatively easy-to-use rig.

KM can be downloaded from the Blender Swap repository at www.blendswap.com (perform a search for "KM") or more directly from www.blendswap.com/3D-models/characters/km.

It has a root control (for moving everything but the feet) around the waist, and a lot of nice facial controllers for different expressions.

Figure 8–31. KM

You can grab the square in front of the jaw to open and close the mouth, while moving the points surrounding the edges of the mouth to make different mouth shapes. One of the things I really like about the KM rig is the unique disappearing IK/FK switch controls. By selecting the words "IK <> FK" above either arm, and then looking to the bottom of the Properties panel, you will see an option to change whether the arm movement is IK or FK (enter 0 for IK or 1 for FK). Depending on which you wish to use, different grabbable controls will appear around the arm—a nice touch.

Walk Cycles

How do you get a character to walk? This is an easy question to ask, as we walk around without much thought, but in reality it can be a very involved process.

Before beginning a walk cycle, you should be aware of the difference between IK and FK. It is much easier to animate the feet when they are in IK, because you can place each step exactly where you want it. On the other hand, arms are best animated with an FK setup because they should swing from the shoulders in a circular motion. If you animate the arms in IK, their hands tend to move in straight lines and lose the circular swinging effect.

Obviously, the idea is to keyframe the steps and let the computer do a certain amount of inbetweening. However, if you keyframe each step in turn, it is a recipe for creating awkward walks with bad timing. Because viewers of your animation are used to seeing walks every day, they will be very quick to pick out anything odd, whether it be the size of the steps being wrong or incorrect timing. When it comes down to positioning and timing, correcting one fault so easily introduces another—a real animator's nightmare.

Thankfully, there is a process that you can go through in order to get the timing and positioning of the characters' feet at least close to reasonable. It involves blocking out your walk in basic stages, and then building up the details only when you're happy with first stage is as you want it.

Pass 1: Contact Positions

In a walk cycle, a contact position is where the foot hits the ground. You should start off by only keying these positions so that the character appears to be sliding his feet along the floor, as in Figure 8–32.

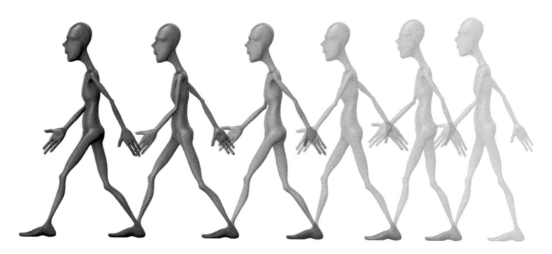

Figure 8–32. Contact positions

Do not key the positions where feet are raised in the air taking a step. The result at this stage should be that the animated character shuffles his feet along the floor as though he has newspaper under his feet, or as though sliding on roller skates.

So why would we want to start the walk like this, without lifting the feet for each step? By doing so, there is still time to change your mind on the timing or the positioning of each step.

If, for example, you decided to alter where the character was walking (if you wanted him to walk in a curved line instead of a straight line), then it would be much easier to change the steps at this point, when they are only the contact positions. If you had keyed the knees being raised as well, then you would have a lot more to adjust, and the task would become much more involved.

The following are some things to watch out for at this phase:

- Keep the pose balanced in terms of center of gravity. With the exception of leaping, characters should be able to freeze in a pose without looking like they are tipping over.

- Don't have the steps so wide as to cause the legs to be straight. When animating, straight legs have a tendency to twitch.

- The arm swinging forward is the opposite one to the leg that is forward.

Press Alt+A to examine your walk often, preferably from different angles. Make adjustments until you are happy with the timing and the positioning of the feet is right.

You should key both feet, both arms, and the root control (where the main spine of the body is) for each contact position. By keying the foot that is not moving, you don't end up with it starting to drift off due to later inbetweening issues.

Pass 2: Passing Poses

Once you are happy with the timing and contact positioning of the walk, you can then move on to keying the inbetween positions where the character lifts his leg for each step, as shown in Figure 8–33.

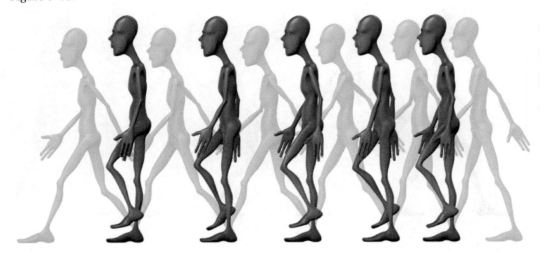

Figure 8–33. *Passing positions*

There are three main things that need to happen here:

- The foot being lifted off the floor needs to be keyed.

- Due to inbetweening, you may find the swinging arms are moving through the body, so they will need to be moved out sideways in order to swing around.

- The root position of the character—that is, the spine—should be raised, creating a head-bobbing motion for each step. Usually you would want to raise the spine enough to nearly straighten the supporting leg, but you should leave a slight bend or else the leg will likely twitch at this position when animated.

Again, make sure each pose is balanced. As the character is supported by one leg, the bulk of the body should be above the supporting foot.

Pass 3: Peeling the Feet

The basic steps are now working, but the feet are landing flat on the floor, and lifting in a similar way, making for very stiff movement. In reality, feet peel as they lift into a step (Figure 8–34) and the foot lands heel-first before flattening to the ground. Work over each step, making the contact positions land heel-first before flattening a couple of frames after. Key in some ball root/toe pivot movements for when the foot is lifting so that it peels as it leaves the ground. The toe tip should be the last part of the foot to touch the floor. This may sound simple enough, but there are certain considerations to be wary of:

- When making the foot peel from the floor, if you simply lift the heel and key it, you will probably find that the inbetweening causes the heel to slowly raise itself up to the point where you keyed it as being up. It is important that you go a few frames before the heel lift and key the foot while it is still flat on the ground. This key, ahead of time, becomes the point at which the heel begins to move. The same holds true for any similar movements such as a toe pivot.

Figure 8–34. The foot peels as it leaves the ground.

- The landing foot in a step should contact the ground with the heel first—with the rest of the foot tilted upward so the toes are in the air—and then slap down to a flat position over about two frames. Now, you could simply tilt the foot upward at each contact position, and then move a few frames forward and key the foot flat to the ground, but it can be time-consuming trying to line up the foot so that it rests perfectly on the floor each time. In our workflow of sliding feet forward, the key positions already have the feet flat on the ground. You can take advantage of this by moving to a point in the timeline a couple of frames after the contact position and then key the foot. Then you can move backward along the timeline to the contact position and tilt the foot so that it is landing heel-first (and key it of course). From here, the foot will slap itself flat in accordance with the position you have just keyed beforehand.

Pass 4: Adding Some Finesse

Your walk cycle should already be looking pretty good, but there are numerous ways to push it even further. You could roll the hips so that they sway from side to side in a swagger (the hip of the back leg about to be lifted normally goes upward). Depending on the style of walk, the arms will act differently. If the character is sad, the arms will droop down low, swinging forward and back. A happy character will have an exaggerated swing reaching high and across the upper torso. Professional animators even go to the extreme of opening the Graph editor window in order to manually control the curvatures of all the movements that are happening. For now, though, the above should be a sufficient workflow to get you started on animating an effective walk cycle.

Shape Keys

Until now, we have animated by either moving whole objects, or by using bones whenever we want something to bend. There is another way of making things change shape: using *shape keys*. With shape keys, you begin with a starter mesh object, which is called the *basis* shape, and then make a library of distortions to this shape, which can then be applied to the original by means of slider controls.

For this example, we're going to add shape keys to the monkey mesh. The first thing that is needed is to create the basis shape key—that is, what the monkey looks like without any changes made.

1. Select the monkey.

2. Go to the Object Data tab.

3. Go to the Shape Keys panel.

4. Click the Add button (the + sign—shown circled in red in Figure 8–35) to add a new shape key. Notice that the first shape key added is called Basis. This is the default shape of the mesh in its neutral state—that is, where there are no distortions made.

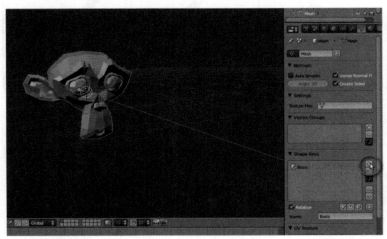

Figure 8–35. *Creating the initial basis shape key*

5. Click the Add button again (Figure 8–36), and you will notice a new shape key gets added, this time called Key 1.

Figure 8–36. *Adding and renaming a new shape key*

6. You can rename the new key if you like, in the Name field below the Shape Keys list, as in Figure 8–36.

7. Now you will want to change the mesh of this new shape key to some kind of distortion to make it different from the original Basis shape key. To do so, with the appropriate shape key selected in the list, click the thumbtack icon, as indicated in Figure 8–37. This locks in the chosen shape key for editing.

Figure 8–37. *Pin the shape key down before editing the mesh.*

8. Then go into edit mode and move vertices around to change the shape. For my first shape key (not the basis shape), I'm making the monkey stretch vertically. You can have any distortion or facial expression you like, as long as you don't add or take away any vertices (see Figure 8–38).

■ **Caution** Do not add or remove any vertices; only move them. Shape keys work by morphing from one shape to another, so each vertex point simply moves elsewhere. If you add or remove any vertices, the mesh becomes inconsistent in terms of Blender knowing which vertices go where.

Figure 8–38. Editing the first shape key deformation

9. When you are done, leave edit mode and deselect the Shape key thumbtack icon. Selecting shape keys from the list should now make the mesh object switch to the corresponding shape.

10. Select the basis shape key, and then click + again to add a second shape, as in Figure 8–39. Edit this as you did the first (click the thumbtack icon and use either Edit or sculpt mode to warp the mesh into a different shape).

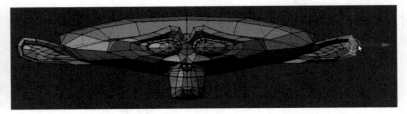

Figure 8–39. Making the second shape key

11. Once both shape keys have been made (and you have deselected the thumbtack icon and returned to object mode), it is time to look at how the shape keys are controlled. Make a new window (split the main 3D view down the center) and assign it as a DopeSheet view (Figure 8–40).

12. In the header, there is a Mode drop-down list, where you can set the mode to ShapeKey Editor (Figure 8–40). This should reveal a series of sliders—one for each of the nonbasis shape keys, as shown in Figure 8–41. Move the sliders, and you will see their effect on the mesh. Not only is it possible to have different shape key strengths, you can also combine shapes together by using different amounts from each of the sliders, as shown in Figure 8–42.

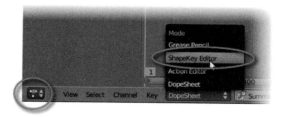

Figure 8–40. Navigate to the ShapeKey editor.

Figure 8–41. Shape key slider controls

Figure 8–42. Using the slider controls, you can control the amount of any shape key.

Shape keys are made for animation. If you slide along the timeline, and then move one of the shape key sliders, the shape is automatically keyed in for that amount at that moment on the timeline.

Once you know how to make shape keys, it is possible to make all manner of facial expressions. Simply break face movements into smaller parts (e.g., an eyebrowlift_L for raising the left eyebrow, eyeslant_L for making the left eye into an angry shape, etc.) and make each part a separate shape key. New expressions are easily made by using different combinations of your basis shape keys. If, for example, you have a frowning mouth with raised eyebrows, the character will look sad or fearful, but if you scrunch the eyebrows in at the nose, the frowning expression will change to one of anger.

Shape keys are automatically keyed to the timeline when the sliders are moved. All you need to do is slide the timeline along to each key pose position, and adjust the slider controls to match the correct expressions at each place. Animate the scene with Alt+A to see your character move through each expression and come to life.

Symmetrical Facial Expressions

Some facial expressions are symmetrical, such as a smile or a frown. Others, like a sneer, are asymmetrical, but you will want to flip the shape over to the other side to make the opposite equivalent. It's no good being able to grimace on one side only, and it would be a lot of work creating mirror images of expressions if you had to do each by hand. Fortunately, there are more efficient ways.

Creating Symmetrical Models

You can use either sculpting or mesh modeling (edit mode) to edit shape keys, so for modeling faces, you can take advantage of Blender's built-in symmetry options when making symmetrical shape keys such as smiles or frowns.

In sculpt mode, you can use the Symmetry XYZ option so that the brush events happen to both sides of a mesh. (Figure 8–43 shows the Tool Shelf with X Mirror active in sculpt mode.)

Figure 8–43. Sculpt mode symmetry options

In edit mode, you can use the X Mirror and Topology Mirror options at the bottom of the Tool Shelf (see Figure 8–44).

The X Mirror option will move vertices that are oppositely positioned against the x axis. This works even if two points are from different parts of the mesh; they merely have to be opposite in terms of their 3D space.

The Topology Mirror option checks to see whether the two X-mirrored pairs are actually from a symmetrical mesh.

Note that these functions are designed to support moving vertices around. Functions that add or delete edges (such as extrusion) are not taken into account.

Figure 8–44. Mirror options for edit mode, at the bottom of the Tool Shelf

There is also the mirror modifier (explained in Chapter 3), but this is not recommended for making shape keys, as it means that everything has to be mirrored all the time. Generally speaking, modifiers should be applied before creating shape keys.

■ **Note** The important thing to remember when making shape keys is that you must never add or delete vertices. Always make a new shape key by moving (or sculpting) the basis points into new positions.

Creating Asymmetrical Shape Keys

Of course, making an asymmetrical shape key for one side is easy; you just sculpt away however you see fit. But how do you create a flipped version of the same shape for the other side?

1. Make a shape key for the right side, as shown in Figure 8–45. With the thumbtack down, modify the shape to a sneer (either edit or sculpt mode will do). Name it appropriately (sneer_R).

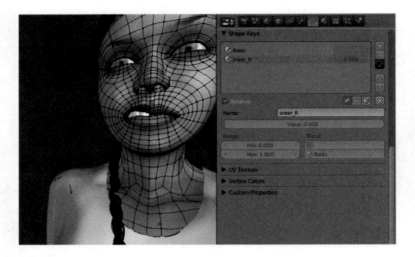

Figure 8–45. Make the first shape key.

2. Back in object mode, select the new shape key. Click the Add button (shown in Figure 8–46) to create a duplicate copy. Rename the duplicate (sneer_L).

Figure 8–46. The Add button

3. The only thing left now is to flip the last shape key, because at the moment it is the same way around as the one it was cloned from. With the new shape key selected, click the down arrow button under the Add/Subtract buttons and choose Mirror Shape Key from the menu that appears (Figure 8–47).

Figure 8–47. *Applying the Mirror Shape Key function*

That's it. As shown in Figure 8–48, your new shape key is now a reversal of the first it was cloned from.

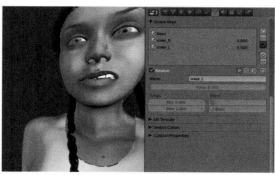

Figure 8–48. *Completed flipped shape key*

Lip Syncing

Shape keys are also an important part of making a character talk. For most rigs, you would make a character open their mouth by carefully weight painting the lower jaw to a jaw bone, as I have done in Figure 8–49. Moving this bone gives a puppetlike speaking action. This becomes more realistic when combined with shape keys that control the mouth into making convincing shapes for individual sounds.

There are no definite rules on which shape keys your character has to have, because not all characters share the same characteristics, and one creature may have completely different mannerisms from another. However, for purposes of a good range of mouth shapes, I suggest using the shapes described in the following sections as a bare minimum.

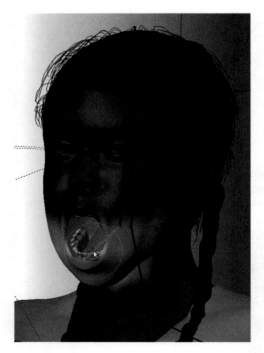

Figure 8–49. Start with weight painting a jaw bone for the main mouth movement.

The Basis Shape Key

This is the default neutral shape key without any particular expression (Figure 8–50). It is the resting position of the face, from which all other shape keys are made. Any changes to this shape key will affect all other shapes, so it is best left alone.

If the topology of the face is good, including the following, then making shape keys that slide smoothly from one to another will be a lot easier:

- A mesh made from quads (four-sided faces) instead of triangles

- An edgeflow that supports the direction of movement, such as having concentric circles around the mouth and eyes

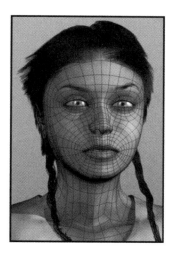

Figure 8–50. *The basis shape key*

Smile and Frown

These are two separate shape keys to control the mouth for basic emotions (Figure 8–51). Note that these do not look convincingly like real expressions. This is because the mouth-centric shape key does not transfer the emotion to other important facial areas like the eyes, which would be controlled by shape keys of their own. That way, it is possible to have eyes and mouths with different variations of emotion, or manipulate the timing of an emotion change (e.g., the eyes express sadness before the mouth does). The smile also looks weird because it mainly includes vertical movement, not horizontal movement, which is taken care of by the next shape key.

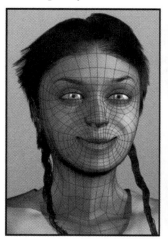 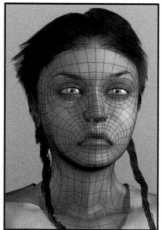

Figure 8–51. *Smile and frown shape keys*

Wide and Pucker

Whereas Smile and Frown contain largely vertical movement, Wide and Pucker are horizontal shapes (see Figure 8–52). Wide looks unnatural by itself, but when combined with other shape keys it becomes very useful (e.g., for making a wide smile).

The Wide shape is used when mouthing "eee" sounds, and Pucker is typically needed for mouthing "w" sounds.

These two shape keys in particular are a good test of effective edgelooping, as they are difficult to form smoothly when edgelooping is bad.

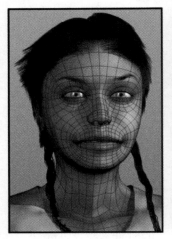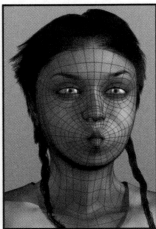

Figure 8–52. Wide and Pucker shape keys

Puff and Suck

Some sounds, such as "puh" and "buh," make the cheeks puff out a little. The Puff shape key is useful in this regard. In combination with the Pucker shape key, Puff can also be used for blowing. The opposite is Suck, which draws the cheeks in (see Figure 8–53). Blender does allow negative values for shape keys (you could type a negative value into the puff slider to get something resembling sucking), but in order to really refine the shape in regard to the cheekbones, I normally make these as separate shape keys.

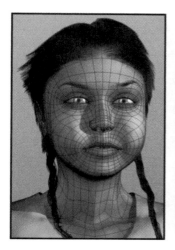
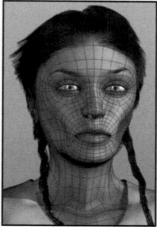

Figure 8–53. Puff and Suck shape keys

Sneer_L and Sneer_R

These shapes allow for a bit of asymmetrical manipulation of the top lip (Figure 8–54). As well as the obvious use in emotional mouth shapes, Sneer is also used when mouthing "n" sounds.

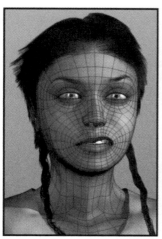
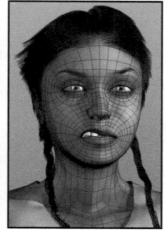

Figure 8–54. Sneer (left and right) shape keys

Grimace_L and Grimace_R

This is the bottom lip's counter to the top lip's sneer (see Figure 8–55). For expressions, the grimace is often used in conjunction with sneer shapes, though having them as four different shape keys allows for a lot of variation.

Grimace is subtly useful in forming part of the mouth shapes for "k," "gih," and "r" sounds.

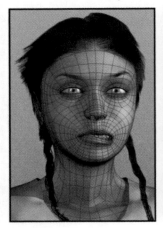 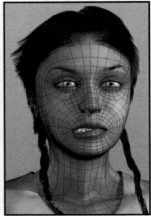

Figure 8–55. Grimace (left and right)

Toplip_out and Toplip_in

These two shape keys allow you to roll the top lip out or to pull it in, as shown in Figure 8–56. Rolling out the top lip out is useful for "s" or whistling sounds, whereas pulling it in helps to define the "m" mouth shape (especially when also pulling in the bottom lip).

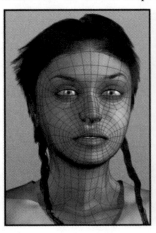 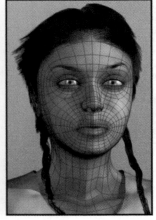

Figure 8–56. Toplip_out and Toplip_in

Bottomlip_out and Bottomlip_in

These shape keys provide curling and tucking motions for the bottom lip (Figure 8–57). Rolling the bottom lip out is useful when making "r" sounds, while pulling the lip in is needed when making "f" sounds. Pull both lips inward when making "puh" and "buh" sounds.

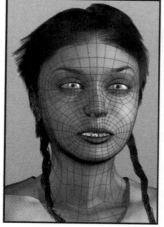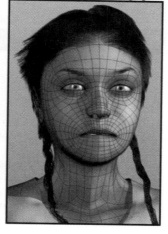

Figure 8–57. *Bottomlip_out and Bottomlip_in*

Preparing the Sound for Lip Syncing

Now that you've made a jawbone and the appropriate shape keys, you are ready to have your character speak. Here are the basic steps.

With the character loaded into the scene, you need to import your sound file (a recording of the voice your of your character). Blender's ability to understand different sound formats can vary from system to system, but it's usually pretty good.

1. Temporarily change the timeline across the bottom of your windows to one of type Video Sequence editor. Pull the top of the window upward, making it taller so its contents are easier to see (or maximize it with Shift+spacebar).

2. Now, with your mouse over this new area, use Shift+A to add a new item. From the choices of Scene, Movie, Image, and Sound, select Sound (Figure 8–58), and when you are presented with a file browser, navigate to the needed sound file.

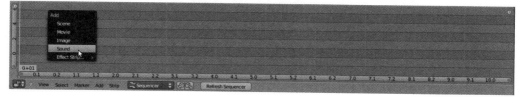

Figure 8–58. *Adding a sound strip to the Video Sequence editor*

3. Occasionally, Blender fails to see files when you hunt them this way, because it has an intelligent filtering to show only the formats it expects. If you happen to be in the correct directory but your file is invisible, try clicking the funnel icon (as shown in Figure 8–59, it is usually either at the very top or bottom of the file search window) to toggle whether Blender should hide unrecognized file types. In some cases, sound and video files that Blender doesn't think it will recognize actually do work well once imported.

Figure 8–59. The Remove File Filter funnel

4. On the file selection screen s with your desired sound file selected, click the Add Sound Strip button to import a selected file (or press the Enter key).

5. Once an audio strip is imported, you should see it appear in the Video Sequence editor as a green horizontal bar. You can right-click it to select this bar and then use the G key to move it into position along the Video Sequence editor timeline. When moving the bar around, tiny numbers appear at either end, allowing you to see the start and end frame number for the strip. Most likely you will want to move the strip into position so that the leftmost end is on frame 1.

■ **Note** Be wary of selecting the ends of the strip, which have arrows on them, because these are designed to resize, or rather to crop, the audio strip. It is better to select audio files from the middle of the strip.

Now that the audio sample is in place, you will want to hear it in order to know that it is working.

1. Change the Video Sequence editor back to a timeline.

2. Press Alt+A to animate. As the animation runs, your sound file should play.

3. You may need to change the start and end animation markers to accommodate the length of your sound strip (these marker are found at the bottom of the standard timeline window, as shown in Figure 8–60).

Figure 8–60. The standard timeline. Note the start and end frame values.

Sometimes, especially in scenes where there is a lot happening on the screen, Blender can't show every animated frame fast enough to keep up with the sound. When this happens, the sound keeps playing on at normal speed, while the action lags slowly behind, and you get to hear things before they happen.

For this reason, the standard timeline has sync options (as shown in Figure 8–61), where you can choose between the following:

- *AV-sync:* The sound tries to match the speed of what is happening on the screen even if it results in choppy audio.

- *Frame Dropping:* Any action on the screen tries to match the speed of the sound.

- *No Sync:* This is the default, where sound and onscreen action each play at its own pace.

For lip sync purposes, the best option is for frame dropping, which will help avoid choppy sound or sound that doesn't match the mouth movements.

Figure 8–61. Timeline sync options

If the sound doesn't work when you animate, try using different sound formats, and ensure that your own system sound setup is working. Go to User Preferences ➤ Sound ➤ System, and check the settings there as well.

For lip syncing, you will want to scrub the timeline back and forth and listen to the sounds as you are watching your animation work. In the standard timeline window, under Playback, check the Audio Scrubbing option to allow sounds to play as you drag the timeline (as shown in Figure 8–62).

Figure 8–62. Enabling timeline-based audio scrubbing

Moving the Lips

Once the sound is working and your character is on the screen, it's time to make those lips move.

As with all animation, it is a good idea to key all bones at frame 1. Otherwise, without being anchored down there, the next movements down the timeline have a tendency to take over as the starting position.

Lip sync animation is not done all at once. Rather, it is better to block out the basic open and shut movements first (the jaw bone), and then return to the animation to add specific mouth shapes. Typically, lip syncing is built up over three workflow stages.

Phase 1: The Jaw Movement

Move along the timeline, using only the lower jaw bone to open and close the mouth like a puppet. Try to match the sound file. Do not try to use shape keys just yet; it is more important that you get the foundation movement of the open/shut timing correct first. Note that when we speak, we don't actually open and close out mouths around every syllable. Instead, we tend to open our mouth for a sentence, shake the bottom jaw at about the half-open mark, and close the mouth only when the sentence is finished.

Phase 2: Refining Mouth Shapes with Shape Keys

Once the jaw is moving in sync with the sound, go over the animation again, adding mouth shape keys to match the shape of the mouth to the sounds. Pull the lips in when the character makes "mmm" sounds, and puff the cheeks a little for "puh" and "buh." Don't worry about expressions at this stage; you're only concerned about the shape keys making the speech look more convincing than the puppetlike motion of only the jawbone. Use some of the previously discussed shape keys for ideas on appropriate shapes for different sounds.

Phase 3: Enhancing with Expression

When you have the lips speaking convincingly, add real life to the scene by finally charging the animation with expression and emotion. Properly placed smiles, frowns, and eye signals will take the character to a whole new level of life.

Summary

Rigging and animation are advanced areas. In this chapter we have gone beyond the simple FK rig setup and into IK, which can be more intuitive for animators wanting precise hand and foot movements.

Much of our rigging has had an emphasis on character animation. I introduced a workflow for effective walk cycles, and examined a few rigs that you can obtain freely from the Internet. We also looked into shape keys and investigated how these can be used in setting up a character for facial animation and lip syncing.

CHAPTER 9

■ ■ ■

Making Movies

Back in 2006, Stephen Colbert issued his first "green screen challenge" to the audience of his American TV show, *The Colbert Report*. After picking up a light saber and rolling about in front of a large green screen, Colbert challenged anyone in the viewing audience to see what they could do to turn his shenanigans into a polished animation. One of the entrants was WeirdHat, who, it turned out, did all his compositing in Blender (shown in Figure 9–1).

Figure 9–1. WeirdHat makes a Jedi of Stephen Colbert

You can see WeirdHat's work at the following: places:

- www.weirdhat.com (WeirdHat's own web site)

- www.youtube.com/watch?v=C8Mkm3QtwgE

Compositing is about mixing movies together, and it's also about color-correcting shots and performing special effects. Just how did WeirdHat go about putting Stephen Colbert into a 3D scene to fight against a CGI Rancor monster that he'd downloaded from scifi3d.com?

To split Colbert from the green background of the original footage, WeirdHat would have used what is known as Blender's *compositing nodes*, which we will be looking at in this chapter.

Before We Begin

Before using nodes, there are a few important concepts you should understand.

Disabling Color Management

Blender has built-in color management, which by default is turned on. Often you will want to use nodes for the purposes of adjusting the lighting of a render. If color management is left on, then Blender will keep trying to enhance the image you are enhancing, and you'll end up fighting each other. When working with nodes, I usually recommend that you turn the automatic color management off. On the Render tab (which has a camera icon), go down to the Shading area and uncheck the Color Management box, as indicated in Figure 9–2.

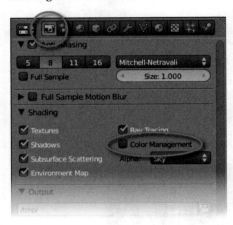

Figure 9–2. The Color Management option. Note that you need to scroll quite far down the panels to get to the Shading area.

Rendering Formats

Until now, I have said you can render using the F12 key. This F12 key is a shortcut to the rendering button, which is actually located in the Render tab (in a section that is itself called Render). Pressing F12 is the same as clicking the Image button you see there (this button is shown in Figure 9–3).

Next to the Image button is a button for rendering an animation, which has the keyboard shortcut of Ctrl+F12. The basic difference is that the Image button is for rendering still images (JPG, PNG, TARGA, etc.), whereas the Animation button outputs movies (QuickTime, AVI, etc.). Of course, there is a little more involved that just selecting Image vs. Animation. It is up to you to specify what size shots you want to take, and you need to inform Blender of a few file type specifics as well.

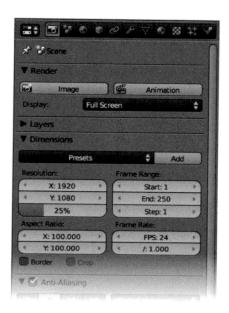

Figure 9–3. The Render and Dimensions areas of the Render tab

To specify the size of the render, go down to the Dimensions section. The main ones here are the x and y resolution settings. If you are unsure of what a standard TV-sized image should look like, you can always opt to choose from the list of presets at the top of this section. For movies, you will also need to specify start and end frames (this updates the same values in Blender's standard timeline). You can also change the frame rate from the standard 25 frames per second (fps) if you so desire.

Look down further and you will see the all important Output settings (see Figure 9–4).

First, there is a file directory given, which is where your movies will go once they are rendered. Note that this area refers to the save path of animations, such as clicking the Animation button at the top of the panel (or the keyboard shortcut Ctrl+F12). For still images, you would normally use a straight render by clicking the Image button (or alternatively the shortcut key F12), and the image would not immediately be saved until you follow with pressing F3 to save the result. This method of saving the still image defaults to saving in the same directory where your .blend file is saved.

Figure 9–4. The Output area on the Render tab

Below this are options specifying what kind of file you want to use. If you want to make a working movie, this is where you would choose AVI or another similar movie format. It is also where you should tell Blender whether your images should render as JPG, PNG, TARGA, and so on.

There are options for BW (black and white), RGB (color), and RGBA (color with alpha/transparency). Only some file formats will support transparency, among them PNG, which makes it a good choice for general purpose renders. Also, if you choose an image format here (as opposed to a movie format) and then tell Blender to render an animation, you will end up with a folder of sequentially numbered images (image001.png, image002.png, image003.png, etc.).

Sometimes that may be exactly what you want to do. For now, know that if your movies don't come out the right size or in the format you are after, then the Render tab is where you should look first.

■ **Note** Not all movies types support sound. Those that do should have appropriate options appear in an Encoding section when their base format is chosen. Blender allows you to mix various codec formats, although you need to work out which ones will successfully produce a working movie with sound.

There is another section you should be aware of on the Render tab: the Post Processing area (Figure 9–5). Under this are two options for Compositing and Sequencer. The techniques in this chapter are about using the compositing nodes (Compositing), after which we will look at the Video Sequence editor (the Sequencer). In order for the techniques presented in this chapter to work, you need to leave these options on.

Figure 9–5. The Post Processing area, which can be found at the bottom of the Render tab

What Is Alpha?

It is important to understand alpha when working with nodes, as it can be important when blending images together.

Images are usually made up of a grid of colored squares known as *pixels*. Each pixel can be any color, and this is usually derived by different mixes of red, green, and blue. This type of image is known as an RGB image. Some images are capable of storing an extra channel known as *alpha*, which records the opacity (the transparency) of each pixel in addition to the RGB color, making the image type RGBA.

When saving images, if you want levels of transparency it is important to know that only some file formats support alpha. JPG does not support alpha, whereas TARGA and PNG do. On the Render tab, in the Output area, there are options for changing the file format of saved images, including whether you want the image to be BW (grayscale), RBG (color without alpha support), or RGBA (color with alpha support).

With these concepts in mind, let's examine nodes and how they can be used to enhance your Blender scenes.

The Compositing Node Editor

The Node editor is a powerful tool for adding special effects to rendered scenes. It is essentially a *post process*—that is, it takes a render after it has been completed and adds enhancements at the end of the rendering pipeline. In a sense, with effects that include blur, brightness and contrast settings, gamma corrections, and more, you could think of the compositor as Blender's equivalent to the filters that you might find in popular 2D programs like Photoshop or Gimp (although some nodes are able to process additional 3D data from the scene, as you shall see when we look into applying a depth-of-field effect, later in this chapter).

To start off, we will add an Invert node to a Blender scene, which will affect the colors by inverting them in the final render.

1. First of all, in order to experiment with compositing node effects, you will want a decent scene to render. The default scene of a cube renders in shades of gray, which does not allow much scope for color correction. Either place some lighting or textures into the scene to inject some color, or load up a scene with an appropriate model. I'm using a model of a mechanical bug, as shown in Figure 9–6.

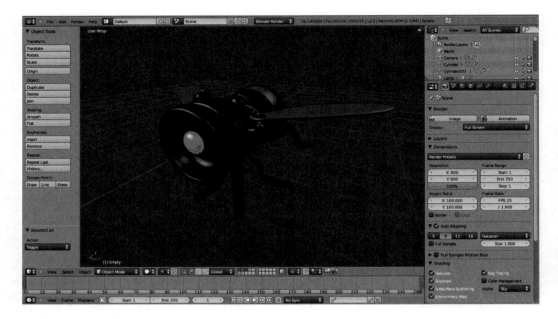

Figure 9–6. Model loaded in and waiting for node work

2. Take a render of your scene (press F12).

3. Now, we need to go into the Node editor. You can split the screen into two and set one half of the screen to be a Node editor (using the editor type menu), or you might like to just choose "Compositing layout" from the layouts listed at the top of the main UI.

4. The Node editor is divided into three parts: material, textures, and compositing nodes. For now, we want the last option, which is the correct choice for making nodes affect the final render, so make sure this option is selected (you can see that the third node icon is selected in Figure 9–7). You then need to click the Use Nodes box. Two node boxes will immediately will appear in the Node editor—the Render Layers node feeding into the Composite node, as shown in Figure 9–8.

Figure 9–7. Compositing nodes and the Use Nodes check box

■ **Note** The nodes sometimes show up blank at first, with no scene preview. If this happens, don't worry; the preview will show on the next render.

---

5. What's the difference between the Render Layers node and the Composite node here? This is a very important point. The *render layers* are the initial raw render, with no added effects, before they hit any nodes. The *composite* is the final render with all effects added. At the moment, one feeds directly into the other so there are no visible changes. Press F12 to render and you will see that there is no difference.

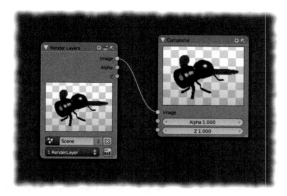

Figure 9–8. *Your first nodes*

6. You may find that the nodes are very small and you need to zoom in to view them up close. As with the 3D view, rolling the MW allows you to zoom the Node editor view in or out. Alternatively, you may find it faster to autozoom by pressing the Home key.

7. We are going to add some nodes in the middle to alter the render image. In the Node editor window, press Shift+A and follow the menu through Color ➤ Invert.

8. A new node should appear. Sometimes the new nodes appear outside the edges of the immediate window area, so you may have to scroll the MW back (zoom out) in order to see them. Alternatively, you can press the Home key to quick-zoom the Node window to fit all nodes. Pull the previous two nodes apart (the top header part of a node can be used to LMB-drag the whole node around) and place this one between them. It is important to use the top header of the node when dragging them because otherwise there is a risk of accidentally LMB-clicking some of the node options and settings.

9. We want to connect the nodes together so that they are like the ones shown in Figure 9–9. Nodes are connected by input (left side) and output (right side) sockets, and it is important that you know how to connect and disconnect them as needed for your own purposes.

    • To join two nodes together, simply LMB-drag from the output socket of one node into the input of the other. They will then be visibly connected by a thin wire. Depending on the functions of the nodes, you may have several different input or output sockets, and it is important to connect the right ones.

    • To disconnect two nodes, you can LMB-drag the very end of a wire out from the input end (the left side) of the node it is feeding into. This does not work from the output side (the right side of a node) because Blender thinks you may be trying to create a new wire. Alternatively, you can hold the Ctrl key down on your keyboard while LMB-dragging across the middle of a wire (as though you were cutting it). Also, an input socket can only receive a connection from one wire at a time (although output sockets can put out multiple wires), so if you try to connect a second wire to an input socket, the first wire will normally be dropped.

Often when new nodes are added, Blender automatically joins them to others (usually to any node you happen to have selected), so knowing how to manually rearrange them is a necessity. See whether you can rewire the nodal setup to include your Invert node, as shown in Figure 9–9.

- LMB-drag a connection from the Image output socket of the Render Layers node to the Color input socket of the Invert node.

- LMB-drag a connection from the Alpha output socket of the Render Layers node to the Fac input socket of the Invert node. (This is optional—it simply tells the nodes to not invert parts of the image that have alpha transparency, such as the background areas behind your model.)

- LMB-drag a connection from the Color output socket of the Invert node to the Image input socket of the Composite node. The Composite node is the one showing the final effect that will be applied when you perform a render.

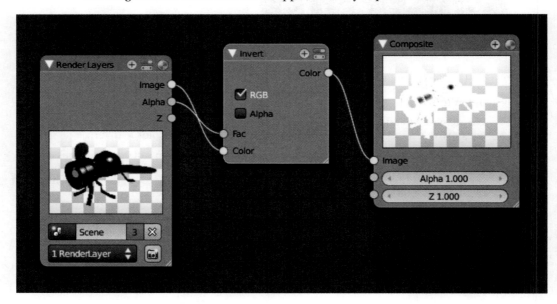

Figure 9–9. *Wiring of the Invert node*

Be aware that the automatic color management, if enabled, will affect your final results, causing the inverted image to be different from what you might expect. As I said at the beginning of this chapter, you are better off disabling color management when using nodes.

And there you have it. When you press F12, your scene should render and then the colors should suddenly become inverted.

Setting Up for Instant Feedback

Normally, when performing a render, the resulting image takes the full screen area, and you need to press Esc to get back to the normal view of your windows. When using nodes, this becomes annoying because

- You don't want to keep pressing F12 all the time to get feedback on the effect of your nodes.

- Pressing F12 is very slow, because it causes the whole scene to render afresh, which can take considerable time with some scenes.

- All that flipping back and forth between the render result and the normal Blender interface is just annoying.

Fortunately, there are some efficient ways of getting instant feedback of the effects of nodes.

Method 1: The F11 Key

Because nodes are applied to a render after it is done, there is no need to actually take the whole render again. Instead of pressing F12 to render everything again, simply press F11, which will bring back the previous render. Blender actually applies nodal changes to the render live, so when you bring the render window up again, the effects of any changes you have made through the nodal pipeline should already be visible. With this method, however, you still need to press Esc (or F11 a second time) to get back to your normal Blender layout.

Method 2: Separate Render Window

If you have a UV/Image Editor open among your other windows, and this same window is set up (in the header strip) as Render Result, then future renders will usually show up there, instead of claiming the full screen as before. You can manually specify this behavior by going to the Render tab (the first tab, showing a camera icon) and then into the Render area, where there is a Display option allowing you to decide if renders should appear in their own new window, in any available Image Editor window, or as full screen. The ability to specify work in an Image Editor window is great for working with nodes because the render is updated while you change node settings, and you don't have to keep switching back and forth between screens for instant feedback on changes you make to the nodes. The Compositing layout from the top header (Figure 9–10) makes use of this technique.

Figure 9–10. Selecting the Compositing screen layout

Method 3: Background Images

You can also have the render result feed back as the background image of the Node editor, as in Figure 9–11. This gives constant feedback on nodal changes as you work on them. Here's how to do this:

1. Click the Backdrop option in the Node editor window header to enable this feature. Nothing will happen at this point, because the backdrop property gets its feedback from a special output node known as a *viewer node*, and you don't have one yet.

2. Viewer nodes don't do anything to the final render, although they are very helpful in showing what is happening at any point of the node chain in order to better control what's going on. Add a viewer node by pressing Shift+A, and then choosing Output ➤ Viewer.

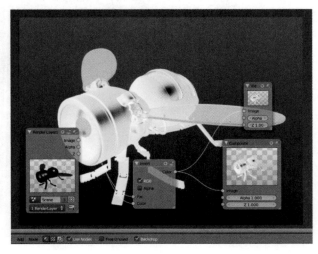

Figure 9–11. Backdrop activated through the viewer node

3. Connect from the Invert node's Color out to the viewer node's Image in. You should suddenly see the background change right behind your Node editor workspace.

You can have any number of viewer nodes, but remember that the Node editor background image shows the results of the last viewer node you selected. This allows you to place multiple viewer nodes at important stages of the node pipeline, and use the background image to check that each stage is applying correctly.

Managing Node Clutter

From here, working with nodes is actually a fairly simple concept, although they do tend to go all over the place once you've daisy-chained a few together. Once you are happy that a node is performing as you would like, there are a few buttons you can use to hide parts of the node that you no longer wish to see (Figure 9–12).

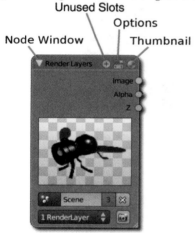

Figure 9–12. Node minimize buttons

You can close the node box by clicking the triangle to the left of the node name so that your main view is less cluttered. The other buttons along the top of a node perform various functions, such as showing only connected in/out plugs, minimizing settings, and turning off preview thumbnails.

Give It a Go

Now that you've seen how the Invert node works, try adding one of these to the chain:

- Color ➤ Bright/Contrast
- Filter ➤ Blur
- Filter ➤ Glare

Experiment with some of the settings in the nodes themselves to explore how the changes are made. Use viewer nodes, as in Figure 9–13, to help if it's hard to see how effects work out.

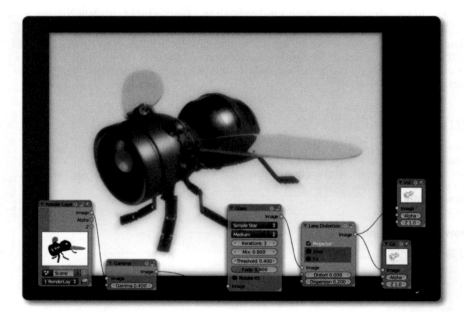

Figure 9–13. Experiment with chaining nodes together for the effect you are after.

Lighting Adjustments

In Chapter 4 we looked at setting up lights to illuminate a 3D scene. Special consideration was taken for setting up a key light source, along with fill lights. We also examined various options to get the shading effects just right. Even after all this trouble, final renders can often turn out as being too light or too dark, or they may simply have the wrong amount of contrast. Changing the lighting itself (e.g., changing the settings for each lamp) to get just the desired amount of brightness could take a very long time, especially when we would have to take a fresh render for every adjustment we wanted to make.

Thankfully, nodes are very good when it comes to tweaking scene renders in terms of adjusting the overall brightness, contrast, and so on. Doing this through nodes is much faster than trying to manually adjust the scene lights.

Using a *Gamma node* is a common method of adjusting the overall tone of a render. You can apply a Gamma node by pressing Shift+A, and then selecting Color ➤ Gamma in the Node editor (as in Figure 9–14). Note that there are a number of useful nodes in this Color submenu, including Hue Saturation Value and Bright/Contrast.

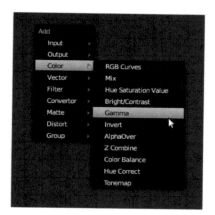

Figure 9–14. Adding a Gamma node

In Figure 9–15, a Gamma node has been added to the render from Chapter 4.

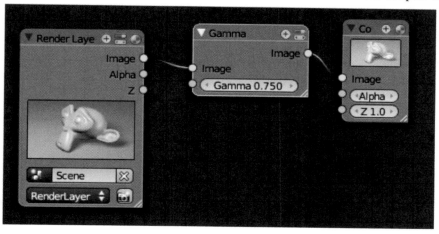

Figure 9–15. Connecting the nodes

Remember to use the previously mentioned techniques for setting the render up for instant feedback when making nodal adjustments; it's a huge time-saver, allowing you to quickly get the lighting balance you are after (Figure 9–16 shows an example of the final lighting balance that was achieved with this technique).

Figure 9–16. Final lit monkey with one key light, two fill lights, and no completely dark areas

Just for clarity, here is a numbered recap of the process:

1. Have your scene correctly lit in terms of key and fill lights, shadows, and so on. Try to get the lighting right, but don't worry too much about getting it perfectly balanced.

2. As explained at the beginning of this chapter, disable automatic color management.

3. Open a Node editor window and enable Compositing nodes. You should set up your window layout to enable one of the techniques mentioned in the "Setting up for instant feedback" section earlier in this chapter. (Simply choosing the default Compositing layout shown in Figure 9–10 will do this.)

4. Take a render.

5. Add a Gamma node through the Node editor window (press Shift+A, and then select Add ➤ Color ➤ Gamma) and link it between the Render Layers node and the final Compositing node.

6. Now, when you change the gamma value of the Gamma node, you will see an immediate effect on the lighting of the shot. For many scenes, a gamma value of 0.75 works well.

This is a speedy way of achieving impressive lighting results. Don't forget that there are other effects besides Gamma you could use, and you can even daisy-chain several of the effects together.

How Color-Mixing Nodes Work

There are a good number of nodes of varying effect available in the Node editor, and it's likely that as Blender continues to develop even more will be added. Some of them are simple single-node filters, such as a Blur and Glare. Others are used to combine two images to get a certain effect, such as the Mix node, which mixes two images (or colors) into one using a range of blending techniques. You can see the Mix node in Figure 9–17, in which the control used to change the blending mode is highlighted. The various mixing methods include mathematical functions such as add, subtract, multiply, and divide.

Figure 9–17. The Mix node

- When two images are mixed by addition, the end result is brighter than either image.

- Images mixed by subtraction typically have a darkened result.

- When images are mixed through multiplication, the results can vary, although the contrast is usually decreased.

We are now going to examine these mathematical mix filters, and how they work in order to gain an understanding of why they give the type of results they do.

Every color on the computer screen is really a combination of different amounts of blue, red, and green light. Blender color notation gives each an amount ranging from 0 (0 percent) to 1 (100 percent), with 0.5 (or 50 percent) being a neutral/gray value. Different shades of gray can be produced, as shown in Figure 9–18.

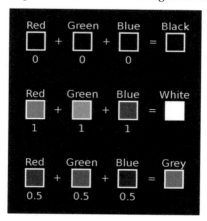

Figure 9–18. Shades of gray are made by having the same amount of each primary color.

Hues of color are created by having different amounts of the three primary colors, which add together to make the new color, as shown in Figure 9–19.

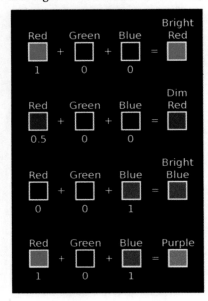

Figure 9–19. *Color hues are created when the amounts of each primary color used are different.*

To get a handle on how this works, add a Mix node, and at the bottom of the node's controllers, click the white panel to bring up the color changer (Figure 9–20). You should then see the values as you use the wheel to pick different colors. Don't forget the lightness slider to the right of the color changer.

Figure 9–20. *The color changer*

When pictures are mixed by adding, subtracting, multiplying, or dividing, the two images are placed on top of each other, and on a pixel-to-pixel basis the RGB values are added, subtracted, multiplied, or divided against each other. Adding makes the image brighter (unless you are adding zero), whereas multiplying can make the image brighter or darker depending on whether the color values are less than or greater than 1.

The following are some examples:

- Adding two dark reds together makes a brighter red

    - 0.5 red + 0.5 red = 1 red

- Multiplying the same values darkens the image because it results in a lower value of the color

    - 0.5 green × 0.5 green = 0.25 green

Because of how this works, adding or subtracting color values results in modifying the brightness, whereas multiplying or dividing tends to affect the contrast.

Mixing Images Together

That was quite a bit of theory, so now let's see it in action. We are going to take two image files and combine them with the Mix node in order to observe the available effects, as shown in Figure 9–21. Of course, it is up to you what images you use, although the original images should be the same size. If one image is bigger than the other, the Mix node won't resize them, and they won't match the way you expect them to.

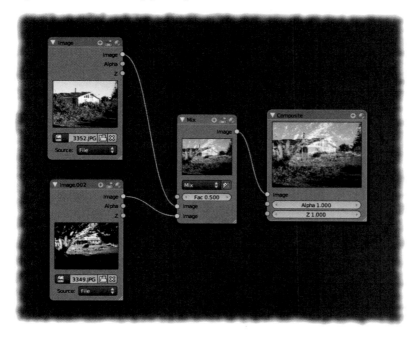

Figure 9–21. Nodes mixing images together

Starting with a new Blender file, create a node setup that combines two photographs, as follows:

1. Organize the Blender windows so that there is a Node editor among them. You can do this by changing the editor type button at the far left of a window header to Node. Alternatively, you could select the predefined Compositing layout from the very top header of the default layout.

2. Add two Input ➤ Image nodes.

3. On each of these Image nodes, click the Open button and link to a picture from your hard drive.

4. Add a new node of Color ➤ Mix.

5. Feed both images into the Mix node, and then feed this to the final compositing node.

6. You can delete the Render node if you like (select it and press the X key), as it is no longer needed for the final result.

7. For instant feedback, add a viewer node and feed the Mix node's Image out socket into it, and then enable the backdrop.

8. Change the properties on the Mix node to explore how the different mix effects look.

The Fac variable controls the amount of mix. Setting Fac to 0 results in only the image from the top socket being visible, and setting Fac to 1 results in the second socket being fully applied according to the type of mix specified. If the Mix node's effect type is set to Mix (which basically fades from one image to the other), a Fac value of 0.5 gives an even balance, although the actual effect varies depending on the mix type. For example, a mix of type Add set to 0.5 will only add half the value of the second socket to the full image of the first. In the case of an Add mix, a visual 50/50 mix (where both images are of equal value to the end result) would actually be a Fac value of 1. For this reason, Fac values can be pushed beyond the limit of 1, allowing you to apply the Mix effect to get the visual balance you want.

Image nodes also support movies. At the bottom of the Image node is a Source field where you can specify whether the input is a still image (the File option), a movie, or even a sequence of images (these would be a numbered sequence—e.g., shot0001.png, shot0002.png, shot0003.png, etc.). When you load in source nodes with animation, you can set on which frame the animation is meant to start, and they will then play along with the standard timeline.

Depth of Field

In photographs, when things are very close to the camera, they often become blurred because they are out of focus for the lens. Likewise, things in the far distance also blur. Adding a similar blur effect can enhance the realism of the image. This distance-based blurring effect is commonly known as depth of field.

The camera Blender uses is capable of storing distance information, known as *Z-depth*. Through nodes, we can use this information to apply a blurring effect only to the parts of the render where scene objects are very near or far from the camera. In the following steps we will apply depth of field to a 3D scene.

Creating the Scene

For the depth-of-field effect to be noticeable, we need a scene that has a lot of objects of varying distance from the camera. There should be objects very close and very far away from the camera, which will become blurred once the depth of focus effect is applied. There should also be some objects comfortably within the focal range of the camera that will not be blurred. A long queue of objects would be ideal, so here is how I would go about setting up the scene:

1. Add a monkey to the scene and rotate it 90 degrees around the x axis in object mode. If you like, you can also add a subdivision surface modifier to the monkey, and select Smooth Shading from the Tool Shelf so that the monkey renders smoothly.

2. To make a row of monkeys

   a. Select the monkey and add an array modifier.

   b. Change the Relative Offset settings of the array modifier to the following: X: 0, Y: 0, and Z: 1.5 (you will most likely have to change the X offset to 0, as it usually is set to 1 by default).

   c. Increase the Count attribute of the array modifier to about 10 to make a long line.

See Figure 9–22 for where these settings reside.

Alternatively, you could simply select the monkey and duplicate it with Shift+D a number of times, dragging each duplicate along until you have the desired number of monkeys. I like to use the array modifier because it provides a quick way of changing the number of monkeys in the queue, or how spread apart they are from each other, simply by changing the Count and Relative Offset values.

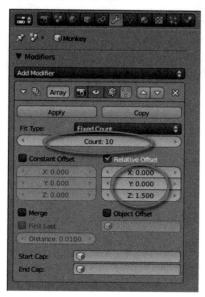

Figure 9–22. *Array modifier settings*

3. Reposition the camera so that it is looking along the array with the front monkeys very close and the others going into the distance. It is probably easiest to aim the camera with the technique discussed in the "Tracking to an Empty Target" section of Chapter 4.

4. Set up lights as needed.

5. Enable nodes and add a Gamma node if you would like one.

6. Select the camera. Go to the Object Data tab, and in the Display area, enable Limits.

7. You will now see a line project from the camera. This line shows how far the camera can see into a scene (it does not make sense to render infinitely, as this would take forever to calculate). Further up the panels in the Object Data tab are entry fields for Start, End, and Depth of Field/Distance. The latter is for where the camera is to be focused (see Figure 9–23). Change its number so that the yellow cross along the line from the camera falls in the middle of the array of monkeys.

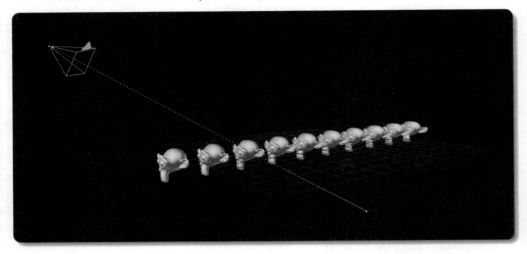

Figure 9–23. *Aiming the camera. Note that there is a yellow cross where the directional camera beam hits the monkey array, marking the depth-of-field distance of the camera.*

8. Finally, add a Depth of Focus node to the nodal setup (press Shift+A, and then select Filter ➤ Defocus, as shown in Figure 9–24).

Figure 9–24. *Choosing Defocus*

9. Wire the original layer to the Defocus node through both Image and Z, as shown in Figure 9–25.

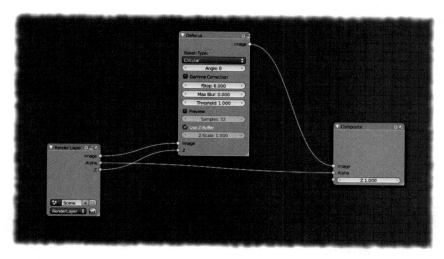

Figure 9–25. *Defocus node*

This Z-buffer contains information about what is close to the camera.

10. Turn the fStop setting in the Defocus node to something low. The lower the fStop, the more intense the focal blur will be. An fStop value of 8 or even 6 is usually plenty for an obvious effect.

That should be it. Remember that you don't have to perform a complete render every time you update the nodes; simply use F11. If everything is in place, your render will be out of focus where things are far off and close to the camera (see Figure 9–26), adding a real sense of depth to your scene.

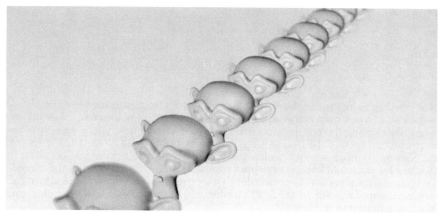

Figure 9–26. *Depth of focus. Notice the blur of the foreground and background monkeys.*

Greenscreen Filtering

Greenscreening, where actors act in front of a mono-hue backdrop for the purpose of being superimposed onto another image, is achievable through matte nodes that selectively affect the alpha channel of the images and combine them into a single image. This alpha channel is a grayscale image (or mask) marking which parts of an image are opaque (solid) and which are transparent. Whiter parts render as solid (strong alpha) and the darker become transparent (weak alpha). The final images, with alpha adjusted on the actor footage, can then be combined via an AlphaOver node.

The greenscreening techniques in this section can be applied to still images or movie shots, although I should point out that animated shots have artifacts like motion blur, which can make accurate masking more difficult than when working with still images.

In the next examples we are going to combine the images in Figure 9–27 through nodes. In the greenscreen image (to the right), I am standing in front of a wall of a local store that happens to be painted a flat green color. You do not have to have an elaborate studio to take your own greenscreen footage. The backdrop doesn't have to be green, but it should be an even color.

Figure 9–27. Two images before superimposing (starring the Blender Foundation's Big Buck Bunny)

Blender has a few nodes that lend themselves to this technique. These are found in the Node editor. Press Shift+A, and then choose Matte, followed by the kind of node you need. Common ones you might use include the following:

- Color Key
- Chroma Key
- Difference Key

These nodes work in a similar way, although the internal algorithm for masking out the greenscreen color (the key color) varies. Each of these nodes has an important Key Color selection area—the color in this area is the target color that the node will aim to convert to alpha transparency. By clicking the colored square at this part of the node, you get a color-picking tool where you can specify the hue of the greenscreen color to be filtered out. This color picker dialog includes an eyedropper tool, which you can use to autoselect the correct color by sampling it with a mouse click (click the eyedropper tool, and then click the part of the image—perhaps within a viewer—that has the desired color). Once the color has been chosen, you can use the sliders within the node to adjust the level of tolerance of the transparent key color, thus fine-tuning how close a match to the key color an area needs to be in order to be made transparent. This options changes depending on which type of node you're using (e.g., Color Key, Chroma Key, Difference Key, etc.).

As an example, look at Figure 9–28 to see how I have used a Color Key node to superimpose one image onto another.

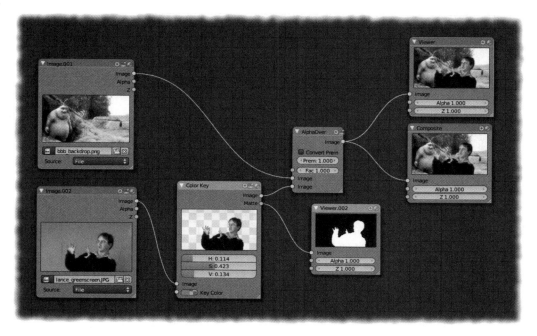

Figure 9–28. Color Key node used to affect the alpha channel in a greenscreen setup

The essential workflow for setting up the nodes is as follows:

1. Insert the reference images/footage (press Shift+A and select Input ➤ Image).
2. Add a Color Key node (press Shift+A and select Matte ➤ Color Key).
3. Connect the Image output socket of the greenscreen footage to the input of the Color Key node.
4. Add an AlphaOver node.
5. Link the image you want to use as the background into the first Image input socket of the AlphaOver node.
6. Link the Image output node from the Color Key node into the remaining Image input socket of the AlphaOver node (the second socket).
7. Link the Image output socket of the AlphaOver node to the Image input of the Compositing node so that the results will pass through to the render.

At the bottom of the Color Key node is a small rectangle representing the color to be made transparent. Click this rectangle to bring up a color selection tool. The color selection options include an eyedropper button, which you can use to get a good match for your key color. Simply LMB-click the eyedropper button, and then LMB-click the background (the green part) of the image in the original greenscreen footage.

Finally, you can adjust the sliders in the Color Key node to get as good a balance of greenscreen color tolerance as you can. My results are shown in Figure 9–29.

Figure 9–29. *The result of the nodes as shown when rendered*

Try experimenting with alternative matte nodes in order to see which works best. Sometimes a node that works well for one shot may not necessarily work with another, and it can depend on the quality of the references images or the footage you are working with.

In Figure 9–30 I've replaced the previous Color Key node with a Chroma Key node. Often, a Chroma Key node will do the job better than a Color Key node, but in this case, I found it was not as effective.

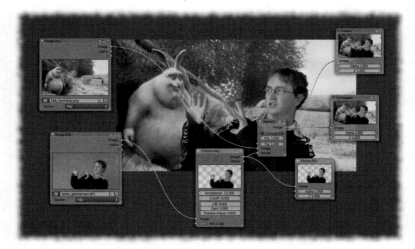

Figure 9–30. *This time a Chroma Key is used with less success than the Color Key. Depending on the material, either approach may have better results.*

Fine-tuning the correct amount of tolerance can be tricky. There could be areas of shadow or highlight on the green screen, and when you increase tolerance for these areas, parts of the actor may disappear. One way to counter this, as demonstrated in Figure 9–31, is to have several different matte keys, each set to different shades of green (one for the main green area, another for the shadowed green, etc.). You can then mix these masks together into one combined output by chaining them through Mix nodes (set to Multiply, which will darken). With each Mix node only receiving two inputs at a time, this method has two major disadvantages:

- You end up with very complex clusters of nodes, which can be difficult to manage.

- Having lots of nodes feeding into each other can cause the computer to strain as it constantly tries to update any changes.

Within reason, mixing different nodes can be a useful solution, but for the sake of efficiency, you should always try to keep the number of nodes to a minimum.

Figure 9–31. A messy node arrangement where alpha masks of different background shades are combined

The Difference node is very good for greenscreen shots. When you put two shots into it, the Difference node uses alpha to generate a new image of the parts that are different in the two images. In theory, this means you could do away with the need for a green screen altogether because you could simply "difference" a shot of actors on a stage against a shot of the stage with no actors. In theory, this would leave you with a resulting image of the actors only, which could then be superimposed into any scene. Figure 9–32 shows my proof of concept of this in action.

For this shot, I took an image of a brick wall with a rubbish bin in front (the actor), and another shot of the same wall with no rubbish bin. I used a camera with a secure tripod to try to get the shots from exactly the same place. Using a Difference node, I was able to combine the two so that I ended up with a shot of the bin all by itself. This resulting image was overlaid onto a third image of the sunny beach where I grew up, and voila! I then had an image of the rubbish bin on the beach, as shown in Figure 9–32.

Figure 9–32. Difference node making a brick wall work like a green screen

In truth, though, I cheated. Even the slightest camera shake causes an offset that makes the fine white lines in the brick wall visible to the difference shot. A more honest result is shown in Figure 9–33.

To achieve the shot, I actually took the picture without the rubbish bin and superimposed the bin onto it, thus creating a perfect pair of images with no camera shake–type differences between them. As long as the backgrounds were exactly the same in the two shots, the Difference node would succeed. However, the results from my more honest shot demonstrate that even with a powerful node like the Difference node, you should still use a green screen (or some kind of flat color background) to get the best results.

Figure 9–33. The real result

A Practical Example of Compositing

Now that you understand how nodes work, you can begin to comprehend how WeirdHat may have gone about some of the techniques he used to put together his short clip of Colbert fighting with a light saber.

With regard to his compositing techniques, WeirdHat also happens to have a tutorial on his web site outlining how compositing techniques can be achieved without nodes, using some old-school techniques (and a much older version of Blender than we are using). You can see the tutorial at www.weirdhat.com/blender/compositing2.

In this compositing tutorial, WeirdHat takes a video of his own room and uses Blender to composite the monkey head primitive onto the floor, complete with matching shadows to blend with the carpet. To add to the realism, in the video there is a moment when he brings his hand in from the left side of the screen and waves it in front of the added monkey, as shown in Figure 9–34.

Figure 9–34. WeirdHat's old tutorial on superimposing a monkey into a video does not use nodes.

WeirdHat's technique involves a clever setup in which a plane is placed in position directly in front of the Blender camera to act as a screen, on which he projects the video footage as an animated texture material. Then he places the Blender monkey in front of this backdrop, and uses special settings on another ground plane to make this new plane transparent except for where it receives shadows. This has the effect of making the shadow from the monkey appear as though it is dropping on the carpet in the original footage. You can see the staging of WeirdHat's scene in Figure 9–35.

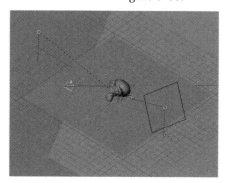

Figure 9–35. WeirdHat's original setup (taken from his tutorial at his web site)

Finally, WeirdHat animates a mask mesh, frame by frame, over the waving hand, and gives it the same footage-projecting properties as the background screen—a clever way of masking a hole in front of the monkey so that it does not appear as though it were really in front of the hand in the original shot.

The technique used by WeirdHat is complex. In the next exercise you'll see how the same procedure might be done using nodes.

Before You Begin

For this exercise you will need the following:

- A movie or a still picture of a suitable room space

- Video footage or a still photo of a hand waving in front of a green screen

Both of these sources should be the same size. For example, you may want them to both be 640×360 pixels.

The final part of the exercise involves using the greenscreen techniques discussed earlier to superimpose the hand over the other elements of the scene. Be aware that if you use movie footage for the hand, it will likely have a certain amount of motion blur and other camera artifacts such as interlacing, which could make the keying difficult, so you may prefer to use a still image for the exercise.

Setting Up Your Windows

You will need windows to at least show a Node editor and a 3D view of what the camera sees. I recommend simply choosing the Compositing layout from the available screen layouts, as in Figure 9–36.

Figure 9–36. Choosing the Compositing layout

As with earlier examples in this chapter, make sure compositing nodes are enabled in the header of the Node editor window (see Figure 9–37).

Figure 9–37. Activating compositing nodes

Setting Up the Background Movie Footage

Follow these steps to set up the background movie footage:

1. Make sure your settings from the camera are the same as your original movie footage. These will likewise be your output render settings. In the Dimensions area of the Render tab, do the following:

    a. Set the x and y resolution values to match the reference of the room that you will be using for the background.

    b. If you are using animated footage (e.g., the hand in front of the greenscreen), be sure to set the frame rate to the same value as this footage.

2. Go to the camera view (press numpad 0), and in the Properties panel, activate and expand the Background Images area. Click the Add Image button and you should see the words "Not Set" with a white triangle to the left of the words. Click the white triangle to reveal an Open button and click this to open a file-finding dialog. From there, navigate to where your background reference (or footage) resides and open it. This should bring you back to the main windows again. If your reference is a movie (as opposed to a still photo), then you should change the Source field from File to Movie so that Blender knows it is an animated background. Your reference should then show as the background for that window. It won't render when you press F12; it is just there to assist you with the layout of the other objects.

3. Use an Image node to replace the background of the render with the image (or movie) of the room. To do this, in the Node editor, press Shift+A and select Add ➤ Input ➤ Image, as shown in Figure 9–38.

Figure 9–38. Setting up an Image node

4.   On this node, click the File selector and navigate to your reference (or footage) of the room. Once it has been located, you may need to specify whether it is a file (a still picture), a movie, or an image sequence.

■ **Note** When importing a numbered image sequence into the Node editor, you only need to select the first image of the sequence when you click Open. On returning to the node, you should then fill in details about the number of frames in the sequence.

---

5.   Add another node (press Shift+A and select Color ➤ AlphaOver).
6.   Wire these nodes together and plug them into the final compositing set up, as shown in Figure 9–39.

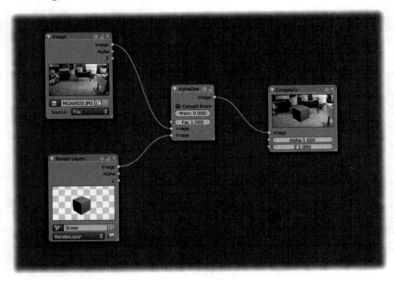

Figure 9–39. The image is now the background in our scene, courtesy of the AlphaOver node.

Now when you render, your footage should replace the usual plain background. The default cube or anything else in the scene will be superimposed in front of the footage. The image from the Node editor would normally replace the render scene completely, but the AlphaOver node has created a mask that tells Blender to work around the cube image.

Positioning the Objects in the Scene

We are ready to set up the actual scene with the monkey positioned on a ground plane.

1. Delete the default cube.

2. Add a plane, and place it carefully in position so that it lies where the floor is supposed to be. You will simply need to be skillful in your placement here. The view from the camera depends on the camera position as much as it does the placement of items. In most cases you will want to have the camera lined up parallel with Blender's floor grid (looking forward) so that you can position the ground plane in a manner that lines up with your footage/reference. Knowing that the ground is flat to the horizon (not tilted at an angle) should help you to line it up so that it overlays the floor in your footage (see Figure 9–40).

3. Place a new monkey into the scene so that it sits on the ground plane in front of the camera (you probably want to add a subdivision surface modifier to the monkey to make it look smooth).

Figure 9–40. Lining up the ground plane with the floor in camera view

Materials and Lighting

Now we are going to change the material of the ground plane so that it turns invisible, except for where shadows fall on it. This way, the nontransparent parts will appear as though they are shadows on the floor of the background image.

1. Set up a key light source based on the light you see in the background image. It should cast a shadow on the ground plane that seems reasonably correct when rendered.

2. Make sure the ground plane has its own unique material, which you can name something like groundshadow.

3. In the material settings for the ground plane, go to the Shadow section and check the box for the Shadows Only option. This pretty much does what we want, as only shadows will now render on the ground plane. Press F12 to test the shadows if you like.

4. Shadows can be tricky to configure, because you have to have the correct material settings to receive them, and also the correct settings in the light casting them. In my own experience, I have found that sun lamps using ray shadows work best when casting shadows on shadow-only surfaces. Sun lamps seem to be the only kind that can cast shadows that are dark enough. If using another type of light, you may like to experiment with whether the lamp casts buffer or ray shadows, as these have differing results (buffer shadows are faster and less accurate, whereas ray shadows are calculated by true raytracing).

5. To give the shadow soft edges, change the Softsize and Samples settings in the lamp settings to something like 5 and 7, respectively. Softsize is the amount of blur on a shadow edge, whereas Samples represents the number of passes, or the quality of the blur.

6. Change the Alpha setting in the `groundshadow` material to alter the strength at which the shadow is cast.

You should be able to move the key light around and change settings until you are happy with the shadow. The shadows on the monkey head will likely be too dark when compared with other shadows in the footage of the scene, so add other lamps as fill lights for the darker areas. Fill lights should have their shadows disabled (using the No Shadow option), as they are only there to illuminate darker areas.

■ **Note** It is important to try to get the light to be the color of the real light source. A good way to get close to this is to select the color of the light (the color square within its settings), and then using the eyedropper tool, select from your screen somewhere in the picture where the light is hitting. The eyedropper steals color from whatever is clicked, so you end up with a close hue.

If you take your time, you should be able to get the lighting so that it really looks like the monkey is in the scene casting a shadow onto the carpet, as shown in Figure 9–41.

Figure 9–41. Comparison between a plain render (with compositing disabled) and a render in which nodes are enabled and the background is added. With the right settings, the monkey should cast a convincing shadow on the floor.

Greenscreening the Hand

Now all that remains is to superimpose the hand into the shot.

1. Add the footage of the hand (press Shift+A and select Input ➤ Image) and specify the correct settings if it is an animation.

2. Add yet another AlphaOver node.

3. Add a Color Key node; or if you prefer, use a Chroma Key or Difference Key node.

4. Rearrange the nodes so that they form the chain going into the final composite output. Be careful to keep the work that you have already done intact (i.e., save your work first!), as it can be easy to make mistakes and lose the essential order of the nodes. Following the logic of the "Greenscreen Filtering" section earlier, you will this time want a couple of AlphaOver nodes. One combines the 3D render of the monkey with the house background reference, and the other combines this result with the greenscreen shot of the hand. Examine Figure 9–42 to see how things should be wired.

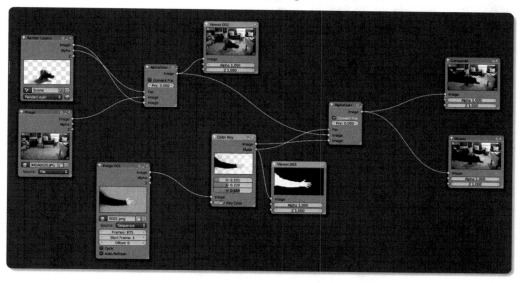

Figure 9–42. Working node sequence

5. Don't forget to use the instant backdrop view and viewer nodes when fine-tuning node settings. You may need to perform an F12 render initially, so that the Render Layers node caches a render of the monkey into the scene.

This setup basically works (see the output in Figure 9–43), but there will be personal refinements you'll want to make, depending on the success of your output. The key is to go through and add/edit/modify as you see fit.

Figure 9–43. The effect

Nodes can get rather messy and complicated when you work on them. Don't try to understand every node you see in someone's work; they can be very different according to the needs of each individual composition. In my own modifications, shown in Figure 9–44, I decided to use blur nodes to soften the edges of the greenscreen/alpha pass, and I used a Color Spill node, which takes away some of the green area that was stubbornly surrounding the hand. Your needs will be different; it's very much a per-shot thing.

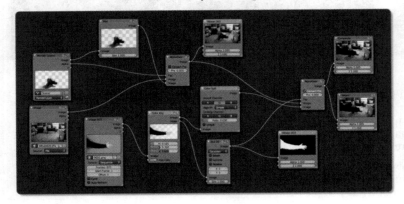

Figure 9–44. My final node setup involves nodes to blur the greenscreen alpha and an extra Color Spill node to eliminate some of the green that forms a halo around the edges of the arm.

The Video Sequence Editor

The Video Sequence editor (shown in Figure 9–45) is where you take all your movie files, cut them up into separate shots, and rearrange them in sequence to form the story you want. It's the ultimate film director's tool. Last chapter we used the Video Sequence editor very briefly to add sound to a lip-syncing exercise. Of course, it's much more than just a sound importer.

To start using the Video Sequence editor, select Video Editing from the available layout options at the top of your screen.

Alternatively, if you like to arrange your own window layouts, split the screen into at least two sections—top and bottom—both of type Video Sequence editor. The bottom half will be your main cutting room, and will stay as the default Video Sequence editor window. We want the top window to be a real-time preview of our editing. You can change this by looking along the header to where there is a drop-down list set to Sequencer (this is the default). Click the list and choose Image Preview. Make sure you also have standard panels over to the right.

Figure 9–45. The Video Sequence editor

One thing you should always do when mixing video is define the frame rate of your movie. The *frame rate* is a measure of how many images are shown per second of film, and this can vary depending on the movie format and quality. For example, TV often has a different frame rate (25 fps for PAL format) from that used in cinema (24 fps). When importing video from external sources, you should set your frame rate to match the imported video, or else it might run at the wrong speed, causing the image and sound to become increasingly out of sync the longer the movie plays. To set the frame rate, go to the Render tab and look down the panels until you see the Dimensions area. There is a slot there headed Frame Rate, where you can type in the rate you want the Video Sequence editor to work at.

Now that your screens are set up, it's time to add some movies for editing:

1. In the bottom Sequencer window, use Shift+A and choose Movie to add a clip from your hard drive. (If you don't have any movies, just choose Image to load in a picture.)

2. When Blender's file-opening dialog appears, direct it to open your movie.

3. A strip now appears along the Video Sequence editor timeline, like the one in Figure 9–46. It is, of course, the movie you have just imported. You can select the strip by RMB-clicking it, and then press G to move the strip to where you want it to be. As you move

the strip, you will see frame numbers appear at either end. It is a good idea to start the beginning of your film at frame 1.

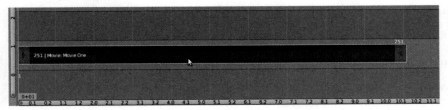

Figure 9–46. Adding a movie strip

4. Now, as you scrub the Video Sequence editor timeline, you should see your movie play in the preview window. Pressing Alt+A should even play the movie in real time (press Esc to quit).

One thing to be aware of, though, is that if you opened the Video Sequence editor through the standard screen, Blender will have placed a standard timeline underneath the main sequence editor window. By default, the end value of the standard timeline is 250. You need to change the frame numbers appropriately to match the frame start and end of your movie. You can obtain statistics for a selected movie strip, such as the start frame and length, by enabling the Properties panel in the Video Sequence editor. If you do this, begin and end frame numbers will appear on the ends of any strip you are about to move (use Esc to cancel the movement).

If you scrub to any point of the timeline and render, you will notice that the rendered image no longer shows the default cube, but whichever frame you are on in the Sequencer. Blender has automatically hit all the right buttons in the Render tab to turn the Sequencer on. Blender does this once you start using a Video Sequence editor window, although, as explained earlier in this chapter, it is up to you to specify the output settings for your video.

Now that you have one video in the Sequencer, use Shift+A to add another movie strip. Obviously, you could chain the strips together so that they play in order, but what about overlapping them? Will they fade in from one to the other?

1. If you've already let the second strip go, reselect it by RMB-clicking the middle of the strip.

2. If the strip also has an audio strip, you may want to Shift-RMB-select that as well.

3. Press G to move the selected strip (note that it's the same as the basic editing keys).

4. Position the second strip over the first, as shown in Figure 9–47.

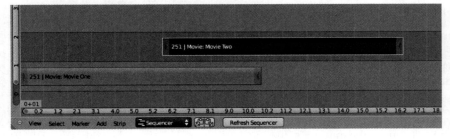

Figure 9–47. Overlapping movie strips

Here we have two strips overlapping. The lower strip (labeled Movie One) is on channel 1, and the upper strip is on channel 2. The channels are labeled numerically at the far left.

If you have overlapping sound, the good news is that Blender plays both samples where the audio strips overlap. As for the video, Blender only plays the top strip, so as soon as they overlap, you only get to see the second strip playing. Of course, there's a simple way to transition between two videos:

1. Press A twice (or the number of times needed to ensure that no strips are selected).

2. RMB-select the middle of the first strip (the leftmost strip, which is also on the lower channel).

3. Shift-RMB-select the middle of the second strip (the one on top channel).

4. Press Shift+A and follow the menu through Effect Strip ➤ Cross (Figure 9–48).

Figure 9–48. *Adding an effect strip*

5. You will notice that Blender places a third strip of its own over the previous two, as shown in Figure 9–49. Scrub this section and you will see in the preview window that a cross-fadeover effect has indeed been added. The effect strip works as though it is a new movie section with just the fadeover part. If you place it underneath the target strips, the effect cannot be seen because it is no longer the topmost strip.

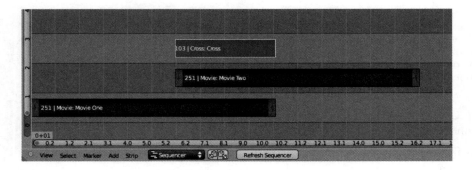

Figure 9–49. The effect strip in place

A Few Things Worth Remembering

The sound is likely to be off when scrubbing the timeline. To turn it on, go to the Playback menu at the bottom and choose the Audio Scrubbing option (Figure 9–50). In some situations, this may cause a speed conflict, as either the sound or video may not be able to keep up with the other. Further along under the standard timeline is a Sync menu allowing you to specify whether movie frames are dropped to match the sound (Frame Dropping), or whether sound is stuttered in order to match the video frames (AV-Sync).

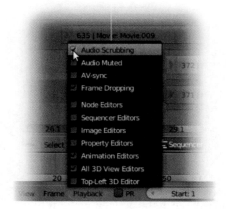

Figure 9–50. Allowing audio scrubbing

You may have noticed that I specifically said to select and move strips from the middle. If you look at the ends of a movie strip, you will see that they have inward-pointing triangles, or arrows, at either end (as shown in Figure 9–51). By RMB-selecting and then moving the ends, you can shorten and lengthen the strip to the cut that you are after. Blender will show how long the imported movie really is with a transparent section at the top, but only the parts of the strip that are between the end triangles will actually play. Don't forget that audio is a separate strip, so if you cut the video by dragging the end, you should do the same to the sound. Using the Shift key while you RMB-select both the end of the video strip and the end of the audio strip causes both to become selected at the same time, so you can then use the G key to slide them along at the same time.

Figure 9–51. *Reshaping a movie strip*

As an alternative technique to sliding the end triangles of a strip you wish to crop, you can place the green vertical time slider at the frame where you want the cut to happen. Pressing K will cause Blender to break the strip into two, on either side of the green line. This is known as a *soft cut* because it is still possible for you to move the end sliders back out again. If you use Shift+K, the cut becomes a hard cut, and moving the end sliders outward (to expand the strip) does not recover cut-off frames.

After a while, the number of strips can stack up and things might get messy. You can combine strips into one *metastrip* to simplify tasks. Select a group of strips and press the M key to merge them into a single metastrip, like the one shown in Figure 9–52. Once a metastrip has been made, you can even enter it to reposition the strips from the inside. Simply select the metastrip and press the Tab key (edit), and you will go into the metastrip where you will be able to continue editing the included parts. Pressing Esc brings you back up a level to the main strips window. Should you want to undo a metastrip, bringing all its contents back into the open again, select the metastrip and press Alt+M.

Figure 9–52. *Metastrip*

Within the Properties panel are various relevant settings for the currently selected strip. As always, setting a name that you'll recognize is a good idea. The name displays on each strip, and this can make organizing busy cuts much clearer (especially for metastrips). Of course, there are other variables in the Properties panel you may like to change as well.

And that demonstrates the basic principle of how the Video Sequence editor works. You add strips, you sort them into order, and you add effects where you might need to integrate them. There are a number of effect strips to play with, some of them working similarly to the effects you would expect from the compositing nodes, although the Video Sequence editor effects are generally very fast. Not all of them require two strips. See what you can find!

Crash Management and Rendering Speed

Unfortunately, crashes are a reality when working with computers. Animation renders can take a long time to process, and it's devastating to return to a computer that was supposed to be churning out a movie sequence to find that it crashed halfway, sending you right back to square one. There is a simple solution to countering such disasters: never render straight to movie. Instead, set your render settings as a quality image format (such as TARGA or PNG). This will result in a folder full of numbered image files. This will make it a simple task to render again, and set the animation timeline to pick up from where the previous render left off. Once all the image files have been generated, simply load them into the Video Sequence editor for re-rendering as a movie. This final pass is very fast because you're not slowed down by complex raytracing, and there is less chance of crashing when simply converting images to movie format.

Another trick to increase rendering speed with movie-making is not to render full scenes, but to have the characters and the background as separate renders, and then output them as image sequences supporting RGBA transparency (e.g., PNG images). When done, you can use the AlphaOver effect strip in the Video Sequence editor to superimpose the characters in front of the background. Not only does it take a lot less time to render characters by themselves (as opposed to a whole scene including the background), but if you need any retakes you can speedily change just the affected layer without having to re-render an entire scene.

Summary

Once we look at the Blender's video-editing capabilities, it becomes apparent that Blender is not just a small part of the pipeline, but it can also be used across many parts of a production. The tools are indeed very sophisticated and can realistically be used for serious production work.

The reason Blender has such amazing tools is largely due to the approach the Blender Foundation has taken in testing Blender with real movie projects (*Elephants Dream, Big Buck Bunny,* and *Sintel*). When you look at these Open Movies, you can enjoy them not only with the knowledge that they were made with free software, but also that the same free software has been directly improved *because* of these movies.

CHAPTER 10

■ ■ ■

Particles and Physics

Particles are difficult to define because they can be used for so many different purposes. They can be fire, dust, water, smoke, and a lot more. Particles are typically lots of items (often thousands) that flow from an emitter object. They can be affected by elements such as the wind (we will look at this early in the chapter). Particles are not editable mesh objects, although it is possible to set them up as clones of other objects.

In this chapter we are going to examine the settings needed to make particles act like the fiery exhaust from a rocket, hair, fluid, and even smoke. I will also give a brief introduction to force fields (such as wind) and how they can be used along with particle simulations. We will also look into soft body physics (e.g., making jelly or foam rubber) and cloth simulation.

Making Particles

To make particles, you create a mesh object and change a few properties in order to assign the mesh as a particle emitter.

1. Start with the default cube.

2. Go to the Particles tab.

3. Click the + sign (shown in Figure 10–1) to add particle emission properties. Lots of different panels will appear.

4. Press Alt+A and watch the particles flow, as in Figure 10–2.

Figure 10–1. Add a new particle system.

The falling dots you see are, of course, the particles themselves. They are going to look different when rendered. Scrub the timeline across a little and press F12 to see the render view.

All that is needed is for you to learn how to change their appearance and their behavior to fit your needs.

Figure 10–2. Particles at default settings

Particle Appearance

Not everything about particles is in the particle panels. The default particles show as something like white spots of light, more correctly knows as *halos*. To change the main appearance, you need to go to the Material tab.

For the material of the object, the very top panel allows you to select whether an object should be rendered as a Surface, Wire, Volume, or Halo shader type (see Figure 10–3). The top shader type options are shown in Figure 10–4.

Figure 10–3. Subdivided monkey showing different shader types. From left to right; Surface, Wire, Volume, and Halo. Note the fuzzy glow of the halo points.

- *Surface*: This is the default for a solid mesh object.
- *Wire*: This shows only the edges of the faces of a mesh.
- *Volume*: This is useful for making a mesh look like smoke.
- *Halo*: This makes the vertices of a mesh appear as halo lights.

Figure 10–4. *Shader type options*

Regardless of which setting you have for the mesh itself, the default form of particles is to render as halo lights. In order to change the appearance of the particles, first choose Halo as the base mesh type. The material preview will now show what the particles look like while you make changes in the material settings. Notice that Halo has different options from the other types. You can experiment to see what the settings do, though here are some of the main options and their effects to get you started:

- *Diffuse (shows as a colored rectangle)*: Changes the color of the halo points.

- *Size*: The basic mass of halo points.

- *Hardness*: Affects the amount of blur/fuzziness of each halo point.

- *Rings*: Gives the halo a number of rings around each point, similar to a lens flare effect.

- *Lines*: A number of lines streaking through the halo points.

- *Star*: Changes the halo to a star shape. You can define the number of tips, but not the color.

Note that Rings and Star both have their own individual color options.

When you've finished setting the Halo properties, click back on Surface so that the object mesh again appears as solid. The Halo settings will be preserved for the particles. If you do not wish to see the mesh in a render or animation, uncheck the Emitter option in the Render area of the Particles tab.

You don't always have to use halos. In the Render section of the Particles tab are a number of alternatives, such as rendering the particles as lines or even another mesh object. By selecting the Object option and then typing the name of a mesh object into the Dupli Object field, the particles will become clones of that mesh, as shown in Figure 10–5. Great for making it rain cats and dogs! Be aware that slower computers may have issues if you are duplicating highly detailed models multiple times.

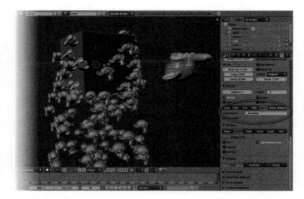

Figure 10–5. Particles can adopt the appearance of another mesh object.

When using the Dupli Object option, the target object (the one that is the real shape of the particles) is disabled from rendering.

Particle Behavior

There are numerous settings on the Particles tab that influence the look and behavior of particles. Experimentation and trial-and-error are the way to go when learning what each option does. For our immediate purposes, the two most important areas of the Particles tab are the Emission area and the Velocity area, as shown in Figure 10–6. The following subsections give a breakdown of the most relevant settings.

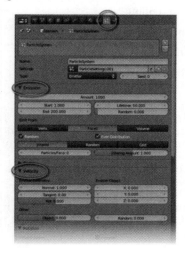

Figure 10–6. Particle settings panel with the Emission and Velocity areas

Emission Area

Within the Emission area you will find options controlling the affecting the distribution of particles, including the number of particles that should appear, the time (in frames) within which they are to appear, and how long the individual particles will last.

- *Amount*: This is the number of particles that will be produced during the predefined generation time (from frames defined at Start and End values). The amount of particles is definite, and will appear more or less crowded depending on the length of generation time.

- *Start and End*: These values define the generation time for which the particles are made. Particles can live beyond this time because they have a separate lifetime setting allowing them to continue beyond the End value, but they are only actually born during the frames between these settings. As stated previously, the number of particles given by the Amount value will spawn over this time.

- *Lifetime*: From the frame that a particle is spawned, this is the number of frames it is allocated to exist.

- *Random*: This value allows for some variation of the lifetime in order to prevent the particles from looking too uniform.

Velocity Area

The main setting in the Velocity area we are interested in is the Normal option. This controls the speed at which particles shoot out from the emitter. It is called Normal because it is dependent on the normal direction of the mesh faces. Each face of a mesh is a surface that has two sides—one side being the inside and the other being the outside. These terms represent which side of the face is on the inside or the outside of the model the face is a part of. Most often, the Velocity ➤ Normal value is a positive number, and particles will flow out from the surface of the emitter, with bigger values resulting in them shooting out faster and potentially covering a bigger distance as they leave. Where negative numbers are used, the particles typically pour inward to the model. If the Normal direction of a face surface is reversed, then this will also change the direction of particles emitted from the surface.

External Forces

As well as having their own settings, particles are also subject to external force, of which there are a number of built-in types. There are two methods of adding an external force.

- By using Shift+A to add items, you should see there is an option to add force field items.

- Alternatively, you can add an empty, and then adjust its force field settings on the Particles tab. This produces the same result as going through the Shift+A menu.

By selecting a force field object and examining the Physics tab, you can access the force field's properties. The first option, Type, allows you to completely change the type of force field. You can experiment with the different types of force fields to see what each does. As shown in Figure 10–7, a force field of type Wind will blow falling particles off in a given direction, depending on which way the force field is facing and whether it has sufficient strength properties to influence the particles (the Strength property is also found on the Physics tab).

Figure 10–7. The effect of wind on particles

Let's try this now:

1. Start with a plane. To represent a sky area, scale the plane four times and lift it upward into the air.

2. On the Particles tab, click the + icon to add a particle system, making the plane (as default) an emitter.

3. Set the Start and End values of your timeline at 1 and 100.

4. Give the plane particles the following properties to make it emit particles that fall like snow:

    *   *Amount:* 2000

    *   Start: 1

    *   *End:* 100

    *   Lifetime: 75

    *   Velocity ➤ Emitter Geometry, Normal: 0

    *   *Velocity ➤ Emitter Geometry Object, Z value:* –4 (this negative value will make the particles go downward)

    *   Field Weights ➤ Gravity: 0.001

5. Start the animation with Alt+A and you should see the particles float down slowly like snow. Keep the animation going. We're going to add a wind effect, and the good news is that Blender 2.5 is capable of adding new dynamics in real time.

6. Press Shift+A to add a force field of type Wind.

7. Pull the wind object off to one side and rotate it inward so that its arrow points toward the falling snow particles. On the Physics tab, raise its Strength property until you are happy with the force it exerts on the snow.

8. Have a go at adding other force field types (e.g., Vortex, Magnetic, etc.) to explore their effects on the particles. You only need to reassign the type of the existing force field on the Physics tab to examine each one.

9. Add more force fields to control the particles and shape their flow where you want them to go.

Exploding Rocket

We are now going to use particles in a short animation. Like the Figure 10–8 sequence, the rocket will launch into space and then explode in a mass of fireworks colors. This will require at least two sets of particle emitters; one for the exhaust from takeoff, and another for the explosion. Of course, if you want to really add to the effects, you could have multiple emitters for the explosion, perhaps having different kinds of sparks (e.g., different colors), or one emitter could be fire while the other takes the role of smoke. For now though, we're keeping things very simple.

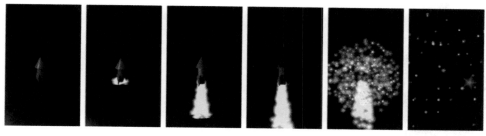

Figure 10–8. Animation of rocket launching

In brief, the rocket (firework) begins on the ground as sparks begin to emit from its exhaust. After a second, it shoots into the air and explodes.

In such an animation, where there are different elements playing together (the rocket, the exhaust particles, and the explosion), timing is critical. Table 10–1 shows the frames in the rocket animation.

Table 10–1. Plot of the Rocket Animation

Frame	Event
1	The rocket is on the ground.
10	Exhaust particles begin to emit sparks.
25	The rocket launches.
50	The rocket disappears, the exhaust particles cease, and the explosion begins.
75	The animation ends.

Here is my workflow for creating the animation:

1. Set the timeline to have the animation running from frame 1 to 75 (as the frame rate value on the Render tab is usually set to 24 fps, this would be about three seconds).

2. Start with the rocket standing on a ground plane at frame 1 (Figure 10–9).

3. Keyframe the rocket location so that at frame 25 it is still on the ground, but at frame 50 it is high in the air.

4. Play the animation and you'll notice that the rocket takes off slowly, and then slows down again as it reaches its height. This is hardly a proper launch, because by default, Blender automatically eases in and out keyed movement.

5. To fix this, change the timeline to a Graph editor, showing the curved lines of the animation. Use A to select all lines, and then follow the menu through Key ➤ Interpolation Type ➤ Linear (or use Shift+T ➤ Linear as a shortcut). Now the rocket should launch with a more convincing swift motion.

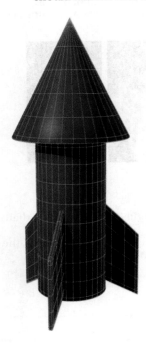

Figure 10–9. A simple rocket for launching

6. Now we want the rocket to disappear at around frame 50. You could just keyframe the size of the rocket down to zero (e.g., key the scale at normal size on frame 50, and then move to frame 51, scale the rocket to size zero, and then key the size again), but a better way would be to make the rocket disappear by moving it to another layer. At frame 50, right-click the layers boxes and choose Insert Single Keyframe (recall from Chapter 2 that the layers are in the 3D view header).

7. Go to frame 51. Press M to move the rocket to the next layer and choose Insert Single Keyframe a second time.

8. On pressing Alt+A, the rocket should now animate as we would like. Now we can move on to the particles.

9. For realism, the particle sparks from the rocket exhaust shouldn't just pass through the ground surface; they should bounce off it, spreading out as fire. Select the ground plane and enable Collision on the Physics tab (click the Add button), with a Particle Dampening factor of 0.75, which will prevent the exhaust particles from bouncing too high.

10. To prevent particles from coming through the sides of the rocket, also give the rocket body collision properties, enabled so as to kill particles. Select the rocket and click the Add button in the Collision area of the Physics tab. You can also click the Kill Particles option in the same panel area, which causes any particles attempting to pass through the walls of the rocket to disappear.

11. Place a new plane inside the rocket exhaust, positioned as indicated in Figure 10–10. Note that the plane should not be encased inside the rocket mesh (or the particles won't be able to get out), but just outside in order to appear as though they come from the rocket.

Figure 10–10. Placing an emitter plane inside the exhaust

12. Parent the plane to the rocket so that as the rocket launches, it takes the plane with it. (Select the plane, Shift-select the rocket, and then press Ctrl+P)

13. The plane in the exhaust needs to be set as a particle emitter with the following particle properties on the Particles tab:

   - *Amount*: 1000

   - *Start*: 10

   - *End*: 50

   - Lifetime: 10

   - *Velocity* ➤ *Emitter Object* ➤ *Z*: –2 (this makes the particles shoot downward)

- *Velocity* ➤ *Random*: 3 (this makes the particles spread out a little, rather than going straight down)

14. Change the material settings on the Material tab to give the exhaust particles a yellow color and any other properties you see fit.

■ **Note** With the emitter object (the plane in the rocket's exhaust) selected, go to the Cache area of the Particles tab. Here, there is a Cache Step setting for the particle emitter that defaults to 10, but I have found it helpful to drop this down to 1. Without doing this, scrubbing between frames and pressing F12 for test renders can give odd results, showing particles at the wrong frames.

---

15. Finally, let's make the explosion. Place a UV sphere over the area where the rocket blows and resize it appropriately for the starting shape. See Figure 10–11 as a reference for this.

16. Set the sphere particle emission properties as follows:

- *Amount*: 500

- *Start*: 50

- *End*: 52

- Lifetime: 10

- *Velocity* ➤ *Normal*: 30 (fast moving)

17. In the Render panel in the Particles tab, make sure Emitter is turned off so the sphere itself is invisible.

Figure 10–11. *The final animation setup. Note that the explosion emitter in the air will not be visible until the particles kick in at frame 50.*

18. In the material settings, give the explosion particles a color and any of the appearance tweaks you like. Rings and Star settings make useful firework effects.

19. Render your animation as a movie and enjoy the result.

Making Hair

Blender's particle-based system for making fur and hair received a generous overhaul during the production phase of the second Open Movie, *Big Buck Bunny*. It is now straightforward to use and comes with some amazing tools allowing the artist to literally comb hair into place. It's almost like the particle version of the mesh sculpt-editing mode.

Hair is actually the same as the animated particles that we have looked at, except that by telling Blender that we want the particle base to be of type hair instead of emitter, Blender knows to draw a fiber along the path of each particle instead of animating the particles over time. Some of the settings of hair and emitter are different, so the path won't literally be identical for both hair and emitter; nevertheless, this method of tracing particles to make a strand is how Blender's particle hair is generated.

Separating the Wig

The first thing we need to do is create a wig for the hair to grow out of. When we enable hair to grow, it will grow from all over the base mesh, so unless we want the model to have whiskers, it is necessary to isolate the areas of the mesh that we want hair to grow from, and make a new wig mesh of just these parts.

1. In edit mode, select the faces that are in the area for the base of this wig (Figure 10–12).

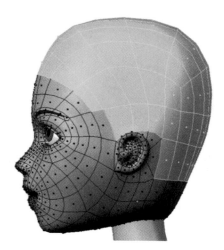

Figure 10–12. Selected faces ready for duplication

2. Duplicate the faces by pressing Shift+D, 0 (the zero key), and then Enter to make sure you don't drag the duplicated faces around. (Alternatively, you can press Shift+D to duplicate and then just press Esc.)

3. With the duplicated faces still selected, press P to tell Blender to separate them as a new mesh. Choose Selection from the pop-up menu, as shown in Figure 10–13.

4. The duplicated wig area you just made is no longer part of the head but is now a separate mesh object. Go back into object mode and select this new wig mesh. If you are tidy in your workflow, this is a good time to name the mesh object wig. At the moment, it has the same skin material as the head we got it from. The danger of having them share the same material is that if you change the properties of this material on either mesh it will affect the other.

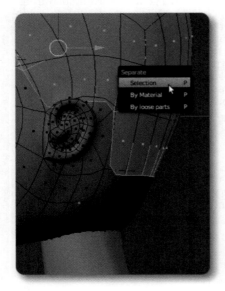

Figure 10–13. Separating the duplicated faces

Creating a New Material Ready for the Hair

Let's fix the material problem.

1. Go to the Material tab and you will see a list of materials with the current skin material chosen. Below this is a text box where you can change the name of the material. This also contains a number showing how many objects are sharing the material. With the wig selected, click this number to make a brand new single-user copy of the material, just for the wig. The new material is likely to have been renamed something like skin.001 (see Figure 10–14), but you can use the text area to rename it to something more sensible, like hair.

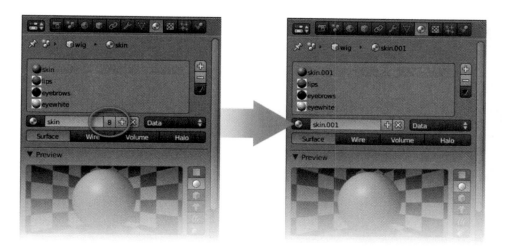

Figure 10–14. Click the number next to the material name to break it off as a newly created, unique material.

2. Now that the material is unique, you can change its diffuse setting (this means color) without fear of affecting other parts of the mesh. Make the new hair material the color that you would like to use for the hair that will grow out from the wig. If you have followed the preceding steps correctly, you should be able to do so without the color of the skin on the other head mesh being affected.

Making the Hair Strands

Let's make the hair.

1. Go to the Particles tab.

2. Click the Add button to add a particle system to the wig.

3. By default, the type is set to Emitter. Click the drop-down list and change this option to Hair, as shown in Figure 10–15. In an instant, hair strands will spring out from the wig base, as shown in Figure 10–16. There are a number of things to change in order to get the hair the way you want it, so let's look at the essential ones first.

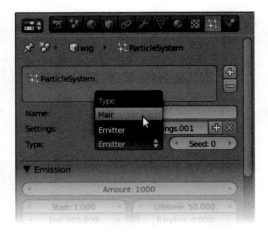

Figure 10–15. Make a new particle system of type Hair.

Hiding the Wig, and Strand Render

On performing a render, you can see that the mesh of the wig is showing. You probably want to hide this so you can only see the hairs. To do this, go down to the Render area of the Particles tab and uncheck the box for Emitter .The wig mesh is the emitter of the particles, and this option is for whether is should be rendered.

Figure 10–16. A new head of hair (in 3D view)

Not far below the Emitter option is the Strand Render option. By enabling this, you cause Blender to use a special strand primitive for the hair particles, which makes them faster to render. It is useful when rendering a lot of hairs, although it does not render with raytraced shadows.

You can see both these options—the Emitter option and the Strand Render option—in Figure 10–17.

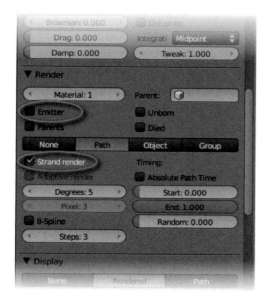

Figure 10–17. Render setting to enhance the default hair strands

Hair Texture: Creating Fine Ends

When rendered, the default hairs look like stiff strands of spaghetti; not much like real hair, which should taper away at the ends.

There are a couple of methods you can use to define hair strands with fading ends.

- You can specify the physical shape of the strands so they are thicker at the roots, or thinner at the tips.

- You can use an alpha-based texture to make the ends of the hair strands fade.

You can choose which of these methods you prefer, or even apply both at the same time if you like.

Strand Thickness Variation

Below the Material tab, the Strand area contains settings to modify the shape of the hair strands (see Figure 10–18). You can change the root of the hair to make the base thicker, or the tip to make the ends thinner.

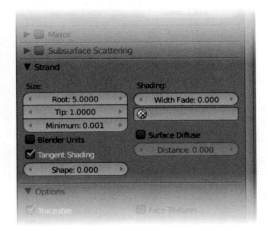

Figure 10–18. Strand options

In Figure 10–19 I have made three wigs for three monkey heads with roots of different thickness. The first monkey wears a wig with a Root setting of 0, which is the default value. The middle monkey has hair with a Root setting of 5, and the third monkey has a Root value of 10, making the base of the hair strands a lot thicker than the others.

Figure 10–19. Hair strands with different Root settings

Note that the Preview area of the Material tab has an option to show how a material will look as particle hair (this is circled in Figure 10–20). This preview allows you to see the effect of the strands without having to perform a full render, which might take some time.

Figure 10–20. Material tab preview of particle hair

Alpha Material Blend

You can fade the ends of the hair strands by assigning them a material with alpha (transparency) settings, and have that material run from root to tip in order to just fade the ends of each hair. Let's see this in action.

The first requirement of this approach is to set up the hair material so that it can accept the transparency from the alpha texture.

1. Select the wig and go to the Material tab.

2. Go down the panels to the Transparency area. Enable transparency by clicking the option box.

3. Within the Transparency area (you may have to expand it by clicking the black header triangle), make sure that Z Transparency is on, and slide both the Alpha and Specular sliders down to zero, as has been done in Figure 10–21. Doing this means that the current material settings won't override the same values when the texture tries to influence them.

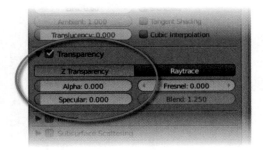

Figure 10–21. Enabling transparency settings. Don't forget to slide the Alpha and Specular levels down to zero.

Currently, if you perform a render, you will see that the hairs are now invisible regardless of you still being able to see them in the 3D view. Now it's time to set up the alpha texture.

1. With the wig object still selected, go to the Texture tab.

2. The list of textures is probably blank right now. Click the New button to add a new texture, which you will use to determine the transparency of the hair. You can name the texture by typing in the appropriate entry box near the top of the Material tab (Figure 10–22). Call this texture hairstrand.

Figure 10–22. Naming the texture

3. On clicking the New button, the default type of the new texture is Clouds. Change this to Blend.

4. To work properly, fading only toward the tip end of the hair, the texture will need a sense of direction for the hair strands. In the Mapping area, change the Coordinates value from Generated to Strand. This causes Blender to align the texture along the direction of the hair strands.

5. In the Influence ➤ Diffuse area of the Texture tab, you will see that the texture is assigned to influence the color of the hair. Check the Alpha option. This will allow the texture to affect the hair strand transparency.

6. You should leave the Color option checked.

7. If you were to turn off the Color option, the hair strands would get their color from the wig mesh. This may suit your needs just fine, though hair can be made more interesting by changing the color along a strand (e.g., you might like blonde hair with dark roots). As you shall see soon, you can get the same texture, which influences the alpha of the hair, to customize the color of the strands in interesting ways.

8. For now, if you take a render, the hair should be visible, with purple strands, something like Figure 10–23. This color is a result of the current texture taking its color from the default purple color at the bottom of the Influence area of the Texture tab.

Figure 10–23. By default, a blend texture affects the diffuse color, turning the hair ends purple instead of making them taper to transparent.

Maximizing Control Through a Ramp

Certainly, there are a lot of steps to follow. We are nearly done with the texturing part, though. The settings are correct in that the hair supports transparency, which is controlled through a blend texture. The color of the hair is influenced by this same texture also. To finish of the texturing, we are going to add our own custom colorband gradient, like the one shown in Figure 10–24, to the blend texture so that we can manually control the color and alpha levels by hand.

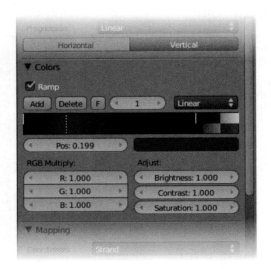

Figure 10–24. More advanced color ramp settings

On the Texture tab, in the Colors section (expand this if it is not already open by clicking the arrow in front of Colors), check the box for Ramp. This creates a new gradient strip, which can be custom generated. By default, this strip is transparent on the left side, which is the wrong way around, as the left side of the colorband influences the root of the hair strands, while the right side affects the tips. To flip the strip, click the F button above the colorband.

Initially, you start with only two predefined positions at either end of the strip, but new ones will appear along the middle each time you click the Add button. Select any position by LMB-clicking it, and then change the color and/or alpha by LMB-clicking the color rectangle positioned below and to the right of the colorband strip. This gives you a lot of control over the gradient. You can position of the colors so that the hair only fades at the very tip (the right side) instead of through the full length of the hair strands. This will achieve a result similar to Figure 10–25. You can also use multiple colors (e.g., red hair that's dark at the tips and blond at the roots).

Figure 10–25. Strands fading toward the ends

Shaping the Hair

Now it's time for the fun part: shaping the hair. You can do this by first setting up the initial base settings, where you determine the starting values of the hair strands. Then you can use freehand editing, in which you use Blender's combing tools to more specifically shape the hair.

Base Settings

Having set the wig as an emitter, you currently have a host of straight hairs protruding out from the head. There are a bundle of settings to play with that will give the hair different properties in terms various styles of wave and curl.

1. On the Particles tab, locate the Field Weights area (see Figure 10–26).

2. Check the box labeled Use For Growing Hair. Suddenly, you will see the hair drop down as though it is very heavy.

3. Further up, there is a field called Gravity, which is at the maximum level of 1. Change this value to 0.02 or thereabouts. Your hair should now have a slight sag reflecting its weight.

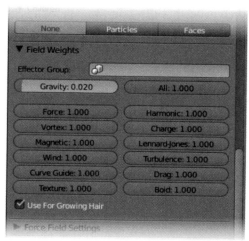

Figure 10–26. The Field Weights section

■ **Note** To change the overall length of the hair, adjust the Normal field of the Emitter Geometry panel in the Velocity section. This works because, as explained earlier in this section, hair is generated by tracing the path of a particle to represent a hair strand. Raising the velocity of this particle means that the hair strands extend further away from the surface.

Children

Before we get into the freehand editing, it pays to cut down the number of hairs the need to be tweaked so that we don't end up trying to edit a tangle of too many hairs to efficiently control.

1. If we are going to have children hairs, we don't need as many real hairs for a full head. At the top of the Particles tab, under Emission, you'll notice that Blender is using (by default) something like 1,000 hairs (the Amount value). Cut this down to about 50.

2. Now go down to the Children panel. Currently the option of None is selected, which means there are no child hairs Select Faces to make the faces of the mesh emit child hairs. Each hair is now multiplied by a certain number to form a group of child hairs.

3. When you click the Faces button, a few new fields should appear, including Display (which is by default set to 10) and Render (set to 100). These variables control the number of child hairs that appear.

    • The Display value sets the number of extra hairs (per parent hair) to show in the 3D view.

    • The Render value determines how many hairs are present in the final rendered image.

There are also a number of settings in the Children panel that affect the general shaping of the hair. Experiment with these to see what they do, taking special note of the effects of the Clumping slider and the Kink options of curl, radial, wave, and braid.

Freehand Editing

With the hairpiece selected, use the Mode menu to enter particle mode (see Figure 10–27). Make sure the Tool Shelf is on display.

Figure 10–27. Particle mode

The Tool Shelf should reveal a number of useful brushes, as shown in Figure 10–28, which can be used to manipulate the hair by dragging the mouse over the strands while holding down the LMB.

Figure 10–28. *Particle hair brushes*

Available brush options include those in Table 10–2.

Table 10–2. *Particle Brush Types*

Type	Description
Comb	Moves hair strands into place.
Smooth	Untangles strands.
Add	Generates new hairs in a specified area. If you change the brush size to 1, you can insert single hairs.
Length	Grows/shrinks hairs.
Puff	Fluffs hair about.
Cut	Chops hair strands at the area of a mouse click.
Weight	Adjusts hair with cloth soft body.

You can change the size of the brush (shortcut key F) as well as the strength, and there are other various options. Styling hair this way has a similar feel to modeling in sculpt mode.

Also note that when freehand editing, child hairs typically disappear, as they are clones of the parent hairs and thereby inherit any changes. Of course, the child kink properties temporarily disappear as well.

When you edit a mesh, you can choose between three modes, for manipulate vertices, edges, and faces, respectively. Particle mode has equivalent settings in the 3D view header, as shown in Figure 10–29. The three modes for particle manipulation do the following:

- *Path edit mode*: Allows you to manipulate hairs as full strands

- *Point select mode*: Allows every point to be seen and selected (similar to vertex select mode in mesh editing)

- *Tip select mode*: Allows you to manipulate just the tips

Figure 10–29. Particle mode buttons

Using these modes, you should be able to freehand edit your hair strands into place (Figure 10–30). When rendering, the Children setting will make the end result look like a full head of hair (Figure 10–31).

Figure 10–30. Combing hair strands into place

Figure 10–31. *A quick render showing the hair taking shape*

Fluid Dynamics

Fluid dynamics are about making liquid simulation. If you want an animation where liquid is poured from a glass, then fluid is the appropriate choice. The process involves assigning a mesh object to act as fluid, and another to be the domain marking a boundary for how far the fluid is able to flow. Blender uses these to create an animated simulation of how the liquid spills. Making fluid is a very taxing task for a computer. For this reason, many high-end computer animation packages still don't have fluid dynamics, and professional production companies are known to have not only specialist programs, but even entire teams dedicated to just getting the water to work. Fortunately for us, Blender has a fairly good engine for fluid dynamics.

Because fluid has a tendency to flow everywhere, it would take too much computing power to check the entire 3D space every frame to see whether there was fluid here or there. You need to have not only the fluid object itself, but also a domain object to mark a finite area within which the fluid simulation occurs. By restricting the fluid simulation to as small an area as possible, you narrow down the amount that Blender has to calculate at any one time.

Here's an example:

1. Start with a new scene and the default cube, which will be the domain. Rename the cube `domain`.

2. Scale the cube about three times, which is sufficient for a small simulation (select it, press S, type **3**, and press Enter).

3. Switch to wireframe mode (press Z). This enables you to see through the cube so you can observe the liquid object you are about to place inside.

4. Add a new object such as a sphere (Shift+A ➤ Mesh ➤ UV Sphere) to represent the starting shape of the fluid. Name the sphere `liquid` and place it inside the cube, perhaps dragging it near the top, as in Figure 10–32.

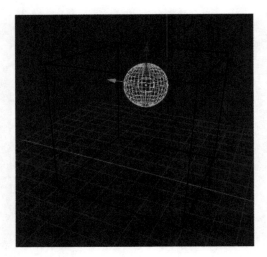

Figure 10–32. Preparing to make a sphere into fluid. Note the outside box marking the simulation domain.

5. The important thing is to make sure the cube completely surrounds the sphere. The resolution (number of vertices) in the sphere is irrelevant, as the liquid (once it is generated) will adopt the general shape of the inner object, but it won't actually take into the account the amount of vertices.

6. Right now, the cube and the sphere are just ordinary mesh objects. It's time to get them to work. Start by selecting the sphere.

7. With the sphere selected, go to the Physics tab.

8. Click the Add button on the Fluid panel. A new Type field with a drop-down list will appear. Choose Fluid from there.

9. Now select the cube.

10. On the Physics tab under Fluid, select the Add button again, but this time choose Domain from the drop-down list (Figure 10–33).

Figure 10–33. The Physics tab

■ **Note** From now on, when I refer to fluid physics of a certain type, I am referring to the Fluid panel on the Physics tab you have just used.

---

11. After you set up the domain, a number of new options appear. One of them reveals a cache directory, most likely /tmp, which is where the calculations of the fluid spill are going to be stored. This is an important option because it means that while fluid simulation can take some time to calculate, by caching to a specific area for a given project, you can eliminate the need to recalculate every time the file is opened because Blender will simply load in the results from the previous session from this directory. Therefore, you should select this slot and direct it to a new folder set aside for storing the fluid animation for your project. By defining your own directory, you can easily clear the simulation cache by simply going in and deleting the generated files.

12. You might want to change the End value under the timeline to 100 frames, giving four seconds of animation for this example. This way you won't have to wait too long for the animation to calculate.

13. You should see a Bake Fluid Simulation button further up the panel. Click this button and wait a few minutes while Blender calculates the movement of the fluid. You will see a progress bar like the one in Figure 10–34 at the top of the window as Blender works out where the fluid will spill. Depending on the size of the domain, Blender can sometimes take a while to calculate this stage, although our scene is relatively small and should only take a few minutes.

Figure 10–34. Progress bar showing fluid bake in progress

14. When the calculations are finished, press Alt+A to run the animation. Note that you can actually scrub the timeline while the animation is being evaluated. You should get a result similar to the sequence shown in Figure 10–35.

Figure 10–35. *The resulting fluid animation*

Looking at the animation, you will notice a couple of things:

- The domain mesh (the outside cube) seems to disappear. It is not actually vanishing—rather, it is changing into the liquid itself. So it's not the mesh we originally named `liquid` that becomes the fluid at all. Rather, the domain object becomes the fluid and only uses the other mesh as a starting shape.

- Once its shape has been referenced, the mesh originally set up as the `liquid` object is actually useless to the animation (unless you want to bake afresh, so don't just delete it). It just sits there throughout the animation, and may as well be taken away from the scene by moving it to another layer (RMB-select it in object mode and press the M key). Alternatively, you can hide it with the H key (press Alt+H to unhide objects).

Press Z to get back out of wireframe mode; the liquid looks good as a solid. You might also want to set the shading to type Smooth in the Tool Shelf.

■ **Note** You can have multiple liquid objects within a single domain. As long as they are within the boundary, the domain will calculate all of them, although this will increase processing time. Having liquid objects that start with an overlap can cause undesirable artifacts.

Exercise: Tsunami Simulation

Now that you have an idea of how fluid works, take it to the next level by adding obstacles. Normally, Blender's fluid will simply travel through other objects. To make a mesh act as an obstacle, so that fluid flows around it, simply do the following:

1. Select the object.

2. Go to the Physics tab.

3. Click the Add button in the Fluid panel.

4.   For the Type option, choose Obstacle (as in Figure 10–36).

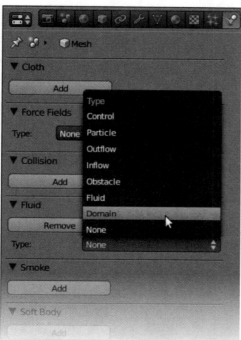

Figure 10–36. Activating an obstacle

5.   On a ground plane, create several boxes to represent buildings. To make things easy, start with one cube set as an obstacle and then press Shift+D duplicate it to make the others. This way you won't have to manually set up the physics for each one because they will have copied the Obstacle property from the first.

6.   Resize and position each box until you have something like the buildings in a city.

7.   Make a wall of water off to one side and set its physics to a fluid type. Add a final cube to encompass the scene and set it up as the domain.

8.   Animate the scene and enjoy your results (Figure 10–37). This will take more time than the previous example, as there is more involved.

Figure 10–37. Flood simulation

To speed up the processing time, you could do the following:

- Avoid making the animation longer than necessary.

- Avoid having too much detail in the buildings; using simple blocks is fine.

- Avoid making the domain too large. If necessary, scale the whole scene down so it is a miniature model, as opposed to a full-size city.

Pouring Liquid from a Cup

You will need a fairly capable computer for this exercise.

1. Make a cup or a bottle. It does not have to be fancy, but its walls need to have thickness for the physics to work.

2. Set it up to be of type Obstacle.

3. Place a volume of liquid inside.

4. Animate the cup (or bottle) so that it upturns, pouring out the liquid.

There are a number of things to watch out for here. Make sure the liquid mesh does not go through the walls of the cup in the starting position. The liquid is likely to be pretty thick at the default settings, so you may need to play with the Resolution settings (just under the bake button; see Figure 10–38) in order to thin the fluid. Likewise, the Viscosity setting under Domain World on the Physics tab should be set to Water.

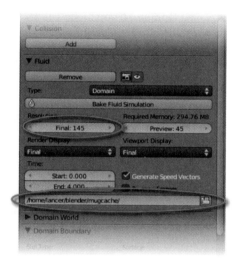

Figure 10–38. Fluid resolution settings

The animation will take some time to generate and you won't want to renew it every time you open the file, so I highly recommend you set up a folder to save the cache. Also, if Blender crashes, doing so will enable you to load the scene and scrub through however much of the animation was calculated. See whether you can complete an animated pouring sequence, as shown in Figure 10–39.

Figure 10–39. Pouring cup animation

Smoke

Smoke is similar to fluid, in that an animation is generated within the bounds of a physical domain, which is defined by another object. Of course, the settings for modifying the behavior of fluid and smoke are going to differ, and smoke needs special attention in order to make sure it renders properly.

1. Start with a new scene and, in object mode, expand the default cube about three times (press S, type **3**, and press Enter). Name the cube domain.

2. With the domain object selected, go to the Physics tab, and in the Smoke area click the Add button. From the buttons that appear below, select Domain. If you are in solid viewport mode, you should notice that the domain cube now displays as a wireframe.

3. We need an object to act as the source of our smoke. Inside the cube, place a UV sphere or some other object you want to act as the smoke emitter. Move it down to the bottom of the domain cube, but make sure it is inside the area as shown in Figure 10–40. Name this new object smoke.

Figure 10–40. *Positioning the smoke emitter inside the domain*

4. With the smoke object selected, return to the Smoke area of the Physics tab (Figure 10–41) and click the Add button. This time, select Flow from the list of buttons, which is a way of saying that the selected object should be a smoke emitter.

Notice that there are a few options there:

- The Temp. Diff. value affects the speed the smoke will billow out.

- The Density value allows you to control the thickness of the smoke (higher values mean thicker smoke).

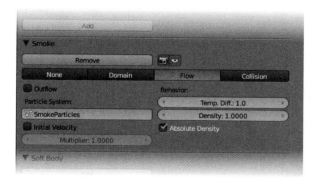

Figure 10–41. The Smoke area of the Physics tab

If you now go to the Particles tab, you will notice that a new emitter-type particle system has been made for the smoke. The smoke is in effect another form of particles. You can change settings here, just like you did earlier. For example, you could change the Start and End values to define when the smoke gets omitted.

If you don't want to see the emitter sphere as the smoke rises, you should uncheck the Emitter option in the Render area of the panels of the Particles tab.

Like fluid, smoke can take a long time to evaluate, and it is worthwhile to make a *cache*, which is a series of files stored on the hard drive to record the smoke animation. This way, Blender won't have to recalculate the smoke physics every time it is animated; it will just replay what was recorded the first time. We will soon set up this smoke cache, but first it is best to save the current Blender file, because Blender will then know where the cache should be saved (by default, a separate directory within the same directory as the saved .blend file.)

So, if you haven't done so already, you should save your work now. Blender will automatically make its own cache for the smoke, so for the impatient, you *could* press Alt+A to see the smoke animating. It is better that you know how to set up your own cache, however—which is as follows:

1. Select the domain object and go to the Physics tab.

2. Go down the panels until you find the Smoke Cache area, which is shown in Figure 10–42. You may need to expand this by clicking the black triangle to the left of the Smoke Cache heading.

3. Depending on your animation, you can change the Start and End values to determine when (in frames) the particle smoke is emitted. These values are separate from the standard animation Start and End values (the timeline values found in the Dimensions area of the Rendering tab under Frame Range), and you should always ensure the two sets complement each other.

4. Type a unique name into the File Name field. (In Figure 10–42, it's named Smokey.)

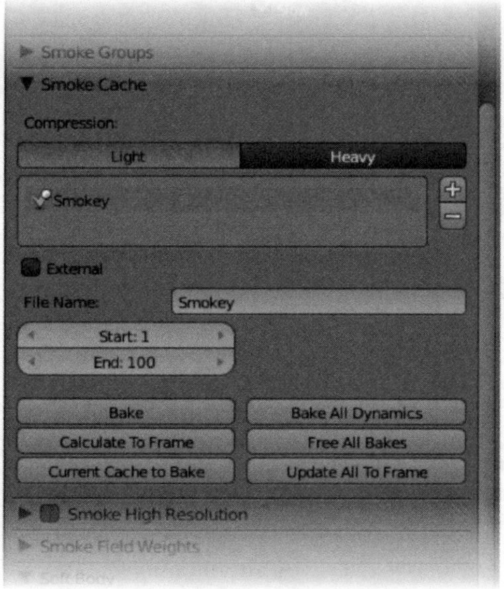

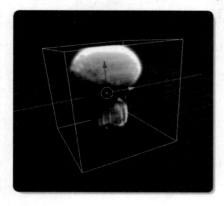

Figure 10–42. The Smoke Cache area of the Physics tab

5. Now we are ready to calculate the smoke animation into the cache, and then view the animation. Click the Bake button and wait while Blender generates the animation. This is the point where Blender records all those cache files.

6. Scrub the timeline or press Alt+A to observe the result.

You should now see the smoke billowing out from the emitter object within the confines of the domain object, as shown in Figure 10–43. The animation is fast because it has to be prebaked, and you can select anywhere along the timeline to instantly see what the smoke is like at that frame. This is thanks to the power of caching.

Figure 10–43. Smoke physics

If you look through your files, where the Blender file was saved, you should see a new directory called blendcache_yourcachename. Inside this directory are a number of files, each representing the cache record of the smoke for a specific frame.

Once you have baked the smoke animation, the Bake button changes to become the Free Bake button. Should you wish to cache the animation again, click this button to ready the cache afresh. This will not actually delete the cache files; it simply allows Blender to make new ones.

Rendering the Smoke

The smoke looks pretty good in 3D view, but if you scrub the timeline to a frame where the smoke looks good and then to press F12 to render, you won't see the smoke you might expect. Instead, all that can be seen is the domain object rendering as a large cube (see Figure 10–44).

Figure 10–44. With incorrect Material settings, smoke renders as a cube.

In order to render the smoke, both the domain and the emitter object need to undergo changes to certain settings. It is a good idea to make the background dark in order to see the light-colored smoke in front of it.

1. First go to the World tab.

2. Change the horizon to a dark color or even black.

3. Next, to stop the domain object rendering as a solid cube, you need to change its material settings. Select the domain object.

4. Go to the Material tab. If it does not have one already, make a new material for the domain. Name the material smoke_mat. It might seem strange that we are naming the domain material as opposed to the smoke item, but changes to this material will directly affect the look of the smoke itself.

5. Change the material type to Volume.

6. Rendering the cube now results in a cube full of smoke, as shown in Figure 10–45. You will need to clear this smoke or it will get in the way of the final smoke we are wanting to create.

7. In the Density area of the Material tab, slide the Density value down to zero.

8. If you render now, the cube of smoke will have gone (since it has no volume).

Figure 10–45. Smoke-filled cube

We now need to add a texture and link it to the smoke object, which will add density to the parts where we want the smoke to be seen.

9. With the domain object still selected, go to the Texture tab.

10. Add a new texture to the domain (or if there is one already there, you can adapt it).

11. Name the texture smoke texture.

12. Set the Type to Voxel Data.

13. In the Influence area, check the Density option.

14. Go down to the Voxel Data area of the Texture panels.

15. Set the File Format field to Smoke (it should be the default).

16. In the Domain Object field, select the name of the domain object (it should be domain).

17. For the source, choose Density (it should be the default).

Now the render should work, showing your smoke. The result at this stage will be fairly smudgy, as can be seen in Figure 10–46.

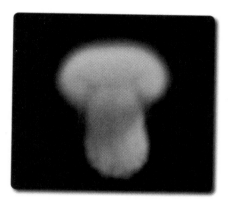

Figure 10–46. A smudgy start

Improving the Smoke

Here are a couple pointers on making the smoke look better:

- On the Material tab of the domain object, in the Density area, increase the Density Scale to make the smoke thicker. I recommend a setting of about 3.

- In the Shading area, increase the Scattering value (again, I would suggest a value of 3).

A fresh render will now result in more vivid smoke, although it is still blurry and lacks definition (see Figure 10–47).

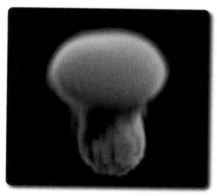

Figure 10–47. Density Scale and Scattering improve the look.

With the domain object selected, go to the Physics tab. In the Smoke area there is a Resolution field, which is set to 32 by default. The resolution is directly relative to how detailed the smoke is, and is taken from the domain boundary. You can bump up this value for better-looking results, as in Figure 10–48 (try doubling it to 64), although this will be more taxing on CPU power and RAM. You will need to click the Free Bake/Bake button a couple of times in order to renew the cache at this higher resolution. The bake will take considerably longer than before.

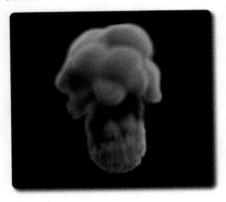

Figure 10–48. Increased number of resolution divisions

Because the resolution is taken from the size of the domain, a useful strategy you can use is to scale the domain down, in object mode, so that it is a closer fit for the smoke. This way, Blender does not have to waste too many calculations on non-smoke areas. If you can halve the size of the domain cube, it's like doubling the resolution, and you get great results without the long waiting time.

Finally, you might want to pay some attention to the Smoke High Resolution area, which is the next panel down from the Smoke Cache area. When you want a highly detailed cloud, you can enable this option and tweak the settings within (particularly adding to the Resolutions/Divisions field).

Note that Smoke High Resolution has its own cache, which appears below as a new panel when Smoke High Resolution is enabled.

This option can give some very detailed results (the one in Figure 10–49 uses a Divisions level of 2), although it is very RAM intensive and requires a powerful computer to work well.

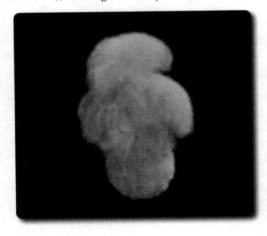

Figure 10–49. The effect of the Smoke High Resolution option

Smoke is one of the newer additions to Blender, so play with it and see what you can do.

Soft Body Physics

Soft body physics enables us to give properties to a solid mesh in order to make it behave like foam rubber and other not-so-solid substances. In this exercise we are going to use the settings to change the monkey into wobbly rubber.

1. Delete the default cube.

2. Add a monkey mesh. Rotate it 90 degrees around the x axis (make it upright), and then raise it up into the air a little (you can raise it 1.5 units by selecting the monkey and pressing G, pressing Z, typing **1.5**, and pressing Enter).

3. Add a ground plane, and scale it about three times (press S, type **3**, and press Enter).

4. We don't want the animation to last for too long (because this also means Blender will take some time to bake the animation), so change the End value of the timeline from 250 to 100 frames.

Now we are ready for some soft body physics fun. We are going to make the monkey act like it is made of soft foam rubber, and have it drop onto the ground plane, coming to something of a wobbly halt.

1. Select the ground plane.

2. On the Physics tab, click the Add button in the Collision panel. You shouldn't need to change any of the settings, as the defaults will be fine. This will ensure that the monkey will be able to collide with the ground when it falls, as opposed to passing right through it.

3. Next, we'll change the properties of the monkey. Figure 10–50 shows the changes outlined following. Select the monkey, and on the Physics tab, click the Add button in the Soft Body panel. Numerous new options will appear.

4. Uncheck the Soft Body Goal option. This allows for vertices to be pinned in place, which would result in the monkey being restricted from falling.

Figure 10–50. Soft Body settings

5.   Check that the Soft Body Edges option is enabled (it probably is enabled by default). Expand this panel and change the Bending value to 9. This makes the mesh act stiff, so it won't crumple too much on impact.

6.   Finally, expand the Soft Body Field Weights panel and change the Gravity setting to 0.85.

7. At this stage, you could just press Alt+A to animate, but it will be very slow. Instead, it's better to prebake the animation while you go and have a coffee or something and let Blender do all the calculating work.

8. Near the top of the Soft Body panels, expand Soft Body Cache.

9. Change the End value to 100 (if it is not that already).

10. Click the Bake button and wait while Blender calculates the animation.

When Blender is done, animate and watch the show. As in Figure 10–51, you should see the monkey drop down to the ground plane and flop around like rubber. Its eyes, which are not actually attached to the main mesh, will even pop out of its head!

Figure 10–51. *The final result (with coloring added to clarify what happens to the eyes)*

Cloth Dynamics

The soft body physics we have just used is the old way of making cloth. Indeed, if you experiment a little with different values, you'll discover that changing certain values (e.g., Bending) will create a mesh that collapses like Obi-Wan Kenobi from the original *Star Wars*. But Blender now has a more sophisticated approach to making cloth simulation.

1. Start a new scene. Leave the default cube where it is.

2. Create a new grid (Shift+A ➤ Mesh ➤ Grid), and at the bottom of the Tool Shelf, specify that the X and Y subdivisions should be 45.

3. Scale the grid three times.

4. Pull the plane above the cube, to something close to a z value of 2.3, as in Figure 10–52.

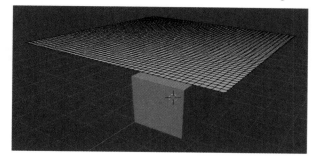

Figure 10–52. *Grid positioned above the cube (in edit mode so you can see the vertices)*

5. Now all we need to do is add the right dynamics and bake. Select the cube.

6. On the Physics tab, add a collision to the cube.

7. Select the plane/grid.

8. On the Physics tab, add a cloth dynamic.

9. You might also want to enable Self Collision in the Cloth Collision area. This prevents the cloth from going through itself.

10. In the Cloth Cache panel, you can click the Bake button. Blender will work out the cloth dynamics, and soon you will be able to animate with Alt+A to see the results (see Figure 10–53).

11. Click the Bake button (which now reads Free Bake) to reset your cloth dynamics.

12. Cloth usually looks better if you set its shading to Smooth in the Tool Shelf. You won't need to rebake, as this only affects the how the shape is rendered, not how it moves.

Figure 10–53. The final animation of cloth dropping over the cube

Summary

We have spent some time looking at the particle system in Blender and also the physics properties that are useful for simulation animations. These are complex features that even many expensive 3D programs lack (forcing production teams to use specialized packages for these tasks). Blender's physics is a work in progress and does not pretend to have anything over industry-level proprietary applications for these tasks. However, we are offered a very sophisticated toolset to work with.

As you read through this chapter, you no doubt noticed many options I didn't explain. I gave only a brief introduction to physics, which is in itself a specialist field of computer graphics.

Most of the techniques examined in this chapter are cache based. That is, the computer takes some time to calculate the animation, baking the result for playback at a later time. Blender is also capable of real-time physics simulation, but this involves looking into the Blender game engine, which is the topic of our next chapter.

CHAPTER 11

■ ■ ■

The Game Engine

In the last chapter, you studied some of the things Blender can do in terms of physics. In this chapter, we are moving on to look at the Blender game engine, which has a common link in that it also uses physics—although for game purposes, the physics used needs to be much less intensive than some of what we were looking at before, because game engine physics needs to be able to perform in real time.

In modern games, cars race around tracks slipping and sliding realistically around corners. Boulders tumble down slopes, and players stumble over with rag-doll precision. The Blender game engine is capable of all these things.

Given that you should now be familiar with physics, I will start off introducing the Blender game engine in a similar way, by showing you how to set up objects and then use the Blender game engine to simulate them tumbling in real time. Bear in mind that Blender can't make your machine perform faster than it is—it is a good idea to have a reasonably fast machine if you want to get serious about real-time physics simulations.

The Blender game engine is not just about physics, of course. Games involve interaction with a player, and I will dedicate much of this chapter to showing you how to create a keyboard-controlled robot that you can drive around, and also how you might go about making a simple two-player game.

Game Engine Physics

To start using the Blender game engine, we are going to use it with something we are familiar with from the last chapter: a physics engine. Much of the physics done then, including that involving fluids, is slow to work out and may even require baking. Game engine physics is designed to be simple and speedy. In this next exercise, we will create a simple scene where an object tumbles around reacting to gravity while deflecting off other objects.

1. Start with the default cube. In edit mode, select one of the top edges and pull it down near the bottom to create a ramp.

2. In object mode, create a ground plane.

3. Finally, add as sphere, (either a UV sphere or an icosphere are fine) and position it in the air above the top of the ramp in a position where it is set up and ready to roll down, as shown in Figure 11–1.

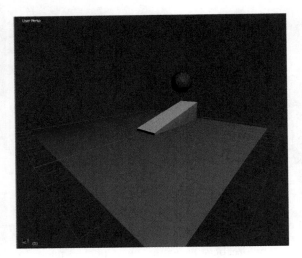

Figure 11–1. The ramp and ball in position

4.   Now you will apply the real-time game engine physics. Select the sphere and go to the Physics tab, where you found many of the soft body physics features in the last chapter.

5.   The game engine physics is hidden, though. To access it, you need to change the render engine (the menu is normally located at the top of the screen) from Blender Render to Blender Game, as in Figure 11–2.

Figure 11–2. Changing the render engine

6.   On changing this menu, you will notice that the available physics options have changed (likewise, the panels on the Render and World tabs are different). There is a Physics Type value set to Static and several new properties, such as whether the selected object should be an actor, a ghost, or invisible, among a host of others. As demonstrated in Figure 11–3, when you have the UV sphere selected, change the Physics Type from Static (which means the object is a nonmoving object) to Rigid Body (which means it can now move).

Figure 11–3. *Rigid Body selection*

7.   Now, in the main 3D view, press P to enter Blender's game play mode.

Voila! You should see your ball drop and roll down the ramp in real time! Press Esc to exit game play mode.

■ **Note** There is a problem that can occur in the Blender game engine resulting in some objects displaying as bright, white, shadeless forms. This problem seems to happen in GLSL display mode, when the shading mode of the 3D viewport is also set to Solid. To fix the issue, do either of the following: In the Properties panel, in the Shading area, choose either Multitexture or Texture Face instead of GLSL. Or, change the viewport shading mode of your 3D view to something other than Solid (Textured would be a good choice).

Exercise: Marble Slide

Make a marble slide like the one shown in Figure 11–4 by creating planks for the marble to roll down. Try to position the planks so that the marble does not fall off the edge until it hits the bottom.

If you want obstacles that react when they are hit (instead of being stationary), then you will also need to change their physics state from Static to Rigid Body. Experiment with different settings, such as Mass, to see the effects on your world.

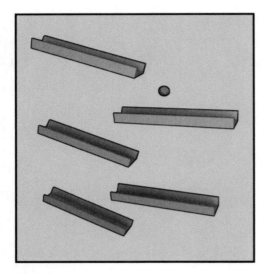

Figure 11–4. The marble slide challenge

Creating Your Own Droid

The game engine is of course more than a physics simulator. In order to live up to its name, it has to be interactive.

The game engine gets its interactive abilities from *logic bricks*, which provide a visual way of programming instructions and decision-making capabilities into Blender objects. Blender also supports Python scripting, although we won't be going deep into Python in this book. In order to start learning how logic bricks work, we are going to use them to program our own simple droid-bot, which we will be able to control through the keyboard.

Step 1: Making the Droid

Let's start making the droid:

1. Start a new scene and delete the default cube.

2. Insert a monkey and rename it Player.

3. Go to side view (numpad 3), select the monkey, and enter edit mode.

4. Select all vertices (press A) and rotate the monkey so that it is positioned in a way that will allow it to sit flat to the ground, as in Figure 11–5.

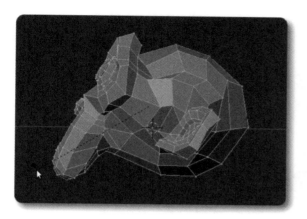

Figure 11–5. Rotating the monkey

■ **Note** The x, y, and z directions are critical to the game logic. By rotating the monkey in edit mode, you move the vertices of the mesh but not the actual object itself, so local z stays in an upward direction while the local y axis points straightforward or back.

5. Once you have rotated the monkey, enter object mode.

■ **Note** Just in case you used object mode instead of edit mode, select the monkey and press Ctrl+A to go to the Apply menu. From the list that shows, choose Rotation. This will cause the axis coordinates to reset even if you had rotated the monkey object in object mode. I know I'm being heavy handed here, but I really want to make sure the local coordinates of the monkey are correct; otherwise, the game engine could make the monkey fly off at odd angles.

6. Add a ground plane via Shift+A ➤ Mesh ➤ Plane.
7. Scale the plane so that it is large enough to resemble a floor (press S, type **7**, and press Enter).
8. Name the ground plane ground.
9. Raise the monkey a little above the new ground plane (in the z direction).
10. Give the monkey a new material, and change this to a bright green color (see Figure 11–6). Likewise, give the ground plane a new material and change it to a bright yellow (see Figure 11–7).

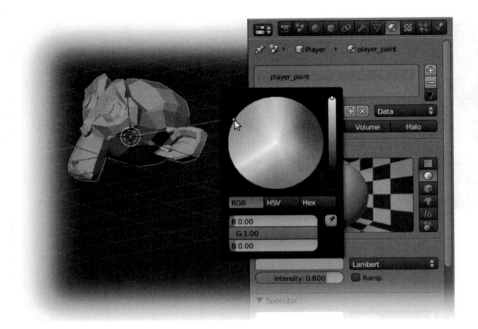

Figure 11–6. *Selecting a color*

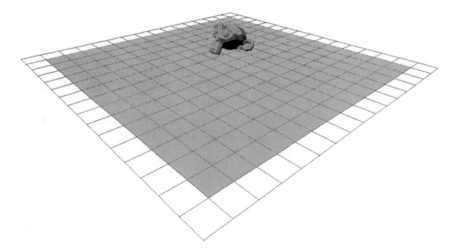

Figure 11–7. *The green monkey positioned over the yellow ground plane. The squares are Blender's viewport grid.*

11. Now we are going to add some user interaction to the monkey, so that we can move it around through the game engine. It is going to become our own remote-controlled droid! In the top header, change the rendering engine type to Blender Game (See Figure 11–8).

Figure 11–8. The rendering engine menu

12. With the monkey selected, go to the Physics tab and change the Physics Type from Static to Dynamic, as shown in Figure 11–9.

Figure 11–9. The Physics Type menu

13. Now press P to play the game engine (make sure your mouse is over the 3D view when you do this), and you should see the monkey fall to the ground plane. Press Esc to exit when done. It may not fall all the way down, and you might like to change its Radius setting in the Physics panel to 0.5 or thereabouts to get convincing results. This is a very rough spherical estimate of its size.

14. If you want more accuracy, go further down the Physics tab, and in the Collision Bounds panel set the bounds as Triangle Mesh. Doing so causes Blender to take the full mesh shape into consideration, whereas until now Blender had only roughly worked out the size of the monkey as a spherical estimate. Calculating the full mesh is more difficult for the computer to work out, considering that everything needs to be calculated in-game on a per-frame basis. Of course, this also depends on the complexity of the mesh.

15. Now that your monkey droid is physically active (it responds to gravity, at least), it's time to plug in some controls. Split the windows and make a new view of type Logic editor. This window needs to be fairly large, taking up the lower half of your screen. Alternatively, in the Screen menu in the main header, there is a ready-made Game Logic layout setup that lays everything out nicely (see Figure 11–10).

Figure 11–10. Choosing the Game Logic layout

■ **Note** Choosing a predefined Game Logic screen doesn't set the render engine, so double check that it is displayed as Blender Game (as shown previously in Figure 11–8).

Step 2: Setting Up the Logic Bricks

The Logic editor is the brains behind the game engine. It provides instructions to each active object on an individual basis. Whether it be a spaceship moving to player key presses or an alien bouncing from side to side while shooting missiles at random intervals, each item has its own individual set of game logic instructions to follow, making it possible to have multiple events happening all the time.

The Logic editor works as a list of instructions. Each instruction is normally broken into three parts: a sensor (to the left), a controller (in the middle), and an actuator (to the right), as shown in Figure 11–11.

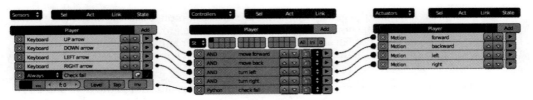

Figure 11–11. A stack of logic bricks

For a breakdown of the three categories of logic bricks, study Table 11–1.

Table 11-1. *Definitions of Logic Brick Types*

Logic Brick Type	Description
Sensor	This is the *if* or *what if* part of the instruction. It's the trigger. For the instruction *If the player presses the spacebar, then launch a rocket*, the sensor would be the ability to detect whether the spacebar is being pressed.
Controller	Between the *if* of the sensor and the *then action* of the actuator, controllers are a bridge where extra conditions may be evaluated in order to properly evaluate the correct resulting task. In most cases, controllers acts as a big *or* gate, allowing data to pass from the sensor straight through to the resulting action of the actuator. Sometimes, though, there may be several conditions that need to be met for an actuator action to happen. For example, we might modify the instruction from *If the player presses the spacebar, then launch a rocket* to *If the player presses the spacebar* **and** *their ship is still alive, then launch a rocket (resulting action)*. In this case, two sensors—the *spacebar press* sensor and the *player alive* sensor—would feed into the controller, which will only allow the signal to the actuator if both conditions are met. Similar logic would be applied to a vehicle in a game. Pressing the accelerator button warrants that we want the car to move forward, but this should only happen if the wheels are also touching the ground.
Actuator	This is the final action of an instruction/decision. It could be anything from making an object turn around or change speed, to bigger events such as restarting a game level or broadcasting a signal to spark off other sensor/controller/actuator reactions.

With that knowledge, let's make the monkey into our own remote-controlled droid-bot.

1. Make sure the monkey is selected.

2. We are going to use a sensor to detect when the up arrow of the keyboard is pressed. Go to the Sensors panel. In the Add Sensor pull-down menu (Figure 11–12), choose Keyboard from the list of available inputs.

Figure 11-12. *Add a new sensor.*

3. Among the new options that appear, click in the Key field. You should be greeted with the message "Press a key" in the Key field. At this point, press the up arrow on your keyboard, and "Press a key" will become "Up Arrow."

4. Change the name from Keyboard to "UP arrow" (this will be all you see when the sensor is minimized).

5. Sensors, controllers, and actuators can really build up over time, so it pays to minimize them in order to prevent overcrowding the screen. Minimize the sensor by clicking the top-left button, as shown in Figure 11–13.

Figure 11–13. Completed "Up arrow" sensor with minimize button circled

6. Add a new And controller by clicking the corresponding Add Controller menu. There are no real changes needed from the default.

7. Add a new Motion actuator in the actuator menu.

■ **Note** The number of options available depends on the type of object selected. For example, if you were to toggle between Static and Dynamic, you would see that there are less actuator options showing when the object's physics type is set Static than when it is set to Dynamic.

In terms of the y axis, the monkey happens to be facing backward, against the direction of the green arrow. Therefore, when we want to move it forward in response to the up arrow being pressed, it will be in the negative y direction.

Be careful not to mix local and global (world) coordinates. Local coordinates change when an object is rotated, whereas global coordinates align to the world space. You can switch viewing modes for global and local in the proper menu in the 3D view window header, as shown in Figure 11–14. With local coordinates enabled, you will see that the manipulator arrows turn with the monkey object if you rotate it.

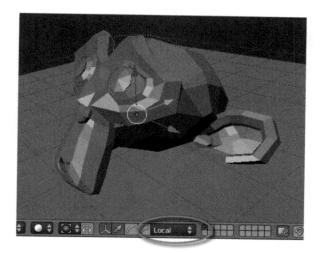

Figure 11–14. The monkey is facing in the local negative y direction (against the green arrow).

There are a number of different motion types available in the actuator options, though for now we want to make the second Linear Velocity value –5. The three different values correspond to the speed in the x, y, and z directions, respectively; hence the Y value is the speed in the y direction. Check the *L* to the right to let Blender know it should apply the force to the local axis of the monkey (as opposed to the global y axis). These changes are circled in Figure 11–15.

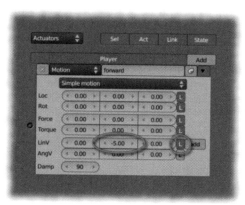

Figure 11–15. Use local linear velocity to control the forward movement.

The sensor, controller, and actuator are all set, but you need to connect them together. At each end, there are small dots for linking them. Simply LMB-drag from one dot to the next to combine the logic bricks. Should you ever need to disconnect the logic bricks, hold down the Ctrl key and LMB-drag a line through the connecting wire.

If you have everything set up right, the expanded logic bricks should resemble that shown in Figure 11–16.

Figure 11–16. Logic bricks (expanded) for the up arrow/forward movement

Let's give it a go:

1. Put the mouse over the 3D view.

2. Press P to test the play and see whether the up arrow makes the monkey move forward. If everything is OK, press Esc.

3. If anything goes wrong, check the logic brick connections and also that you have set up a value different from zero in the velocity field.

4. Now you need to set up the other conditions for moving the monkey in the other directions. First, minimize the previous logic bricks to preserve vertical space.

5. Add another sensor, controller, and actuator.

6. Configure the new sensor so that it utilizes the down arrow.

7. Configure the new actuator so that it feeds a value of +5 into Linear Velocity. Check the *L* to ensure this is a local translation.

8. Link the three new logic bricks together.

9. Press P and test that the forward and backward movements are both working.

10. Finally, add another two rows of logic bricks for turning the player left and right. Assign the sensors to the side arrow keys. This time, instead of having the actuators feeding into the Linear Velocity values, have the actuator feeding from the left arrow key add 0.1 to the Rot Z value (this is the third column of the Rot row, given that the values represent x, y, and z, respectively). Likewise, the right arrow key should be wired to a Rot Z value of –0.1.

Figure 11–17 shows the full setup of your current logic bricks.

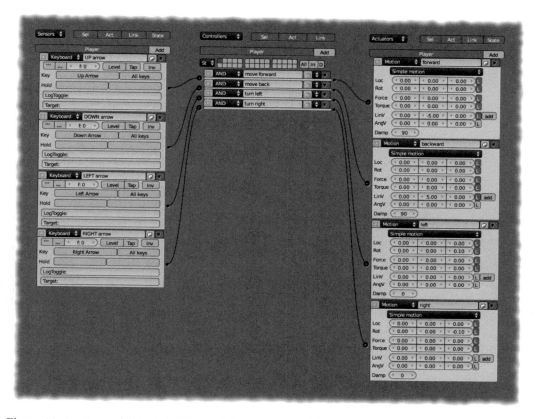

Figure 11–17. *Expanded logic bricks of all four directional keys*

Press P to play with your new droid. Hopefully it drives well, although you can change settings to adjust to your own taste.

Step 3: Dealing with the Falls

The problem with the current setup is that when you drive the droid over the edge of the ground plane, it just falls away and disappears. It would be better if it were reset to the starting position when it goes over the edge. There are a couple of ways to accomplish this:

- Creating a logic brick safety net
- Using Python

We need a way of detecting when the droid falls over the edge, and of putting it back at the starting position.

Method 1: Creating a Logic Brick Safety Net

One of the available sensors is Touch. Using this sensor, we can create an invisible safety net that sends a signal to reset the droid back to the starting position whenever it falls over the edge and collides with (or touches) the net. The touch sensor works by detecting whether an object has made contact with a specific material. Let's add it now.

1. Create a new plane, and resize it about 20 times, so that it's big enough to ensure it will catch the falling droid. Place it in position below the ground plane, as shown in Figure 11–18.

2. Create a new material for the new plane. Give the material the name death.

3. On the Physics tab for the death plane, check the Invisible property. This will ensure that you don't get to see it during game play.

Figure 11–18. *Under the yellow ground plane is a much bigger safety net, ready to catch the falling droid.*

4. Now to set up the logic bricks. With the monkey selected, set up a sensor of type Touch.

5. In the Material field of the sensor, type death (or whatever name you gave the material of the safety net). Notice that as you type into this field, Blender gives a list of suggested materials, so you only need to LMB-click from the list.

6. Set up an And controller and an actuator, and link the three logic bricks together.

7. Set the actuator to type Game. Then, where the actuator reads "Start new game," change this to "Restart this game."

8. Of course, make sure the sensor, controller and actuator are linked like the ones in Figure 11–19.

9. The "Restart this game" actuator works by reloading the file, so save the game before playing.

Figure 11–19. *Touching the death material forces a game restart.*

Now, when you press P to run the level, you can see that when the droid leaves the ground plane, the level restarts, allowing you to continue play. This is good for checking that your sensor and setup actually work, but restarting the whole game isn't the most elegant method to reset the player.

We're going to use an actuator that repositions the droid back at the start, but since it only handles one of x, y, or z, we're going to need three of them.

1. Back in the logic bricks, change the existing Game ➤ "Restart this game" actuator to one of type Constraint. (Click the primary menu button reading Game and choose Constraint from the list.)

2. Add another two actuators of type Constraint. By default, constraint actuators are set up to control location, which is what we want. The three Constraint actuators will be used to adjust the location of the monkey to send it back to the starting position.

3. Within each of the three actuators is a Limit field, currently reading "None." Change this on each of the actuators so that the first one is Loc X, the second is Loc Y, and the last is Loc Z.

4. For refreshing the droid in the middle, it's fine for x and y to be set to zero. However, we want the droid to restart slightly above the ground, perhaps falling downward onto the ground plane as it reenters the scene. On the third actuator (with the Loc Z property), change both the Min and the Max values to 1.5.

5. Connect the sensor to the controller. Also connect the controller to each of the three actuators, as shown in Figure 11–20.

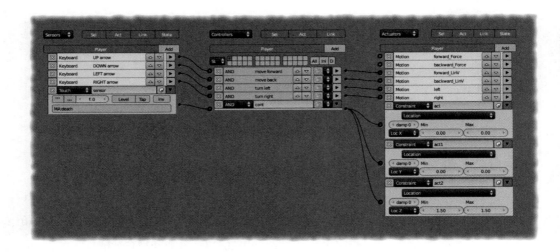

Figure 11–20. *Logic bricks modified so that now touching the death material resets the ball xyz location*

Constraint actuators work by setting minimum and maximum boundaries for how far an object can move along a given axis. By setting the boundary limits to the starting position (we have set definite x, y, and z limits), the monkey object is forced to return to the physical space within that area. Once the monkey droid is back to the starting position, it is no longer touching the death material, and the constraint restriction is lifted, allowing the droid to freely move around again.

Finally, press P once more to test your level.

Method 2: Using Python

The method of adding a safety net mesh with a Touch sensor and constraint actuators works, but it's long winded and not the most efficient way of working. Surely it would be simpler to just tell Blender, "When the z value of the object hits –3, reset the x, y, and z values to 0, 0, and 1.5," all in one simple sentence . Sooner or later, there are going to be things you want Blender to do in a game, but the actuators you are wanting won't have been implemented.

Blender users who use the game engine a lot rely on a powerful scripting language, Python, to code the game and make the game engine do exactly what they want it to do. We are not going to study Python in any real depth in this book, although I'll show you enough to use it as an alternative to the safety net method.

■ **Caution** The following steps assume you have *not* made any of the actuators outlined in the previous method (e.g. making a net with special death material to catch the fallining Player).

To write Python code, you need a text editor window open. If you used the standard Game Logic layout, then this will already be open at the top right of your screen; otherwise, make a new window area and set the window type as Text Editor.

In the header of the text editor, follow the menu through Text ➤ New, and then carefully type the following into the main text editor window:

```
import bge
object = bge.logic.getCurrentController().owner

if object.worldPosition2 < -3:
        object.worldPosition = 0, 0, 1.5
        object.linearVelocity = 0, 0, 0
```

■ **Caution** When you are typing Python code, the indents (tabs or spaces before a line) are important! In the preceding example, the last two lines are both indented the same amount after the if statement. This indentation means that they are both conditional to the if statement. If you take away the indentation from the second line (object.linearVelocity = 0, 0, 0), then it is no longer part of the if statement, and therefore gets evaluated constantly, dragging the monkey item down to a crawl throughout the game.

The code works by assigning the owner of the current logic brick—that is, the *player*—to the variable object. It then checks whether the z position of the object is less than –3, and if so, resets the x, y, and z location values to 0, 0, and 1.5, respectively. It also sets the linearVelocity, or the speed of the object, to 0 in the x, y, and z directions, so that the monkey does not enter the scene already moving with the momentum it had when it left the playing field before. Note that Python arrays read the first value as 0 instead of 1; hence, the object.positionnumber reference refers to x as 0, y as 1, and z as 2.

The name of the code block you have written is reported in the header of the text editor window: by default, it will be called Text, but you can change it to whatever you like.

All that is needed now is for you to activate the Python script for use in the game.

1. Create a new sensor of type Always.

2. After sensors are activated by an event, they usually send only one *True* signal to the controller, but Blender can also *pulse* signals at a specified regular frequency if we need. By clicking the True Level Triggering button (labeled as "'''"), we tell the sensor to keep pulsing a True signal with the frequency set by the Freq value further to the right of the sensor. So click the ''' button now.

3. Add a new controller of type Python Script, click in the field to the right of the Script menu, and choose the Python script you have written in the text editor (most likely this will just be "Text," although you can rename it). Your setup should look something like Figure 11–21.

■ **Note** The Python controller doesn't need to link to an actuator because it is the controller script and takes the action (see Figure 11–22).

4. Press P to test your result.

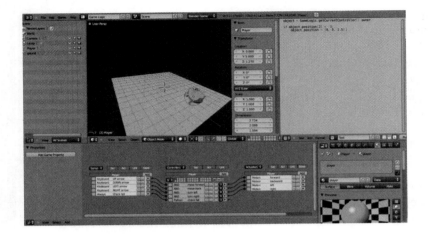

Figure 11–21. The Python layout with a working script

Figure 11–22. You do not need an actuator to call Python scripts. It is done in the controller.

Step 4: Debugging the Movement

A little experimentation reveals that the linear velocity movement of our droid is less than ideal. For example, if the player keeps the forward button pressed, then the droid moves forward without dropping down much until the button is let go. If you have used the safety net method for detecting falling, this makes it possible for the droid to overstep the net.

Fixing such issues is a normal part of game design. In this case, there are three immediate solutions:

- You could extrude the safety net edges upward into walls that are higher than the floor. Now there is no way for the droid to glide over them.

- At the same time as manipulating the `linearVelocity` value for the local y direction, you could add a `linearVelocity` for the z direction, making the droid move downward. This will have little or no effect while the droid is on the ground, because it can't move through the ground plane, and yet it will ensure that the player falls when the forward key is being pressed.

- Instead of using `linearVelocity` to move the droid forward and back, you could use the Force value. This works with more of a pushing action and does not affect the downward movement like the `linearVelocity` method. Because force builds up, this method of movement has a tendency of accelerating.

Step 5: Setting Up a Chase Cam

By pressing numpad 0 you change the 3D view to the camera view and the game will play from the point of view of the camera. A useful trick is to now make the camera follow your droid around. Blender has a built-in chase cam function that you can use for this.

1. Select the camera.

2. Add an Always sensor to the camera, an And controller, and a Camera actuator.

3. In the actuator, choose Player from the Camera Object option. This is the target that the actuator will follow.

4. Now the camera will follow the droid, but it will be far too close. In the Camera actuator, define the distance the camera is to stay behind the droid. Set the Min and Max values in the actuator so that the camera keeps a sensible distance (e.g., a Min of 10 and a Max of 15).

5. You should also set the Height field to something like 5 so that the camera looks slightly down on its target from above. See Figure 11–23 for the final setup.

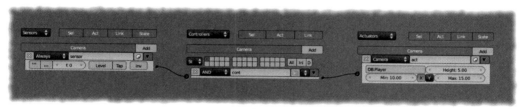

Figure 11–23. *Setting up a chase cam*

Silly Soccer Game

We are now going to make our first game: a simple soccer simulation between two players who try to hit a ball into the goals at either end of the playing field.

Step 1: Making the Playing Field

The first thing we need to do is make the playing field.

1. Start with the default cube.

2. Scale the cube seven times along the x and y axes (press S, press Shift+Z, type **7**, and press Enter). Note that pressing Shift+Z tells Blender to scale perpendicular to the z direction, meaning that it scales in both the x and y directions.

3. In edit mode and face select mode, select the outer faces of the cube (the walls, but not the ceiling or floor faces). Extrude these outward in the following way:

    a. With all four faces selected, press E and then Esc. This will create an extrusion all around, but pressing Esc means you won't move the faces at all, so you won't see any clear difference in the shape as yet.

    b. Scale the extrusion outward by pressing S, pressing Shift+Z, typing **1.05**, and then pressing Enter. The result should resemble what is shown in Figure 11–24.

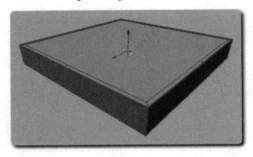

Figure 11–24. The extruded walls (highlighted in red) have been scaled outward along the x and y axes at distance of 1.05.

    a. Press A to ensure no faces are selected.

    b. Shift-RMB-select only the top edges of the extruded walls.

    c. Press E, type **1**, and press Enter to extrude them exactly one unit upward.

Written instructions like these are often difficult to follow. The main thing is you should have a playing field with walls similar to Figure 11–25.

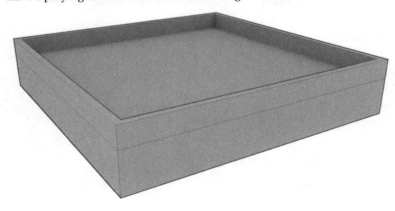

Figure 11–25. The completed Silly Soccer game field

Step 2: Making the Ball

Now we need to add a ball to the game:

1. In object mode, press Shift+A, choose Add Mesh ➤ Icosphere, and name it `ball`.

2. Scale the ball to half size (press S, type **0.5**, and press Enter).

3. Make sure the render engine is set to Blender Game.

4. On the Physics tab for the ball (Figure 11–26), choose a physics of type Rigid Body so that the ball will be able to rotate.

5. Still on the Physics tab, change the mass of the ball to 0.05 (make it light) and set the dampening values for both rotation and translation to zero. The dampening value recognizes that in the real world, objects don't instantly stop, but decelerate. How heavy an object is (and how much momentum it has) will affect the time it takes to slow to a halt. By turning the object's mass (weight) and dampening factor down, we cause the ball to change direction very quickly so the game doesn't appear sluggish.

6. Give the ball a new material, colored bright white.

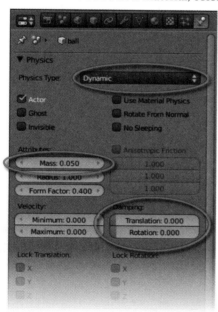

Figure 11–26. Ball physics settings

Step 3: Making the Players

There are going to be two players for this game, but in order to save time, we are going to make one character first, give it some movement controls, and then duplicate the whole character to make the other. This will save us the tedious tasks of manually re-creating a whole set of logic bricks all over again.

1. Create a cube and name it player1. The naming (including the case of letters) is very important to the game engine logic, so take care to always name things properly.

2. Scale the cube to half size along the x axis, and quarter size along its y axis. You could do this via the usual keyboard-shortcut method, but it might be easier to type the values right into the Scale fields of the Properties panel, as shown in Figure 11–27.

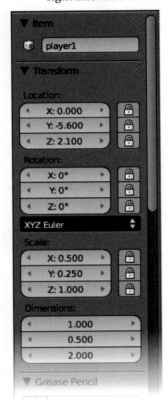

Figure 11–27. player1 scale settings

3. Pull the player1 cube back to the edge of the game field (to about an x value of 5.6) and slightly above the ground surface.

4. Set the physics of player1 to Dynamic.

5. Give the cube a bright green color to distinguish it for player1.

6. If you test the game by playing it (P key) you may find that the player drops through the floor a little. Change the Radius setting on the Physics tab to correct this. Most likely it needs to be set to 0.5.

7. Now it is time to add logic bricks to player1 so that it can move and push the ball around. Set up the player to move with arrow keys in a similar way to the droid in our earlier exercise. Forward and back movements should be given local linear velocities of 20 and –20, while the side arrows should turn the player through a Rot Z of 0.1 and –0.1. The logic bricks should look as shown in Figure 11–28.

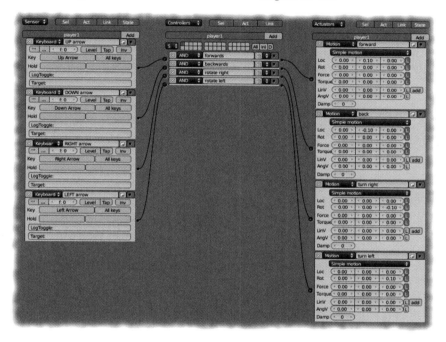

Figure 11–28. Player 1 movement

8. Test your game. You should be able to move around and bounce the ball of the walls.

Now, to make player 2, you could create another cube, resize it, reposition it, and add all the logic bricks for another set of keys—but it's much easier to just duplicate player 1 and make player 2 modifications.

1. Select player1.

2. Press Shift+D to duplicate.

3. The new player is, by default, called player1.001 (as shown in the Properties panel). Change this to player2.

4. Move player2 to the other side of the playing field.

5. Rotate player2 180 degrees around its z axis to make it face inward, toward the game.

6. Make a new color for player2—bright red—so that you can easily tell the players apart.

7. Go into the logic bricks of player2 and change the arrow movement to read from the following keys instead: W for forward movement, S for backward movement, A for turning left, and D for turning right (or use other keys of your own choosing). The sensors should resemble those in Figure 11–29.

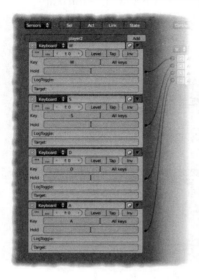

Figure 11–29. player2 movement sensors

8. Test your game, and you should be able to move both players around to chase the ball in competition.

Step 4: Making the Goals

Of course, it's not really a game unless we have some goals and are able to keep score.

1. Make a new cube, which will be a goal for player1 to hit. Give the goal a new material of a unique color (I suggest blue).

2. Name the blue-colored material for this object player1_goal (this is important!).

3. Scale and position the goal so that it pads the wall immediately behind player2, as shown in Figure 11–30.

Figure 11–30. Blue goal positioned behind player 2

4. The goal doesn't have to actually do anything other than have the appropriately named material. It is there for collision detection for when the ball touches it. The logic bricks to get the ball working are within the ball itself. With the ball selected, set up a touch sensor. Have this feed through to a controller, and then feed the controller out to two actuators (see Figure 11–31).

5. Have the touch sensor set up to detect the material `player1_goal`.

6. Set the resulting actuators up as constraint controllers: one for Loc X (location X) and the other for Loc Y (location Y). Both of these should have zero values, as this is where the center of the game field should be.

Figure 11–31. Logic bricks to reset the ball once a goal is scored

The game should now work so that the ball resets its position when a goal is scored.

Step 5: Setting Up the Score

All that is needed now is a score.

1. Select the `player1` character.

2. To the left of the Game Logic window should be a Properties section with a button reading Add Game Property. Press N to toggle this display if it is missing.

3. Click the Add Game Property button and change the name of the field reading "prop" to "score."

4. The type of property is currently Float. Given that scores don't need decimal places, change this to Integer, as shown in Figure 11–32.

Figure 11–32. Adding a "score" game property

5. Finally, LMB-click the blue "i" icon toward the end of the score property values. This makes it possible for the score to show on the screen once debug properties are enabled. The debug properties are normally used by game developers to keep track of various variables within a game so they can tell how things are working. We are taking advantage of this feature by using it as a simple means of displaying the score on the screen.

6. Go to the top of the screen and activate Show Debug Properties from the Game menu, as shown in Figure 11–33. Alternatively, you can also activate this setting in the Render tab, in the Performance area. The score, which has been marked to show for debugging, will now appear onscreen when the game is played. All that remains is to add up the points.

Figure 11–33. The Show Debug Properties option

7. Select the ball and go to the logic bricks. You already have a sensor/controller/actuator set for detecting when the ball has hit and for resetting the ball. You need another controller to message the player to increase their score by one point.

8. Add another controller and a new actuator.

9. Have the original goal-hit sensor connect to this new controller, and then to the new actuator.

10. Call the new controller `message p1`.

11. Assign the actuator as a Message type. In the To field, type **player1**, and set the Subject to "goal."

With the logic bricks now arranged like those in Figure 11–34, when the ball hits the goal, its position is reset, and it sends out a goal message to player1 so that its score can be increased. Incidentally, you may be wondering why I made another controller for this instead of just branching out from the previous controller. For now, that would work, but I'm thinking ahead for when we add the logic bricks for player2. The ball will reset its position on the field for either player scoring, but only one player will actually score each time, depending on which of the touch sensors has been triggered. For this reason, there needs to be a divide in the logic flow, so the reset position can be called every time, but the scores only at certain specified times. There are usually several different ways of achieving similar results, and my method should hopefully be very clear at the end.

Figure 11–34. Actuator for announcing a goal

Now that we know a message will be sent to player1 when it scores, we still need to make sure that player reacts by actually adding a point to its score total.

1. In the logic bricks for player1, add a new sensor of type Message, a new controller, and a new Property actuator, and have them feed into each other.

2. Set the sensor Subject field to "goal." This way, when the actuator sends the message we made before, this sensor will pick it up.

3. Change the actuator's first field type to Add. Set the Prop field to "score," and the Value field to 1. The Logic Bricks for player1 should be as shown in Figure 11–35.

Figure 11–35. player1 is set up to add the score on receiving a message from the ball.

4. Play the game and you should be able to score points with player1.

Set up `player2` in a similar fashion:

1. Give `player2` a "score" property.

2. Add a sensor/controller/actuator chain to `player2` where, just as with `player1`, the sensor of type Message receives the subject "goal," and passes a signal to a Property actuator that increases the score by 1. (Note that `player2` will not accidentally pick up on `player1`'s goals because the message from the ball is sent privately to a specific player as opposed to broadcast).

3. Make another goal for `player2` and place it over the other end of the field. Just be sure to give it a unique color (I suggest purple) with the material name `player2_goal`.

4. In the ball logic bricks, add the necessary bricks so that when the ball touches the `player2_goal` material, it will send the appropriate "goal" message to `player2`.

5. As stated before, the reset position for the ball needs to be triggered when either of the players scores a goal. To have each of them working, connect both goal sensors to the controller for the ball reset, and change the controller to an Or gate. Don't use And because this would require the impossible feat of both goals being hit at the same time.

Figures 11–36, 11–37, and 11–38 show my logic bricks for you to study, should your arrangement not work for some reason.

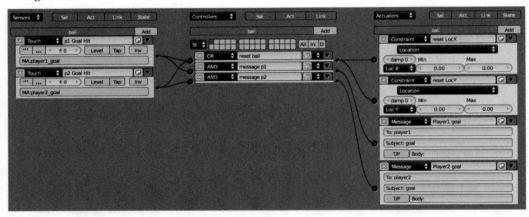

Figure 11–36. Logic bricks for the ball

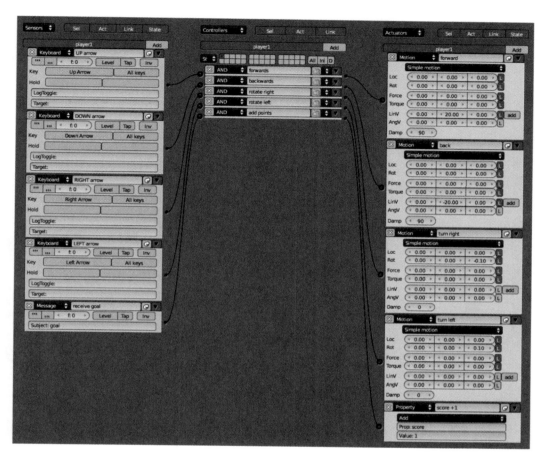

Figure 11–37. *Logic bricks for player1*

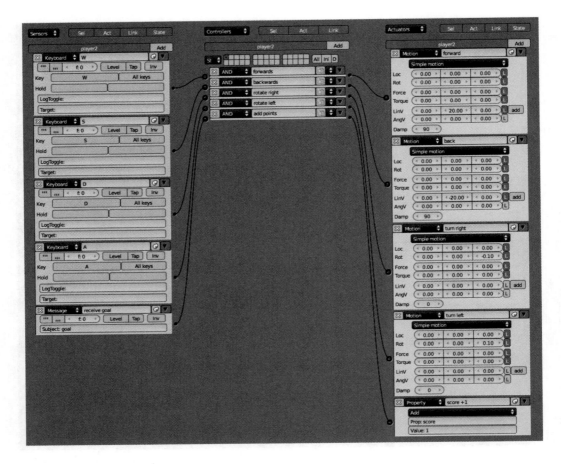

Figure 11–38. *Logic bricks for player2*

Step 6: Setting Up the Camera

Place the camera up high where it can see most of the field. By adding an Edit Object actuator set in track-to mode, you can make the camera follow the ball. Have it delayed by 1 second (25 frames) and the game will seem as though it is being followed like those on TV. You should also click the 3D button at the bottom of the Edit Object/Track To actuator to ensure the tracking works properly in 3D space; otherwise, the camera will only swing horizontally like a compass needle, as opposed to looking up and down toward its target. See Figure 11–39 for the logic bricks for the camera.

Figure 11–39. *Setting up a spectator camera*

Finally, you may notice that the ball occasionally leaves the field and falls, ending the game in an awkward way. Should this happen, you might like to employ the techniques we used in the droid exercise to make the ball reset in the middle of the playing field so the game can resume. Alternatively, you could place some Always constraint actuators on the ball (one each for x and y) to make sure it can't go beyond the walls of the playing field.

The game is now complete. You should have two goals and a ball, as in Figure 11–40. Grab a partner and play the game—have fun.

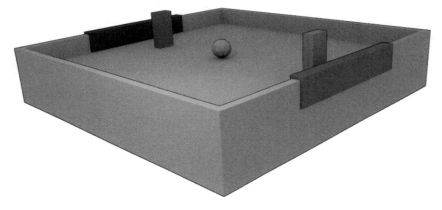

Figure 11–40. *The finished game*

A Change of Scene

Most games aren't just one scene; they can be many. Games often have progressive levels. These are *scenes*. There are often separate screens to jump to, like the title screen, the game screen, and the game-over screen. These also are different scenes.

Scenes are created in the main header. By default, there is one scene named Scene, and you can add others by clicking the + button to its right (see Figure 11–41). A new scene is like creating a new Blender file: Blender asks whether you would like to link or copy objects from previous scenes across to new ones, so they don't always have to start empty. (You can also access this option through the Object ➤ Make Links menu).

Figure 11–41. Make a new scene by clicking the + button.

To make scenes useful, you simply need to control their interaction through logic bricks. For example, you could have a special scene that the game jumps to when one of the players earns five goals. This might be set up as shown in Figure 11–42.

Figure 11–42. Logic bricks to trigger a scene change

1. Create a new scene from the top menu and call it game over.

2. Add some items so that you can recognize the scene. A couple of hints here: the "text" object tends not to show up in the Blender game engine, so go through the Object ➤ Convert ➤ Mesh from Curve/Meta/Surf/Mesh menu (or use the shortcut Alt+C) to convert any writing you want to display into polygons. Also, the Blender game engine tends to take its point of view for a new scene from the available camera, so make sure there is a camera in the scene and aim it appropriately.

3. In the first scene, select player1, add a new set of sensor/controller/actuator logic bricks, and link them together.

4. Set the sensor up to be of type Property, with a function of Equal (the default). In the Prop field, type **score**, and set the Value field to 5.

5. Have the actuator set as type Scene. Change its function to Set Scene, and in the SCE field, type in the name of the destination scene (game over).

Now, when player1 scores five goals, the game will jump to the game over scene. Of course, you will need to also set things up for player2. You could have different scenes for when each player wins, or you could have them both go to a generic scene. In that scene, you could have Blender wait until a key is pressed to restart the application.

Shooting Things

So far, what you have learned gives scope for games consisting of objects that bump into each other and may be controlled by different keys on the keyboard. Many games involve the option of shooting things, and the chances are that you will want to know how to make some kind of a gun that fires a bullet, so I thought I should write a section explaining how you might go about that.

The basic idea behind making a bullet is that it spawns inside the gun barrel when the fire key (e.g., the spacebar) is pressed, and continues to move forward, shooting out from the gun to wherever the gun is aiming when the fire key is pressed.

Step 1: Creating the Bullet

The first thing we need to do is make a bullet that constantly shoots forward. This might seem like a premature action for the bullet to be taking (it hasn't even been fired yet), but the idea is that later on, whenever the fire key is pressed, a new bullet will be spawned from the gun; so in effect, if a bullet is there, it should always be moving.

1. Create a small bullet item (a tiny cube will do) and name it `Bullet`.

2. Select the bullet object so you can add some logic bricks.

3. We now need to make the bullet so that it shoots forward. First, with the bullet selected, go to the Physics tab and change the physics type from Static to Dynamic. This will allow the bullet to move in the game.

4. Check the Ghost option to ensure that the bullet won't bounce off other objects at odd angles (the Ghost option means that it would go through them, which is the lesser of two evils in most cases).

5. In the logic bricks, create a new Always sensor, an And controller, and a Motion actuator. Wire them together.

6. Set the linear velocity of the Motion actuator to make the bullet fire. New Blender users often find it difficult to figure out which axis (x, y, or z) should be used for the forward direction of the bullet. You can get an idea by looking at the manipulator arrows for the bullet object when the Transform Orientation is set to Local, or you can use trial-and-error. In my case, I set the linear velocity to –40 in the local y direction (make sure it is local by clicking the L at the end of the Linear Velocity row in the Motion actuator).

7. If you press P now, the bullet should shoot forward, moving on forever. While it is fine to have the bullet moving, we don't want it to keep going nonstop like this. If we let this happen, the game will soon be filled with many bullets, and before long it will start to lag as it constantly tries to keep track of them all. Therefore, it's a good idea to have the bullet disappear a short time after it has been fired, perhaps about 2 seconds.

8. Add a Delay sensor, an And controller, and a new Edit Object actuator to the bullet object, and wire them together.

9. Set the Delay field at the bottom of the Delay sensor to 120 (this is measured in *logic ticks*, which are taken at a rate of 60 per second).

10. In the Edit Object pull-down list of the Edit Object actuator, choose End Object. The logic bricks for the bullet object itself should look like those in Figure 11–43.

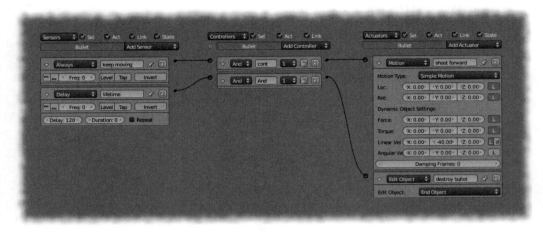

Figure 11–43. *Logic bricks for the bullet object*

11. On pressing the P key, the bullet now moves as before, but this time it disappears after a couple of seconds.

12. Now that the bullet object is made and working, place it onto layer 2 or another hidden layer (use the M key).

Step 2: Setting Up a Bullet Emitter Object

It is important that the bullets come out of the gun barrel, so they need to be lined up properly. One way of doing this is to add an empty (a nonmesh object, therefore invisible) that sits inside the gun and emits the bullets. By parenting this bullet emitter to the gun itself, the bullets will change direction according to how the gun is aimed.

1. Create a new empty object (Shift+A Add ➤ Empty) and rename it to `Bullet_Spawn`.

2. Position the `Bullet_Spawn` object so that it resides inside the gun barrel (Figure 11–44). You can resize it if you like, as the size will not affect the bullets; the empty is here only to influence the initial location and direction of the bullets emerging from the gun.

3. Parent the `Bullet_Spawn` empty to the gun object so that in object mode or when playing the game, if the gun moves, it takes the empty along with it, including the direction of aim. To do this, RMB-select the `Bullet_Spawn` empty, and then Shift-RMB-select the gun, press Ctrl+P, and choose to parent to object when prompted.

Figure 11–44. Positioning the empty at the gun (the mouth) of my spaceship

4. With the `Bullet_Spawn` empty selected, add the logic bricks of a Keyboard sensor, an And controller, and an Edit Object actuator, and wire them together.

5. For the Keyboard sensor, click the Key field. When it reads "Press a key," press the spacebar (or whatever key you wish to use as the fire button).

6. The Edit Object actuator should already have a default Edit Object field of Add Object. If not, change the value to this.

7. Click the Object field box and select Bullet from the list of objects that appears.

The final arrangements for the logic bricks of the `Bullet_Spawn` empty are shown in Figure 11–45.

Figure 11–45. Logic bricks for the empty object/emitter

And that should be it. Now when you play the game, each time you press the fire key, the gun (or ship) should fire another bullet. By giving the bullets a unique material, you can make other items detect whether they have been shot through the Touch sensor.

Note that this technique only works when the original bullet is on a hidden layer; if you show both layers, the bullet spawning will no longer happen.

Exercise: Shooting Spaceship

Now that you know how to make firing bullets, see whether you can make a spaceship that flies around shooting bullets at the same time. You will probably want to include a chase cam to follow your ship around while you fly it.

Summary

This chapter has covered enough of the Blender game engine for you to make simple games using logic bricks. This is, however, only scratching the surface of the real capabilities of the game engine, as it would require something more of an entire book to do it real justice. Many Blender game developers would agree that to get real value out of the game engine, you should learn the Python scripting language.

Still, I'm hoping that you found the experience fun, and that it will give you the confidence to explore more of Blender. Blender does seem to get bigger and bigger the more you look into it. While I have tried my best to explain things in simple steps, it is likely there are areas we have looked at that are still a little unclear. In the next chapter, I'm going to address the more common problems beginners have when they start using Blender, and I'll be suggesting some great free resources to help you further your knowledge beyond what this book has covered.

CHAPTER 12

■ ■ ■

Going Further

I would like to say thank you for purchasing this book and for taking the time to read through the material. As I write these chapters, I have an increasing awareness of what I'm *not* saying. There are things that I might have been able to explain in more detail, or simply things at the back of my mind that I know I have missed.

No doubt, as you explore further, you're going to discover a number of things that have not been discussed so far. This is good, because I want this book to point you in the direction for self-learning.

Considering Blender's modeling capabilities, its powerful texturing tools, what it can achieve in terms of rigging and animation, its complex physics engine, its capabilities as a powerful video-editing suite and advanced node-based compositor, and its sophisticated game engine, Blender is a very big program.

For certain, when you use a complex package like Blender, you will immediately begin to hit problems here and there. This is normal, and even very experienced Blender artists have regular problems to solve. It's part and parcel of creating in 3D.

So, in anticipation that you will have some hurdles along the way, I've collected some common problems and their solutions to help you.

Once I have worked through the answers to these common issues, I am also going to give you a good list of resources from which you can continue to develop your knowledge of Blender.

Common Problems

When I first started looking at Blender, I had been searching the Internet for programs to make computer games with. My search resulted in some interesting finds, and Blender was cited as being a package for making 3D games. I liked the sound of that. Being the sort of person other people turn to in order to troubleshoot their word-processing issues, and someone who has taught himself programming from the age of ten (my Sinclair ZX81 days), I was confident that I'd soon be able to figure out this new Blender program by experimentally punching each button to see what it did. How hard could it be?

Needless to say, Blender is one of the only computer programs I've ever faced that caused me to go away in the frustration of not being able to quickly master even the basic idea of its interface. It was only when I humbly returned (months later) with some tutorials that I was actually able to start making sense of Blender. And now, I'm hoping this book has been a door-opener for your own experience.

But what can I do, now that you have read the preceding chapters, to help you where you might next get stuck?

In order to solve this question, I visited the public BlenderArtists.org forums and posed the following question:

What are the most common troubleshooting problems people run into when they start using Blender? The sorts of things experienced users often overlook explaining?

I told them that I was writing this book, and that I wanted to end with a final chapter on troubleshooting the most common problems.

So, here is a summary of what the users of the BlenderArtists forums have said you'd most want to know.

Interface-Related Problems

This section outlines many common problems related to the Blender interface.

I'm trying to select items, but they won't select, and this funny circle keeps snapping to my mouse clicks.

In Blender, items are selected by RMB-clicking them. The circle you mention is likely to be the 3D cursor, which is repositioned with LMB-clicks. The cursor is good for marking where the next new object should appear; it can be used as a reference point for moving objects around with the snapping menus (Shift+S), and it is the center rotation point when performing spin functions. You can reset the cursor to the center of the main 3D grid by using Shift+C, although this also resets the overall point of view of the 3D window.

Can I select multiple items?

Yes, you can—by Shift-selecting them, or by using the B key to select a rectangular region of items (block select), or by holding down the Ctrl key and dragging the mouse around while holding down the LMB to perform a lasso select. Another interesting method of selecting is to use the C key. This causes the mouse to act like a brush, and selections can be made by LMB-dragging before pressing Esc to exit selection paint mode.

Can I edit multiple selected items?

This depends on what you mean by editing. By selecting multiple objects, you can perform a certain amount of object mode editing—that is, scaling, rotating, changing location, and so on, will work on all items as a group.

The last selected item is the *active* object of the group, and if you enter edit mode, you will only be editing the active (last selected) item—so the answer here is no, you cannot apply edit mode to two different objects at the same time. Workarounds for this would be to join objects together with Ctrl+J, but then you would need to break them apart afterward if you wanted them to remain separate. Joining objects and then breaking them apart can alter the location of their pivot point center (the orange dot, which represents the object's center).

You also need to be aware that objects inherit location, rotation, and scale transforms from any object they are parented to. This means that if the legs are parented to a body, then they will transform with that body at the object mode level.

What is the orange dot in the middle of my object?

It's the object's pivot point center and is really the heart of the object. All the vertices and faces of the mesh itself are simply additions to the center point unit. Take care not to move the mesh away from the center (which is easy to do in edit mode), or else you may find that object mode rotation appears to be off center, as the pink dot is the default pivot point for the rotation, scale, and location of any object. If you delete all vertices in edit mode, the pink dot still exists in object mode, and you know the object itself was not really deleted properly

For some reason, I can move my objects but not rotate or scale them. I haven't put on rotation constraints or anything like that.

You may have clicked the "Manipulate object centers only" button, next to the Pivot Point pull-down list (shown in Figure 12–1). This button is used to align selected groups of objects relative to each other. For example, when this button is active, if you have several objects selected and you rotate them, the result is that they orbit each other without any of the objects actually changing their own individual rotational orientations. Again, if this button is active and you select a group of objects and scale them, the objects will spread apart (or conversely move closer together), but the sizes of each individual object won't change. Because of the functionality of this button, rotation and scale of individual objects in the local sense becomes disabled when it is active.

Figure 12–1. The "Manipulate object centers only" button

Where did my window header go?

Normally, the window should have at least one header, either across the top or along the bottom. You can RMB-click this bar to switch its position or choose Maximize Area to expand it to full-screen (the same as holding down Shift with the mouse pointer over the window and pressing the spacebar). To revert from full-screen mode, RMB-click the header and choose Tile Area.

If you LMB-click and drag the header border into the header itself, you can sometimes completely collapse the header, virtually hiding it. When this happens, a little cross in a white circle will appear in a window corner where the header or panel used to be. When you need to make the header come back, just click the cross.

This same mechanism is used also for the Tool Shelf and the Properties panel.

The button or menu I'm looking for is missing.

There are two things that you should do:

- Check which mode you are in (edit mode, object mode, etc.).

- Check whether you have the necessary item selected; some options will only show when it is clear what they will be applied to (in Blender terminology, this is called *context*).

In the case of weight painting, you should select a bone in pose mode first, then Shift-select the mesh (which should have been in object mode the last time it was selected), and then change to weight paint mode. If you get this order wrong, the option to weight paint may be missing, or the bone will not be selected when you try to paint weights.

Viewport-Related Problems

My objects disappeared.

There are a number of reasons why objects or even entire scenes can suddenly disappear. Most of them are due to wrong key presses and are easily remedied.

- *Hiding/unhiding*: The Blender hide function is activated when you press the H key. The current selection—whether it be a full object or parts of an object, such as a few selected faces in edit mode—will disappear. With objects, the Outliner reveals whether something can be seen or whether it is hidden with an eye icon (click to toggle). To unhide everything, simply press Alt+H.

- *Layers*: Another reason things may disappear is if you accidentally skip to a layer different from the one you mean to be working on. Layers are represented by a group of squares in the 3D window header, like the ones in Figure 12–2, for all modes, with the exception of edit mode. The numeric keys along the top of your keyboard are shortcuts to navigate to the corresponding layers. Therefore, if things disappear (especially if a whole scene disappears), it makes sense to check which layer you are on.

Figure 12–2. *Layers*

- *Zoom out*: In the case of having simply moved your view too far away from objects to be looking at them, press the Home key to recenter all items into view.

- *Undo*: Failing the above, press Ctrl+Z (undo) a few times in the hope that if you actually did delete things it can be reversed.

- *Local view*: While the default view globally shows all objects, there is another local view that functions to make everything except selected items disappear from view, so that you can focus on just the chosen item(s). The shortcut for this is the numeric key numpad / (forward slash). As this key is a toggle, click it a few times to see whether missing items appear. The window description at the top left of any 3D view should read "(local)" when the local view is active. Also, in local view you will notice that the layers are not displayed in the header.

My model has gone all see-through.

The two most likely causes of this problem are

- The Occlusion button

- Viewport shading mode

Figure 12–3 shows three mesh objects as they might appear in the 3D view window while in edit mode. The leftmost object appears solid with no transparency. The middle object has partial transparency and is caused by releasing the Occlusion button. The rightmost object is very transparent and is the result of setting Viewport Shading to Wireframe.

Figure 12–3. Different types of transparency as shown in the 3D view

A more complete explanation follows.

- *Occlusion button*: The Occlusion button, also known as the "Limit selection to visible" button, is active (pressed down) by default. This button only appears in edit mode, and is located in the header of a 3D window, as shown in Figure 12–4. If the Occlusion button is deactivated, then any mesh in edit mode becomes partially transparent, allowing the user to select vertices that would otherwise be hidden on the far side of a mesh object. For most cases, it is better to leave the Occlusion button activated so you don't accidentally select vertices from the opposite side of a mesh. Accidentally deselecting this button may be the reason your mesh has become partially transparent.

Figure 12–4. The Occlusion button

- *Viewport shading mode*: If your mesh appears totally transparent, the most likely cause is that you've activated wireframe view mode by pressing the Z key, which is a common mistake when users try to move objects along around the z axis but fail to press G, S, or R beforehand (e.g., pressing G and *then* Z allows you to move selected items along the z axis, whereas just pressing Z activates wireframe mode). To get back to solid mode, either press Z a second time or use the Viewport Shading menu at the bottom of the 3D view window and select either Solid or Textured, as shown in Figure 12–5.

Figure 12–5. *Changing the viewport shading mode*

How do I easily move the view around to look at what I want?

Navigating the main view is done mainly with the mouse wheel (MW). Table 12–1 describes some of the main viewport functions.

Table 12–1. *Navigation Basics*

Viewport Function	Description
Roll MW forward and back	Zoom in and out of view
Shift-MW	Pan view up and down vertically
Ctrl-MW	Pan view across horizontally
Hold MW down and move mouse around	Trackball the main view
Shift-MW, and move mouse with MW held down	Pan in all directions
Ctrl-MW, and move mouse vertically with MW held down	Controlled zoom
Home key	Zoom out to look at all objects in the immediate layer
Numpad . (decimal point)	Zoom to view and center viewport on selected item (objects or mesh elements —vertices, edges, faces)

Table 12–2 illustrates the number pad shortcuts.

Table 12–2. Number Pad Shortcuts

Keyboard Shortcut	Description
Numpad 5	Switches between perspective and orthographic modes
Numpad 0	Camera view
Numpad 7	Top view
Ctrl+numpad 7	Bottom view
Numpad 1	Front view
Ctrl+numpad 1	Back view
Numpad 3	Left view
Ctrl+numpad 3	Right view
Numpad 2, 4, 6, 8 (numpad arrow keys)	Rotate view in steps

Note that the rotational shortcuts are positioned strategically, so that if you were in a four-way view, the positions of the number pad keys would correspond to the typical screen layout views. There is a dedicated "Toggle Quad view" button in the Properties panel that honors this setup.

How do I line the camera up to where I want it?

If you position your view so that you are looking at the render as you would like the camera to view the shot, simply press Ctrl+Alt+numpad 0 to make the camera switch to your view.

Alternatively, you can set the camera up to always view an empty with TrackTo. Select the camera first (the object in Figure 12–6), and then select the empty and press Ctrl+T, choosing "old track" when the option is asked. The camera will probably go off center in its rotation, so select the camera afresh and press Alt+R to reset its rotation. Now the camera will follow the empty, which you can then aim at whatever you want the camera to be looking at. When lining up a camera manually, it is a good idea to split the view to make a window for what the camera can see (press numpad 0 over this window to show the camera's point of view).

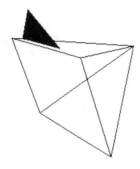

Figure 12–6. *The Blender camera*

File Management Problems

This section details many common file management problems.

Where did my saved render actually go?

For images, after you render with the F12 key, you'll be presented with the rendered image. From here you can press F3 to save the image to your hard drive. (You may then have to press Esc to get out of the render view and return to the normal Blender layout.) In a similar way, if you want to look at an previous render, press F11 to bring it back to your screen, and then press F3 to save the image. By default, Blender will try to save files where the .blender file resides.

For movies (rendered with Ctrl+F12), Blender will save in the result in a temp directory (e.g., /tmp/) unless otherwise stated (see Figure 12–7). On the Render tab, check the Output settings to specify a destination directory. You can also select the animation type (e.g., the format of image or movie to use) from this panel.

Figure 12–7. *Output settings for the render*

Blender never told me my work wasn't saved when I closed it! How can I get it back?

Blender shows an asterisk in the window title bar when current work is unsaved, but it does not warn you to save work when closing the file. If you do close a Blender session prematurely (without saving), Blender attempts to save a `quit.blend` file into a temporary directory (e.g., `C:\Documents and Settings\Local Settings\Temp\`, or `/tmp/`—different systems can vary). On the next run of Blender, if you follow the menu through File ➤ Recover Last Session, as shown in Figure 12–8, then you can often rescue the most recently worked-on file.

Figure 12–8. The Recover Last Session option

Should Recover Last Session fail, you may still be able to get some of your work back, as shown in the answers to the next two questions.

I've noticed there are .blend1 files in my project folders. What are they and can I delete them?

The correct extension for a Blender file is `.blend`, with no number afterward. Having a backup of files is one thing, but with complex 3D art, it's also wise to have successive backups in case you find yourself regretting changes you've made a few saves back. For this reason, Blender has a feature whereupon saving a file, the newest save maintains the ordinary `.blend` extension, while the previous version is renamed as extension `.blend1`, the save before that becomes `.blend2`, and so on, with the highest number representing the oldest save.

Blender will make up to 32 backup saves this way. You can specify the number of backups by going to the User Preferences window (use the leftmost button in a window header and choose User Preferences from the resulting menu), clicking the File tab, and entering the maximum number of backups into the Autosave/Save Versions field.

An alternative method for making multiple backups is when saving files (press Shift+Ctrl+S), press numpad + (i.e., the number pad "plus" key) when performing a repeat save. This will add a number to the end of the file name, or increment the number by 1 if it is already there. A file named `mymonster001.blend` will be renamed `mymonster002.blend` when numpad + is pressed.

How else can I recover work after a crash?

Blender has facilities for backing up your work at regular intervals. In the User Preferences window just mentioned, click the File tab and check Auto Save Temporary Files. This will cause Blender to maintain a regular backup of your work in the temporary directory, as specified in the Temp box in the same panels. These backup saves will have unusual names (i.e., `somenumber.blend`) and can be reopened afterward directly by Blender.

If your Blender session does crash, back these files up, and if the previously mentioned File ➤ Recover Last Session method does not work, you may at least be able to recover to an autosave that may have been taken not long before the crash. Note that you can also set the Timer value to specify how frequently you want the backup saves to occur (see Figure 12–9).

Once a file is recovered, don't keep it in the temporary directory. Save it in a secure place while you can.

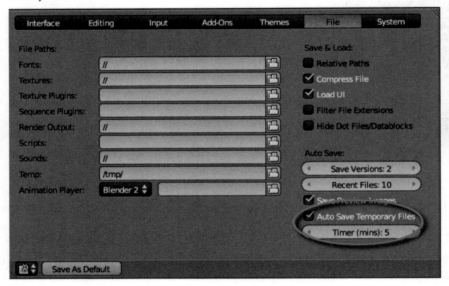

***Figure 12–9.** Settings to make autobackup files*

Can I combine Blender files into one?

Yes—although it requires a somewhat advanced understanding of what is inside of a Blender file. On the File menu, Blender has options to append or link objects from other files. Using these will allow you to navigate through any Blender file and select the components you wish to import from one file to the other.

What's the difference between appending and linking files?

- Appending will make a copy of the chosen element(s).

- Linking will create a link into the file itself, which will be updated whenever the corresponding element in the original file is altered.

You generally should append or link files by whole-object data rather than one piece of object data, because the full object contains multiple pieces (materials, modifiers, etc.) that are needed for the complete object.

Appending a file. To see how this all works, we'll now perform a simple example of appending a cube from one file to another. Begin by creating the first scene with the object you wish to append elsewhere.

1. Start a new scene.

2. Name the default cube `mymodel`. This will be the object we will add to the next file.

3. Give the cube a new material of a green color, so that it will stand out for this exercise.

4. Move the cube upward so that it is not at the default starting position. When we append/link files, their location/rotation/scale data can also be included as part of the append/link data. We are moving the cube so that it is not hidden from view if another object in the next scene happens to be taking up the same location in 3D space (e.g., the other default cube).

5. Save your work, naming the file `model01.blend`.

■ **Note** It is very important that you name the cube object. Not only will this make it easier to find, but if Blender is asked to import an object into a scene where another object of the same name already exists, the importing process will fail.

Next, we will create another file, and then follow the steps to append the `mymodel` cube from the first.

1. Create a brand new Blender file (File ➤ New).

2. Save this file near the previous one. For the purposes of this exercise, it will be easier to locate the target components from the first file (the `Mymodel` object) if both files are conveniently saved next to each other.

3. Follow the menu through File ➤ Append (press Shift+F1).

The next part can be tricky because not all readers will have directories in the same place. When the file dialog opens, you need to direct it to the directory where the two files were saved. There is a good chance that file path will start inside one of the files, and you will need to direct upward to the base directory. Don't click the Link/Append button yet; we still need to find the model we wish to import.

1. Direct the file dialog to the base directory where the files are stored (see the preceding paragraph).

2. Still in the file-finding dialog, LMB-select the `model01.blend` file.

3. Various internal Blender file directories will appear. Enter the one called Object.

You will see the available objects in the Blender file. Thankfully, we named the object we want to import, so it is easy to identify.

4. LMB-select `mymodel` and click the Link/Append from Library button.

You should now be back in the second file with the green cube from the first in plain view. The append has worked, and you should now have a copy of the green mymodel cube from the first file. The cube here is a copy of the one in the first file. You can do whatever you like to the cube in this scene; it won't affect the other file and vice versa.

Linking a file. To link the file (as opposed to appending), follow the same steps as before. However, instead of choosing File ➤ Append, choose File ➤ Link (or press Ctrl+Alt+O). Do not try to link the file into a scene where it has already been appended, as there could be a clash in the naming of items. Start with a fresh file.

When you have followed the steps by linking, you will end up with a similar result to when you used appending, except that you will not be able to move the linked object. Why is this? Because the new object is a direct link to the object in the other scene, and if that one hasn't moved, then neither will this one. That's all very fine if you want to link in unmoving objects like scenery, but there's a good chance you do actually want to move the linked object. To do so, simply do the following:

1. Select the linked object.

2. Follow the menu through Object ➤ Make Proxy (or press Ctrl+Alt+P).

After asking for confirmation, Blender will replace the linked object with a proxy object, which appears the same, but this time is able to be moved around (its location can be changed, it can be scaled and rotated, etc.) just like any other local object. The form of the proxy (the shape of the mesh, materials, etc.) is still linked to the original file, so you are unable to make edit mode–level changes. You can only perform object mode–type manipulations.

The really neat thing about linking files is that if you alter the original source file (e.g., the mymodel object from within the first file), then those changes will be carried through into the files linking to them. In a production pipeline, you could link models to a final scene so that modelers can make modifications to the individual props as separate files. When changes to the prop files are made, the result is immediately observable when reloading the final scene.

Using groups to manage linked files. The chances are you will not want to link one or two objects from a file, but several or even many. Importing them one at a time is a tedious business. Blender has a grouping system that can make the task a lot more straightforward. The idea is that you define a collective group of objects you want, and then in the destination file, you import the group instead of individual objects as before.

To create a group (in the source file with the objects you wish to export as linked or appended items), do the following:

1. Shift-select all the objects you want to be a part of the group.

2. Press Ctrl+G or follow the menu through Object ➤ Group ➤ Create New Group.

3. At the bottom of the Tool Shelf will be an area where you can change the group name. Type in something that sensibly describes the items you have in the group.

If you forget to include an item to the group, simply select that item, and on the Object tab, look down the panels for the Groups area. Here you will see an Add to Group button, as in Figure 12–10. Click this and you will be able to choose which group the item should be a member of. There is also a + sign to the right of this button that allows you to make a new group.

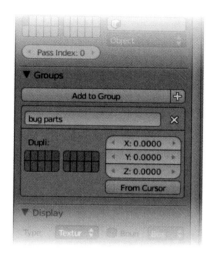

Figure 12–10. *The Groups area of the Object tab*

When your groups are made, remember to save the file before exiting. To append or link to the groups

1. In another file, go to File ➤ Append or File ➤ Link, as before.

2. This time, instead of following the Object folder within the Blender file, enter the Group folder, and you should see the groups you have named.

When linking to grouped items, you should not need to make a proxy, as this is done for you. There will be an empty in the center representing the group, and you should be able to perform object mode changes (e.g., location, scale, and rotation changes).

Surface Texture Problems

This section describes some common problems many users face with regard to surface texture.

I have black lines/faces on my mesh.

There are two main reasons for black lines or faces on a mesh:

*   Inverted face normals
*   Double vertices

Inverted face normals. The most common reason for black surfaces on mesh are that normals have been reversed (see Figure 12–11 for an example). Every face has a correct inside and outside. Given a strip of human skin, you can tell that the outer side has hairs on it. Computer skin is the same—it is meant to be textured from the correct side. When this is reversed, lighting reacts to the surface in the opposite of the intended way, causing strange black artifacts that may show up in the 3D view (depending on which view mode you are using) or even the final render, especially where the face settings are set to Smooth. When the view mode is set to texture, faces with reversed normals can appear invisible, as Blender only tries to color faces from the outside.

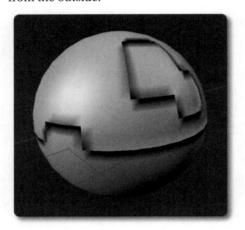

Figure 12–11. Black artifacts caused by reversed normals

Mesh normals are calculated from the direction of the closest face to the pink object center dot. If this dot is moved outside of the mesh or the closest face to the dot is facing inward instead of outward (e.g., it may be the model of a character's gums), then the normals could be miscalculated.

To remedy the situation, do the following:

1. Go into edit mode.

2. Select all faces.

3. Follow the menu through Mesh ➤ Normals ➤ Recalculate Outside (as in Figure 12–12).

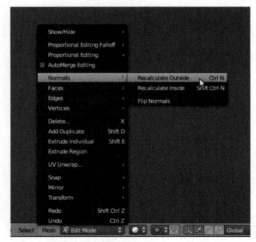

Figure 12–12. Recalculating normals

An alternative method is to go to through the Tool Shelf, which has a Normals area when you are in edit mode, with Recalculate and Flip Direction buttons. The Recalculate option works as described, whereas the Flip Direction allows you to reverse normals of selected faces manually.

You can see which way normals are facing by going into the Properties panel while in edit mode. In the Mesh Display area, there is a Normals part with options for displaying normals on faces or of vertex points. Normals work on a per-face basis, so for most purposes you would only need to enable the Faces option to see them. That done, Blender will display your object with normal vectors sticking out of each face, making your model look something like a pin cushion. A face with correct normals will usually have the normal vector sticking out of the face, whereas a face with incorrect normals will often have the normal vector going inward to the model.

Double vertices. The second common reason for black faces is having doubled-up vertices, or two or more faces sandwiched tightly together. If two faces are in exactly the same place, Blender may not know which face should be rendered, and weird artifacts will result. Both surfaces are likely to receive shadows from each other, and the surface area will become blackened. This happens a lot when users decide to extrude faces but then press Esc to cancel the move. The faces are extruded, but pressing Esc does not actually delete the extrusion—it merely prevents it from lifting from the mesh surface.

To fix doubled-up faces and vertices, select Mesh ➤ Vertices ➤ Remove Doubles (see Figure 12–13). You can also access this function from the Specials menu by pressing the W key.

Figure 12–13. Removing doubles

Having doubled-up faces can cause mesh normals to miscalculate. Therefore, when you notice black artifacts on the surface of your mesh, a good workflow is to

1. Select the full mesh in edit mode (press A).
2. Select Mesh ➤ Vertices ➤ Remove Doubles.
3. Select Mesh ➤ Normals ➤ Recalculate Outside.

My UV textures aren't showing in 3D view.

This is a big question, and was covered in Chapter 5. The things to look out for are that when unwrapping, you should have all vertices selected. After this, you need to be in a view mode that supports textures (e.g., textured mode or solid can both do it). Also, it can make a difference which shading options are selected in the Properties panel.

You may get better results with GLSL, Multitexture, or Texture Face, depending on which graphics card you are using. Make sure Textured Solid in the Properties panel is active if you want to see the texture in solid view (see Figure 12–14).

Figure 12–14. *Textured Solid option at the bottom of the Properties panel*

How do I get alpha (transparency) to work?

The important thing here is to check the Transparency box on the Material tab. Without this, alpha only fades to sky color, instead of true transparency, which allows you to see objects through each other. Once activated, transparency has two methods: a fast Z-based method that basically fades an object and a full-blown raytracing method, where transparent surfaces refract light, so a transparent sphere could be used like a lens, with the amount of distortion depending on the IOR value (Z transparency is much faster because it does not take light refraction into consideration). An example of this distortion is shown in Figure 12–15.

A common mistake with raytracing transparency is in having the depth value too low. This value is the number of times a single ray of light will refract (bounce) through the transparent items. If it is too low, then light may enter the material (e.g., glass), bounce around a bit, and never come out, leaving black splotches of darkened material.

Figure 12–15. To create distorted refractions in transparent materials, adjust the IOR values.

Shadows will also be very dark, even when they come through transparent objects, unless the material they fall on is set up to receive transparent shadows in its own Shadow option. It is easy to overlook needing to change the transparency properties of the transparent object material *and* the shadow properties of the shadow-catching material.

Physics-Related Problems

This section discusses common physics-related problems.

Why do my particles stop at frame 250?

There are two lots of time settings you need to be aware of when using particles. One is the time allocated in the particle settings, which includes Start and End for the emission time of the particles (in frames), as well as a Lifetime parameter for how long the particles last (see Figure 12–16); the other one is for the Start and End values of the standard timeline editor. If you adjust one set, you may need to fix up the other accordingly.

Figure 12–16. Particles have their own time-based settings.

Beware that editing the time range in the timeline is the same as editing it on the Render tab.

Can I Make a Self-Running Application with Blender?

I left this part out from Chapter 11, because while it is possible to make self-running applications, the process is not entirely complete in the latest official release of Blender 2.5, and there can be dependency issues when trying to port the final application to other computers. Nevertheless, it is an important question to those who would ask, so I'm including it now in the knowledge that there are likely to be people who will benefit from having the question answered even though there are some uncertainties with various parts.

Blender has until recently had an option to create self-running applications where all that was needed was to load your game file into Blender, and then follow the menu through File ➤ Save Game As Runtime.

At the time of writing, this feature has not yet been ported to the latest version of Blender. However, there is an add-on you can install to get this working. This add-on relies on your version of Blender including an executable called `blenderplayer`, which is only included with the Windows versions at this time.

If you have a compatible set up, here is how you can get the add-on to work:

1. Download the following add-on by Mitchell Stokes (Moguri):
   `https://svn.blender.org/svnroot/bf-extensions/contrib/py/scripts/`
   `addons/game_engine_save_as_runtime.py`.

2. In Blender, open a window of type User Preferences. Along the top, navigate to the Add-Ons tab.

3. At the bottom of this section, click the Install Add-On button, and locate the downloaded file.

4. The Add-Ons tab contains a list of add-ons currently available. You should now be able to find Game Engine: Save As Runtime included on the list. Check the box to the right of this entry to enable it.

5. Optionally, if you want the ability to saving self-running applications by default, click the Save As Default button at the bottom left of the window.

6. Load the Blender game file you wish to make run.

7. From the File menu, choose Export ➤ Save As Runtime to complete the operation.

This should result in your being able to save a self-running application of your game. Note that the created self-running app may not be truly portable. When using it on another computer, you may be greeted with an error that certain files are not found, like the one shown in Figure 12–17.

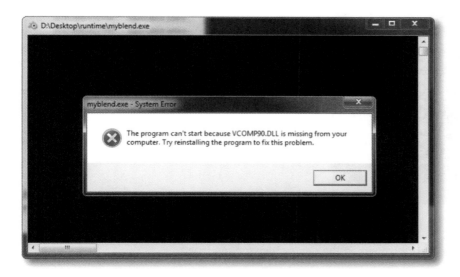

Figure 12–17. Dependency error

If you see these errors, go to the directory where Blender is installed (e.g., `C:\Program Files\Blender Foundation\blender-2.54-beta-windows32`) and you should be able to locate the missing files within. Simply copy them to the directory containing the self-running application.

On a Windows system, the files you need may include `avcodec-52.dll`, `avdevice-52.dll`, `avformat-52.dll`, `avutil-50.dll`, `SDL.dll`, `swscale-0.dll`, `vcomp90.dll`, `wrap_oal.dll`, and `zlib.dll`—but these requirements will vary depending on the system (Blender installations can vary even across Windows platforms).

Migration Problems

There have been a number of essential interface changes since the redesign of Blender. Many users have questions regarding certain features they used in the older versions of Blender but cannot seem to find in the newer versions. The following questions are among the most commonly asked when users try to migrate to the newer versions.

What happened to the old spacebar menu?

Using the spacebar to bring up the Add menus was common practice for many users prior to Blender 2.5. However, the spacebar ➤ Add menu has since been swapped with a new search feature where you can type in commands.

The old Add menu has not gone away, though. Instead, use Shift+A to bring up the Add menu (see Figure 12–18).

Figure 12–18. The Add menu is now accessed through Shift+A.

How do I merge/split windows in the newer Blender versions?

The older method of RMB-clicking window borders is now defunct. To split or merge windows in newer versions, place the mouse over the top-right or bottom-left corner of a window at a point where the mouse becomes a crosshair symbol. Hold the LMB down and drag the corner. If you drag outward, Blender will decide to merge windows, whereas dragging inward to the window makes Blender split the window. Once Blender is merging or splitting a window, you can still change the direction in which a merge/split occurs by then moving the mouse the other way. Pay attention where you click though, because you could accidentally LMB-click in the scene and move the cursor.

Can I open an old file without it spoiling my window layout?

When you load a file through the Blender menu, uncheck the Load UI option on the Recent list on the left (Figure 12–19). Then, when you load the file, Blender will load the scene, but won't make any changes to the UI layout.

Figure 12–19. The Load UI option

Resources

Throughout this book, I have refrained (within reason) from introducing too many programs, other than Blender itself. However, there are plenty of useful programs out there that will enhance your work with Blender, and so accordingly deserve a mention.

The next few pages outline some of the software that will be helpful to your toolkit as an animator or 3D modeler. The ones I am mentioning are chosen not only because they have quality, but also because they are freely available and, for the most part, available for multiple operating systems (e.g., Windows, Linux, and Mac).

After the software, I am also listing various web sites to further your study of Blender. Some of these offer ongoing tutorials, others are Internet forums where you can join a Blender community and get assistance and support directly. Others offer free Blender files you can use in your own projects.

Render Farms

When making a full animated production, it can take some time to render one image, let alone some 25 images for every second of film. If, for example, each image only took a minute to render, then each second of the movie would take nearly half an hour for a single computer render.

Render farms are a way to counter this issue. By using lots of computers, each simultaneously rendering different frames of the film, you can dramatically shorten this time. Just having two computers will halve the time it takes, and if you have dozens, or even hundreds, then it stands to reason that your production will be much more likely to meet its deadlines.

A good render farm will usually have one master computer as the core controller, with the other machines acting in the role of slaves, or rendering clients. The master computer takes the responsibility of giving the necessary files to these clients and allocating which ones are to render which frames of the movie. As clients finish their frames, they are given new jobs from the master until the all of the film is complete. This way, if a client crashes, other computers are given the next available frames, and the stalled client won't result in the project grinding to a halt. For this reason, render farms do not normally render to movie format (MOV, AVI, MPG, etc.), but as image sequence files, which can quickly be recompiled into movie format by other software (Adobe After Effects, Adobe Premiere, or even Blender's Video Sequence editor).

When using render farms, they need to run the same version of the software for consistent results. Also, some effects, such as particles and bullet physics, do not work well with render farms, and need to be baked as finished animations if the render farm is even capable of supporting the effects at all.

Render farms are often owned by industry animation studios with the finances to own enough dedicated computers to handle the task. Alternatively, you can also hire online render farm services that will render your uploaded project files and allow you to download the completed renders once the job is done, usually at a per-use cost.

Fortunately, there are free render farm services available. I have one of each type (a program for my own dedicated network and a community-driven online service).

The BURP Project

BURP (the Big and Ugly Rendering Project) is an online service you can use to render your Blender projects. It can be found at http://burp.renderfarming.net. Instead of paying for the use of the BURP online render farm, you can earn credits (by making your computer available for jobs) so that your own projects have priority in the queue along with everyone who wants a job done.

To utilize BURP's services, you have to download and run a BOINC client, which allows your computer to be included as one of the render farm slaves when your CPU is relatively idle (e.g., the render farm kicks in when you are away from your computer). This means that the more people who use BURP's services and allow their computers to be used as clients, the better the render farm gets! BURP usually includes its own version of Blender to ensure users are using the same compatible versions, so you may need to check that your own Blender files are compatible with the same version. You should also be aware that BURP effectively gives all clients a copy of your Blender files in order that they can help out with rendering frames, so if your project has copyright concerns, then you should seek a commercial alternative.

Loki Render

If you are fortunate enough to have several computers, there are a number of software render farm programs you can use over your own network. My personal favorite is the Loki Render program (http://loki-render.berlios.de), which is shown in Figure 12–20.

Not only does it support multiple platforms (Windows, Linux, and Mac—and these can combine for a single project), Loki Render has to be the easiest render farm I've ever seen to set up.

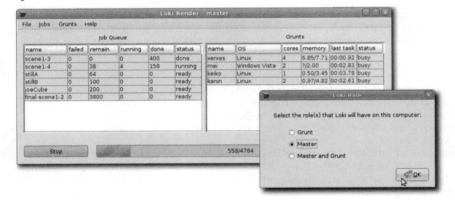

Figure 12–20. Loki Render

Simply create a directory on the master computer that is publicly shared (read and write accessible) by all clients. The Loki software, along with your Blender project files, should go into this directory (that's right—Loki Render only needs to be on the master computer, as long as the slave computers can all see it and use it). Each computer runs Loki Render from there, and is asked whether it is a master or a grunt (slave). The slave computers stand idle while waiting for jobs, whereas the master computer is given an easy interface from which to choose jobs to start rendering. The process of electing which grunts render which frames is automated by the Loki Render program.

Sound Editing

Audacity (http://audacity.sourceforge.net) is an open source sound editing program. What Blender's Video Sequence editor is for movies, Audacity is for sound files. You can make cuts, layer several files together, perform volume corrections, and apply a wide range of filters such as wah-wah, echo, and reverse (to name a few). Audacity imports and exports a wide range of sound formats. I tend to use Audacity alongside Blender as my main sound mixer, giving me a single WAV file for importing into my final animation mix.

Paint Programs

Blender is 3D, but textures are 2D. While Blender is capable of some impressive texturing techniques, such as projection painting, to really touch up your textures you're likely to want a decent paint program.

GIMP

GIMP (www.gimp.org) is a very capable open source paint program, similar to Photoshop (see Figure 12–21). GIMP has a wealth of features like handling layers, a wide range of brushes, and a great number of filter effects. Unless I'm specifically wanting a particular feature from another graphics program, GIMP is usually what I rely on to be able to deliver the 2D tools I am after.

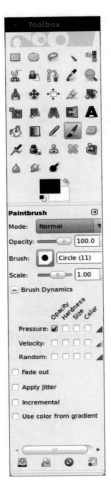

Figure 12–21. The main GIMP toolbox

MyPaint

MyPaint (http://mypaint.intilinux.com) is a paint program with an aim at presenting a canvas and tools that are more realistic than those offered by more standard paint programs. The natural feel of MyPaint makes it ideal for concept art, and it has been used extensively in the development stage of the latest Open Movie, *Sintel*.

Alchemy

Alchemy (http://al.chemy.org) is a rather different art program. This program makes random yet user-definable accidents happen while you paint, in order to create new and unexpected forms. It's strangely helpful in the concept design stage, when you need to come up with some genuinely unique design ideas. Like MyPaint, Alchemy was used to generate some of the concept artwork in the recent *Sintel* movie.

Vector Drawing

Inkscape (http://inkscape.org) is an open source vector drawing program. It differs from paint programs in that the images are made of editable lines and Bezier curves. This makes it ideal for creating blueprint designs, because changing the curvature of a round edge is very easy and precise, and deletions are largely nondestructive when compared to the eraser tool used in paint programs. Traditionally, Blender has been able to import curves made from Inkscape.

Camera Tracking

I had been considering including a tutorial on this in Chapter 9, but then found it's not compatible with the current Blender release. (Note that this is true as of the time of writing—by the time you are reading this, updates may have happened). It is compatible with Blender 2.49b, so you can still use it if you're working in that version, and you can then import the created file to Blender 2.5.

This amazing software (available at www.digilab.uni-hannover.de/docs/manual.html) is able to take footage from a handheld video camera, and generate a Python script that creates a Blender file with the camera moving as it would have been from the footage, as well as numerous tracking points marked (as empties) in the Blender scene. This allows you to position your Blender models in the scene, and they will be perfectly aligned with the background footage, even though the camera is moving. Search YouTube for "voodoo blender" for examples of what can be created with this software.

BlenderArt Magazine

BlenderArt (http://blenderart.org) is a free downloadable magazine on all things Blender in PDF format (see Figure 12–22). It has news, art samples, and quality tutorials covering a range of ability levels, voluntarily contributed by the members of the wider Blender community. BlenderArt magazine is professionally presented, and attempts to address a particular theme each issue, such as texturing, the latest new features, or a particular special topic, such as car modeling. If you've missed issues, you can go into the archives and download all you need. Enough to keep you busy for some time!

Figure 12–22. BlenderArt magazine

Getting Blender

The main Blender web site (www.blender.org; see Figure 12–23) is where the latest official release can be downloaded. Should you want an older version of Blender, you can get it from http://download.blender.org/release.

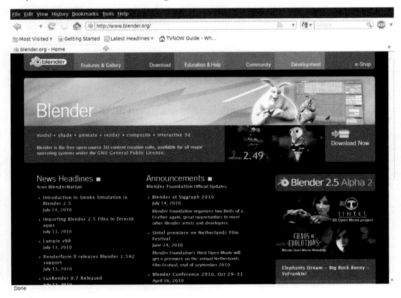

Figure 12–23. The Blender.org home page

You can also see the Blender Manual at http://wiki.blender.org/index.php/Doc:Manual.

Cutting-Edge Releases

The GraphicAll web site (www.graphicall.org/builds; see Figure 12–24) offers cutting-edge compiles of the latest developer versions for most operating systems. These often contain newer features and bug fixes not presented in the official Blender.org release.

Figure 12–24. Graphicall.org features the very latest compiles of Blender

Community

There are a number of Blender community sites.

BlenderNation

BlenderNation (www.blendernation.com; see Figure 12–25) is the prime source for the latest Blender news. Find out about the latest developments and news of how Blender is breaking new ground around the world.

Figure 12–25. BlenderNation

The BlenderArtists Forums

Perhaps the best place on the Internet if you're seeking help with Blender is the BlenderArtists Forums site (http://blenderartists.org/forum; see Figure 12–26). This site is frequented by a huge number of Blender enthusiasts of a wide range of levels. They are generally very newbie-friendly, and with a constant audience from around the globe, you can often find answers to your posted questions surprisingly fast. Sign up and see whether you can also help someone with their Blender problems.

The site also hosts a gallery section featuring some of the very best artwork.

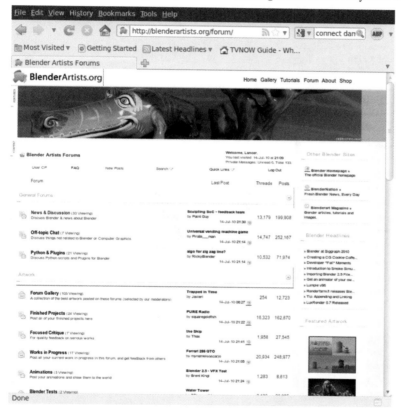

Figure 12–26. BlenderArtists forums

Noob to Pro

The Noob to Pro site (http://en.wikibooks.org/wiki/Blender_3D:_Noob_to_Pro; see Figure 12–27) contains a huge archive of tutorials for Blender. Many are for older versions, although the information is nevertheless still relevant, and new tutorials for recent builds are likely to follow soon.

Figure 12–27. Noob to Pro

BlenderNewbies

If you need some beginner-level tutorials, BlenderNewbies (`www.blendernewbies.blogspot.com`; see Figure 12–28) is a great place to start.

Figure 12–28. BlenderNewbies

Blender Guru

Andrew Price (www.blenderguru.com; see Figure 12–29) is the author of "The Wow Factor," which he markets commercially from this site. As well as this, Andrew has a generous number of well-made tutorials freely up for grabs. There is a mix of readable tutorials as well as video tutorials available.

Figure 12–29. Blender Guru

Blender Cookie

Blender Cookie (www.blendercookie.com; see Figure 12–30) hosts a wealth of video tutorials for Blender. The site is constantly updated with new material, so you are guaranteed to find information relating to the current version of Blender.

The site offers for-pay downloads of its tutorials (plus Blender files used), although you can also see a good number of tutorials for free.

Figure 12–30. Blender Cookie

Free Blender File Resources

This section includes some great free resources for your Blender projects.

Blender Materials (www.blender-materials.org) hosts a large number of mostly procedural materials free for use in your own work. If you quickly need a surface to look like ice, fire, or copper, then this site is worth a visit (see Figure 12–31).

Figure 12–31. Shadeless ice material by Yogyog

Also worth a visit are the Blender Model Repository (http://e2-productions.com/repository/index.php) and the Blender Open Model Repository (www.blendermodels.org; see Figure 12–32).

Figure 12–32. Blender Model Repository

Finally, BlendSwap (www.blendswap.com) is a great resource. It was used for the recent Open Movie *Sintel*.

Summary

I hope that this book has been an encouragement for you and a positive stepping stone in your understanding of Blender. I have said repeatedly in the various chapter summaries that Blender is really big in a variety of ways, and it is. Blender is very complex and can be difficult to learn. I'm hoping that by writing this book, I have given you a good start in using Blender, and that you will continue to develop your skills much further than what I have been able to write down.

At the end of the day, Blender is an art program, and it is useless without an artist to drive it. I would be ecstatic if I were to bump into some amazing Blender artwork in the future, and discover that this book had helped the artist when they were learning the tools.

So have fun, keep being creative, and maybe I'll see you in the BlenderArtists forums.

Lance Flavell (aka Lancer)
www.animator.co.nr

Companies That Use Blender

This appendix provides a list of companies that current use Blender. The content of Table A-1 is based largely on information found at www.blender.org/community/professionals.

■ **Note** This appendix is licensed under the Open Content License, a copy of which is contained in Appendix D. For more information, see http://opencontent.org/opl.shtml.

Table A-1. *Blender Users*

Company/Web Site	Description
Montage Studio www.montagestudio.org	This is a small studio that focuses on providing professional-level training for artists looking to learn Blender. It also provides services such as modeling, rendering, and some animation.
Realworks Studios India www.realworks.in	This is an open source 3D visualization studio.
Cinesoft http://cinesoft.net	Cinesoft provides open source/free software development and customization for the entertainment and media industry.
Blender 3D Architect www.blender3darchitect.com	This site focuses on using Blender 3D for architectural visualizations, with articles on subjects including external renders, CAD drawing with Blender, and precision modeling.
See3D www.see3d.co.uk	This is a team based in a state-of-the-art facility at Aberystwyth University. It provides cutting-edge visualizations services to commercial customers and academics.

Company/Web Site	Description
J. Michael Saunders www.jmichaelsaunders.com	This is the blog and portfolio for Blender user J. Michael Saunders; it includes professional work and personal art.
MetaVR www.metavr.com	MetaVR provides high-performance PC-based solutions for 3D visual systems for simulation and training. MetaVR's software products enable users to build high-fidelity virtual worlds with its WorldPerfect-terrain generation application and render the resulting virtual world with its real-time 3D visualization application, Virtual Reality Scene Generator (VRSG).
instinctive mediaworks www.instinctive.de	instinctive mediaworks performs graphics services for the digital domain, print media, web design, software development, and music production. Some of its modules have been contributed to the official Blender tree, including audio integration into the animation system, mesh beveling, and DTP-like 3D text objects.
3D Verstas www.3dverstas.com	3D Verstas develops techniques to include 3D graphic material in productions, where this type of material is rarely used because of the expenses. In addition to 3D pictures and animations, 3D Verstas produces special effects for marketing and other types of videos .
Damiles home page www.artresnet.com/david	This is the blog of David Millán Escrivá, a developer of Blender nodes who is also involved in the *Plumiferos* movie. He is currently working on a computer vision application project.
IDstudio www.idstudio.it	IDStudio is a multimedia agency.
Pixelarq www.pixelarq.com	Pixelarq offers support in all kind of digital projects related to architecture and web design.
Pikilipita www.pikilipita.com	Pikilipita is a cartoon studio and creates live video performances for handheld video game consoles.
Science Museum of Minnesota www.smm.org	The Science Museum of Minnesota uses Blender to teach adolescents and teenagers 3D techniques; it also uses Blender for professional educational/science content.
IronCode Software www.ironcode.com	IronCode Software is an independent game developer.

Company/Web Site	Description
2gen.Net www.2gen.net	2Gen.Net produces 3D visualizations, animations, and engaging applications.
mke3.net www.mke3.net	mke3.net is an online visual communication portfolio of Blender user and contributor Matt Ebb; it includes both personal and professional work across various media.
MXDSoft Computer Games www.themagicseal.com	MXDSoft Computer Games creates "games for smart people."
TrackTo www.trackto.nl	TrackTo is a 3D animations production studio.
FloatPoint Media www.floatpoint.com	FloatPoint Media is involved in advanced digital design and 3D animation.
CSN Media www.csnmedia.nl	CSN Media provides courses, video, and animation productions.
Studio ZOO www.zoo.nl	Studio ZOO provides digital design and education projects.
imago viva www.imago-viva.de	imago viva creates interactive 3d and animation productions.
Rickert Digital Design www.rickert-digital.com	Rickert Digital Design works in the areas of 3D media concepts and design.
CyberEye Visioneering www.cybereye-visioneering.com	CyberEye Visioneering provides digital imaging for oil and gas exploration.
3D Artworx www.3d-artworx.de	3D Artworx creates audio, video, web, and 3D animation productions.

APPENDIX B

■ ■ ■

Blender and GPL Terms of Use

This appendix is provided as a reference in question/answer format, intended to give you quick answers to frequently asked questions many people have about Blender. For further information, you can find the FAQ online at www.blender.org/education-help/faq/gpl-for-artists, and read the GPL in Appendix C.

■ **Note** This appendix is licensed under the Open Content License, a copy of which is contained in Appendix D. For more information, see http://opencontent.org/opl.shtml.

In a few sentences, what is the GPL?

- You are free to use Blender, for any purpose.
- You are free to distribute Blender.
- You can study how Blender works and change it.
- You can distribute changed versions of Blender. In the last case you have the obligation to also publish the changed source code as GPL.

Can I sell my Blender creations?

Anything you create with Blender—whether it's graphics, movies, scripts, exported 3D files, or the .blend files themselves—is your sole property, and can be licensed or sold under any conditions you prefer.

So I can make games without having to worry about the GPL, right?

Games created in Blender (.blend files) are program output and therefore not covered by the GPL. You can consider them your property, and license or sell them freely.

With standalone games, however, any data that is included inside the actual standalone executable is covered by the GPL. If this is a problem, then you should set up the standalone player so it reads from external .blend files. A common practice is to include a "Please wait, loading . . ." scene in the standalone, and read level files externally.

The Blender standalone player or the game player can be sold commercially too, but you have to make it available under the GPL conditions.

So I own the copyright to all output?

In almost every circumstance for Blender, only the code and other GPL'd files themselves are covered. Any output of such material is copyright the person who produced the output; in this case, the artist.

What about the splash screen and icons?

The splash screen and icons are GPL'd material; therefore, when using them, the terms of the GPL must be followed. Usage of the Blender logo is only GPL too when used within the context of screenshots of the GUI, with or without splash screen.

The Blender logo is a trademark; usage guidelines are here:

http://www.blender.org/blenderorg/blender-foundation/logo

The Blender Foundation logo is also a trademark, and is only used for official Blender Foundation communications.

What if I take screenshots of the Blender interface?

To enable documentation (like books) with author copyrights, screenshots of GNU GPL applications are considered to be licensed as an author wishes. However, this only goes for the screenshot as a "whole," as an illustration of how the software works. Individual items in a screenshot (such as icons) are still GPL'd.

Copyright law in different countries actually differ in this area. Please consult legal advice if you're unsure.

How does the GPL and Blender benefit me?

- The GPL allows for developers to work on Blender without worry that their work could be copied into a closed application. They can keep their own copyright on the code, even reserving the rights to sell or license it as they wish to.

- The GPL makes it so that all contributors must make their code open; this means that if someone distributes a version of Blender with a cool feature, everyone can have access to it.

- The GPL ensures that all future Blender versions will always be available as free software, providing the core freedom users and developers expect from it.

One of the main benefits of Blender is that it's truly "your own software". You or your studio can treat it as in-house software equally to the big powerhouses in the film industry.

Can I distribute the official Blender.org releases under my own branding and name?

Yes, you are free to name Blender whatever you like, and repackage and distribute it under your own branding, provided you still deliver or publish it under the GPL conditions to your clients.

You *cannot* change Blender's copyright notices, nor make claims you wrote or created that program.

Without explicit permission, you then also *cannot* change existing claims or credits that have been published for Blender, such as feature or specification listings on Blender.org, galleries or movies, release notes, screenshots, press articles, reviews, and so on.

If you wish to rename and/or rebrand Blender, you will have to create and use your own credits and achievements as well.

Can I license .blend files myself?

The output of Blender, in the form or `.blend` files, is considered program output, and the sole copyright of the user. The `.blend` file format only stores data definitions.

In case you embed the `.blend` file with Python scripts, and the scripts provide bindings to other libraries or facilities, the next topic applies.

What about my Python scripts?

When a script uses calls that are part of the Blender Python Script Interpreter, the interpreted program, to Blender, is just data; you can run it any way you like, and there are no requirements about licensing that data to anyone.

The Blender Python Script Language is defined here:

`www.blender.org/documentation/249PythonDoc/index.html`

This only applies to the Blender Python API calls. Scripts still have to follow the licenses of other code, bindings, or libraries that they might use.

If you link a Blender Python script to other libraries, plug-ins, or programs, the GPL license defines they form a single program, and that the terms of the GPL must be followed for all components when this case gets distributed.

The bottom line is that we consider everything you can create in Blender as "data," including Blender scripts. But when you extend Blender with "other facilities" you have to follow the regulations of the GPL.

OK is:

Author publishes a Blender script mixed with own code, under own license.

Not OK is:

Author publishes a Blender script, calling a compiled C library with own code, both under own license.

OK is:

Author publishes a Blender script that calls other scripts with own code, under own license.

Not OK is:

Author publishes a Blender binary with own scripts, bundled under own license.

The divider is, "If the script runs in the Blender Interpretor." When the script calls code not running in the Blender Interpretor you are making bindings to other facilities, and the regular GNU GPL rules apply.

Can I give Blender to my coworkers or employees?

Of course, you may give any of the versions of Blender on Blender.org to other people, or share it internally via a server. After 2.25, every version of blender can be freely distributed under the GPL.

Can I change Blender and give it to my coworkers or employees?

Yes, but if you make modifications you must comply with the GPL, and if they request the source code you have to distribute that to them as well. You can charge for the version of Blender you give to your friends even, but it must be licensed under the GPL, and you may not charge an unreasonable fee for the source code.

Can my organization use Blender internally without giving up our valuable changes to our competitors?

The GNU GPL does allow your organization to use a modified version of Blender internally without offering the source code as long as you do not distribute it outside your company or organization.

Can I sell my own version of Blender?

Yes you can, but only if you provide this new version of Blender and the sources to your clients under the same GPL license..The client then benefits from all rights the GPL offers; free to use it, or even distribute it when they wish.

This method provides an essential business model for contracting and support business with Blender. You can freely sell fixed or changed code in Blender, for as long you deliver this as GPL to clients. You don't have the obligation to publish it for everyone.

Can I sell plug-ins for Blender?

Yes you can, but only if you provide the plug-in and the sources to your clients under the GNU GPL license. The client then benefits from all rights the GPL offers; free to use it, or even distribute it when they wish.

Only if the plug-in doesn't work within Blender as "acting as a single program" (like using fork or pipe; by only transferring data and not using each other's program code), you have the full freedom to license the plug-in as you wish.

■ **Disclaimer** This document is no substitute for legal advice and just represents a subset of possible interpretations of the law and the GPL. For a more complete FAQ, please refer to www.gnu.org or www.gnu.org/licenses/gpl-faq.html.

APPENDIX C

■ ■ ■

GNU Public License

This appendix includes the complete GNU General Public License, available online at http://download.blender.org/release/GPL-license.txt.

GNU General Public License

Version 2, June 1991

Preamble

The licenses for most software are designed to take away your freedom to share and change it. By contrast, the GNU General Public License is intended to guarantee your freedom to share and change free software--to make sure the software is free for all its users. This General Public License applies to most of the Free Software Foundation's software and to any other program whose authors commit to using it. (Some other Free Software Foundation software is covered by the GNU Library General Public License instead.) You can apply it to your programs, too.

When we speak of free software, we are referring to freedom, not price. Our General Public Licenses are designed to make sure that you have the freedom to distribute copies of free software (and charge for this service if you wish), that you receive source code or can get it if you want it, that you can change the software or use pieces of it in new free programs; and that you know you can do these things.

To protect your rights, we need to make restrictions that forbid anyone to deny you these rights or to ask you to surrender the rights. These restrictions translate to certain responsibilities for you if you distribute copies of the software, or if you modify it.

For example, if you distribute copies of such a program, whether gratis or for a fee, you must give the recipients all the rights that you have. You must make sure that they, too, receive or can get the source code. And you must show them these terms so they know their rights.

We protect your rights with two steps: (1) copyright the software, and (2) offer you this license which gives you legal permission to copy, distribute and/or modify the software.

Also, for each author's protection and ours, we want to make certain that everyone understands that there is no warranty for this free software. If the software is modified by someone else and passed on, we want its recipients to know that what they have is not the original, so that any problems introduced by others will not reflect on the original authors' reputations.

Finally, any free program is threatened constantly by software patents. We wish to avoid the danger that redistributors of a free program will individually obtain patent licenses, in effect making the program proprietary. To prevent this, we have made it clear that any patent must be licensed for everyone's free use or not licensed at all.

The precise terms and conditions for copying, distribution and modification follow.

GNU General Public License

Terms and Conditions for Copying, Distribution and Modification

1. This License applies to any program or other work which contains a notice placed by the copyright holder saying it may be distributed under the terms of this General Public License. The "Program", below, refers to any such program or work, and a "work based on the Program" means either the Program or any derivative work under copyright law: that is to say, a work containing the Program or a portion of it, either verbatim or with modifications and/or translated into another language. (Hereinafter, translation is included without limitation in the term "modification".) Each licensee is addressed as "you".

   Activities other than copying, distribution and modification are not covered by this License; they are outside its scope. The act of running the Program is not restricted, and the output from the Program is covered only if its contents constitute a work based on the Program (independent of having been made by running the Program). Whether that is true depends on what the Program does.

2. You may copy and distribute verbatim copies of the Program's source code as you receive it, in any medium, provided that you conspicuously and appropriately publish on each copy an appropriate copyright notice and disclaimer of warranty; keep intact all the notices that refer to this License and to the absence of any warranty; and give any other recipients of the Program a copy of this License along with the Program.

   You may charge a fee for the physical act of transferring a copy, and you may at your option offer warranty protection in exchange for a fee.

3. You may modify your copy or copies of the Program or any portion of it, thus forming a work based on the Program, and copy and distribute such modifications or work under the terms of Section 1 above, provided that you also meet all of these conditions:

   a. You must cause the modified files to carry prominent notices stating that you changed the files and the date of any change.

   b. You must cause any work that you distribute or publish, that in whole or in part contains or is derived from the Program or any part thereof, to be licensed as a whole at no charge to all third parties under the terms of this License.

c. If the modified program normally reads commands interactively when run, you must cause it, when started running for such interactive use in the most ordinary way, to print or display an announcement including an appropriate copyright notice and a notice that there is no warranty (or else, saying that you provide a warranty) and that users may redistribute the program under these conditions, and telling the user how to view a copy of this License. (Exception: if the Program itself is interactive but does not normally print such an announcement, your work based on the Program is not required to print an announcement.)

These requirements apply to the modified work as a whole. If identifiable sections of that work are not derived from the Program, and can be reasonably considered independent and separate works in themselves, then this License, and its terms, do not apply to those sections when you distribute them as separate works. But when you distribute the same sections as part of a whole which is a work based on the Program, the distribution of the whole must be on the terms of this License, whose permissions for other licensees extend to the entire whole, and thus to each and every part regardless of who wrote it.

Thus, it is not the intent of this section to claim rights or contest your rights to work written entirely by you; rather, the intent is to exercise the right to control the distribution of derivative or collective works based on the Program.

In addition, mere aggregation of another work not based on the Program with the Program (or with a work based on the Program) on a volume of a storage or distribution medium does not bring the other work under the scope of this License.

4. You may copy and distribute the Program (or a work based on it, under Section 2) in object code or executable form under the terms of Sections 1 and 2 above provided that you also do one of the following:

a. Accompany it with the complete corresponding machine-readable source code, which must be distributed under the terms of Sections 1 and 2 above on a medium customarily used for software interchange; or,

b. Accompany it with a written offer, valid for at least three years, to give any third party, for a charge no more than your cost of physically performing source distribution, a complete machine-readable copy of the corresponding source code, to be distributed under the terms of Sections 1 and 2 above on a medium customarily used for software interchange; or,

c. Accompany it with the information you received as to the offer to distribute corresponding source code. (This alternative is allowed only for noncommercial distribution and only if you received the program in object code or executable form with such an offer, in accord with Subsection b above.)

The source code for a work means the preferred form of the work for making modifications to it. For an executable work, complete source code means all the source code for all modules it contains, plus any associated interface definition files, plus the scripts used to control compilation and installation of the executable. However, as a special exception, the source code distributed need not include anything that is normally distributed (in either source or binary form) with the major components (compiler, kernel, and so on) of the operating system on which the executable runs, unless that component itself accompanies the executable.

If distribution of executable or object code is made by offering access to copy from a designated place, then offering equivalent access to copy the source code from the same place counts as distribution of the source code, even though third parties are not compelled to copy the source along with the object code.

5. You may not copy, modify, sublicense, or distribute the Program except as expressly provided under this License. Any attempt otherwise to copy, modify, sublicense or distribute the Program is void, and will automatically terminate your rights under this License. However, parties who have received copies, or rights, from you under this License will not have their licenses terminated so long as such parties remain in full compliance.

6. You are not required to accept this License, since you have not signed it. However, nothing else grants you permission to modify or distribute the Program or its derivative works. These actions are prohibited by law if you do not accept this License. Therefore, by modifying or distributing the Program (or any work based on the Program), you indicate your acceptance of this License to do so, and all its terms and conditions for copying, distributing or modifying the Program or works based on it.

7. Each time you redistribute the Program (or any work based on the Program), the recipient automatically receives a license from the original licensor to copy, distribute or modify the Program subject to these terms and conditions. You may not impose any further restrictions on the recipients' exercise of the rights granted herein. You are not responsible for enforcing compliance by third parties to this License.

8. If, as a consequence of a court judgment or allegation of patent infringement or for any other reason (not limited to patent issues), conditions are imposed on you (whether by court order, agreement or otherwise) that contradict the conditions of this License, they do not excuse you from the conditions of this License. If you cannot distribute so as to satisfy simultaneously your obligations under this License and any other pertinent obligations, then as a consequence you may not distribute the Program at all. For example, if a patent license would not permit royalty-free redistribution of the Program by all those who receive copies directly or indirectly through you, then the only way you could satisfy both it and this License would be to refrain entirely from distribution of the Program.

   If any portion of this section is held invalid or unenforceable under any particular circumstance, the balance of the section is intended to apply and the section as a whole is intended to apply in other circumstances.

   It is not the purpose of this section to induce you to infringe any patents or other property right claims or to contest validity of any such claims; this section has the sole purpose of protecting the integrity of the free software distribution system, which is implemented by public license practices. Many people have made generous contributions to the wide range of software distributed through that system in reliance on consistent application of that system; it is up to the author/donor to decide if he or she is willing to distribute software through any other system and a licensee cannot impose that choice.

   This section is intended to make thoroughly clear what is believed to be a consequence of the rest of this License.

9. If the distribution and/or use of the Program is restricted in certain countries either by patents or by copyrighted interfaces, the original copyright holder who places the Program under this License may add an explicit geographical distribution limitation excluding those countries, so that distribution is permitted only in or among countries not thus excluded. In such case, this License incorporates the limitation as if written in the body of this License.

10. The Free Software Foundation may publish revised and/or new versions of the General Public License from time to time. Such new versions will be similar in spirit to the present version, but may differ in detail to address new problems or concerns.

Each version is given a distinguishing version number. If the Program specifies a version number of this License which applies to it and "any later version", you have the option of following the terms and conditions either of that version or of any later version published by the Free Software Foundation. If the Program does not specify a version number of this License, you may choose any version ever published by the Free Software Foundation.

11. If you wish to incorporate parts of the Program into other free programs whose distribution conditions are different, write to the author to ask for permission. For software which is copyrighted by the Free Software Foundation, write to the Free Software Foundation; we sometimes make exceptions for this. Our decision will be guided by the two goals of preserving the free status of all derivatives of our free software and of promoting the sharing and reuse of software generally.

No Warranty

12. BECAUSE THE PROGRAM IS LICENSED FREE OF CHARGE, THERE IS NO WARRANTY FOR THE PROGRAM, TO THE EXTENT PERMITTED BY APPLICABLE LAW. EXCEPT WHEN OTHERWISE STATED IN WRITING THE COPYRIGHT HOLDERS AND/OR OTHER PARTIES PROVIDE THE PROGRAM "AS IS" WITHOUT WARRANTY OF ANY KIND, EITHER EXPRESSED OR IMPLIED, INCLUDING, BUT NOT LIMITED TO, THE IMPLIED WARRANTIES OF MERCHANTABILITY AND FITNESS FOR A PARTICULAR PURPOSE. THE ENTIRE RISK AS TO THE QUALITY AND PERFORMANCE OF THE PROGRAM IS WITH YOU. SHOULD THE PROGRAM PROVE DEFECTIVE, YOU ASSUME THE COST OF ALL NECESSARY SERVICING, REPAIR OR CORRECTION.

13. IN NO EVENT UNLESS REQUIRED BY APPLICABLE LAW OR AGREED TO IN WRITING WILL ANY COPYRIGHT HOLDER, OR ANY OTHER PARTY WHO MAY MODIFY AND/OR REDISTRIBUTE THE PROGRAM AS PERMITTED ABOVE, BE LIABLE TO YOU FOR DAMAGES, INCLUDING ANY GENERAL, SPECIAL, INCIDENTAL OR CONSEQUENTIAL DAMAGES ARISING OUT OF THE USE OR INABILITY TO USE THE PROGRAM (INCLUDING BUT NOT LIMITED TO LOSS OF DATA OR DATA BEING RENDERED INACCURATE OR LOSSES SUSTAINED BY YOU OR THIRD PARTIES OR A FAILURE OF THE PROGRAM TO OPERATE WITH ANY OTHER PROGRAMS), EVEN IF SUCH HOLDER OR OTHER PARTY HAS BEEN ADVISED OF THE POSSIBILITY OF SUCH DAMAGES.

END OF TERMS AND CONDITIONS

How to Apply These Terms to Your New Programs

If you develop a new program, and you want it to be of the greatest possible use to the public, the best way to achieve this is to make it free software which everyone can redistribute and change under these terms.

To do so, attach the following notices to the program. It is safest to attach them to the start of each source file to most effectively convey the exclusion of warranty; and each file should have at least the "copyright" line and a pointer to where the full notice is found.

<one line to give the program's name and a brief idea of what it does.>

Copyright (C) <year> <name of author>

This program is free software; you can redistribute it and/or modify it under the terms of the GNU General Public License as published by the Free Software Foundation; either version 2 of the License, or (at your option) any later version.

This program is distributed in the hope that it will be useful, but WITHOUT ANY WARRANTY; without even the implied warranty of MERCHANTABILITY or FITNESS FOR A PARTICULAR PURPOSE. See the GNU General Public License for more details.

You should have received a copy of the GNU General Public License along with this program; if not, write to the Free Software Foundation, Inc., 59 Temple Place, Suite 330, Boston, MA 02111-1307 USA

Also add information on how to contact you by electronic and paper mail.
If the program is interactive, make it output a short notice like this when it starts in an interactive mode:

Gnomovision version 69, Copyright (C) year name of author

Gnomovision comes with ABSOLUTELY NO WARRANTY; for details type 'show w'.

This is free software, and you are welcome to redistribute it under certain conditions; type 'show c' for details.

The hypothetical commands 'show w' and 'show c' should show the appropriate parts of the General Public License. Of course, the commands you use may be called something other than 'show w' and 'show c'; they could even be mouse-clicks or menu items--whatever suits your program.
You should also get your employer (if you work as a programmer) or your school, if any, to sign a "copyright disclaimer" for the program, if necessary. Here is a sample; alter the names:

Yoyodyne, Inc., hereby disclaims all copyright interest in the program

'Gnomovision' (which makes passes at compilers) written by James Hacker.

<signature of Ty Coon>, 1 April 1989

Ty Coon, President of Vice

This General Public License does not permit incorporating your program into proprietary programs. If your program is a subroutine library, you may consider it more useful to permit linking proprietary applications with the library. If this is what you want to do, use the GNU Library General Public License instead of this License.

APPENDIX D

■■■

OpenContent License

This appendix includes the complete OpenContent License, available online at `http://opencontent.org/opl.shtml`. This license applies to Appendix A and Appendix B of this book.

OpenContent License (OPL)

Version 1.0, July 14, 1998.

This document outlines the principles underlying the OpenContent (OC) movement and may be redistributed provided it remains unaltered. For legal purposes, this document is the license under which OpenContent is made available for use.

The original version of this document may be found at http://opencontent.org/opl.shtml

LICENSE

Terms and Conditions for Copying, Distributing, and Modifying

Items other than copying, distributing, and modifying the Content with which this license was distributed (such as using, etc.) are outside the scope of this license.

1. You may copy and distribute exact replicas of the OpenContent (OC) as you receive it, in any medium, provided that you conspicuously and appropriately publish on each copy an appropriate copyright notice and disclaimer of warranty; keep intact all the notices that refer to this License and to the absence of any warranty; and give any other recipients of the OC a copy of this License along with the OC. You may at your option charge a fee for the media and/or handling involved in creating a unique copy of the OC for use offline, you may at your option offer instructional support for the OC in exchange for a fee, or you may at your option offer warranty in exchange for a fee. You may not charge a fee for the OC itself. You may not charge a fee for the sole service of providing access to and/or use of the OC via a network (e.g. the Internet), whether it be via the world wide web, FTP, or any other method.

2. You may modify your copy or copies of the OpenContent or any portion of it, thus forming works based on the Content, and distribute such modifications or work under the terms of Section 1 above, provided that you also meet all of these conditions:

    a. You must cause the modified content to carry prominent notices stating that you changed it, the exact nature and content of the changes, and the date of any change.

    b. You must cause any work that you distribute or publish, that in whole or in part contains or is derived from the OC or any part thereof, to be licensed as a whole at no charge to all third parties under the terms of this License, unless otherwise permitted under applicable Fair Use law.

These requirements apply to the modified work as a whole. If identifiable sections of that work are not derived from the OC, and can be reasonably considered independent and separate works in themselves, then this License, and its terms, do not apply to those sections when you distribute them as separate works. But when you distribute the same sections as part of a whole which is a work based on the OC, the distribution of the whole must be on the terms of this License, whose permissions for other licensees extend to the entire whole, and thus to each and every part regardless of who wrote it. Exceptions are made to this requirement to release modified works free of charge under this license only in compliance with Fair Use law where applicable.

3. You are not required to accept this License, since you have not signed it. However, nothing else grants you permission to copy, distribute or modify the OC. These actions are prohibited by law if you do not accept this License. Therefore, by distributing or translating the OC, or by deriving works herefrom, you indicate your acceptance of this License to do so, and all its terms and conditions for copying, distributing or translating the OC.

NO WARRANTY

4. BECAUSE THE OPENCONTENT (OC) IS LICENSED FREE OF CHARGE, THERE IS NO WARRANTY FOR THE OC, TO THE EXTENT PERMITTED BY APPLICABLE LAW. EXCEPT WHEN OTHERWISE STATED IN WRITING THE COPYRIGHT HOLDERS AND/OR OTHER PARTIES PROVIDE THE OC "AS IS" WITHOUT WARRANTY OF ANY KIND, EITHER EXPRESSED OR IMPLIED, INCLUDING, BUT NOT LIMITED TO, THE IMPLIED WARRANTIES OF MERCHANTABILITY AND FITNESS FOR A PARTICULAR PURPOSE. THE ENTIRE RISK OF USE OF THE OC IS WITH YOU. SHOULD THE OC PROVE FAULTY, INACCURATE, OR OTHERWISE UNACCEPTABLE YOU ASSUME THE COST OF ALL NECESSARY REPAIR OR CORRECTION.

5. IN NO EVENT UNLESS REQUIRED BY APPLICABLE LAW OR AGREED TO IN WRITING WILL ANY COPYRIGHT HOLDER, OR ANY OTHER PARTY WHO MAY MIRROR AND/OR REDISTRIBUTE THE OC AS PERMITTED ABOVE, BE LIABLE TO YOU FOR DAMAGES, INCLUDING ANY GENERAL, SPECIAL, INCIDENTAL OR CONSEQUENTIAL DAMAGES ARISING OUT OF THE USE OR INABILITY TO USE THE OC, EVEN IF SUCH HOLDER OR OTHER PARTY HAS BEEN ADVISED OF THE POSSIBILITY OF SUCH DAMAGES.

Index

■ O

■ P

You Need the Companion eBook

Your purchase of this book entitles you to buy the companion PDF-version eBook for only $10. Take the weightless companion with you anywhere.

We believe this Apress title will prove so indispensable that you'll want to carry it with you everywhere, which is why we are offering the companion eBook (in PDF format) for $10 to customers who purchase this book now. Convenient and fully searchable, the PDF version of any content-rich, page-heavy Apress book makes a valuable addition to your programming library. You can easily find and copy code—or perform examples by quickly toggling between instructions and the application. Even simultaneously tackling a donut, diet soda, and complex code becomes simplified with hands-free eBooks!

Once you purchase your book, getting the $10 companion eBook is simple:

❶ Visit **www.apress.com/promo/tendollars/**.

❷ Complete a basic registration form to receive a randomly generated question about this title.

❸ Answer the question correctly in 60 seconds, and you will receive a promotional code to redeem for the $10.00 eBook.

233 Spring Street, New York, NY 10013

Offer valid through 4/11.